Charles Taylor's Doctrine of Strong Evaluation

Values and Identities: Crossing Philosophical Borders

Series editors: Paul Crowther is Professor of Philosophy at the National University of Ireland, Galway.
Tsarina Doyle is Lecturer in Philosophy at the National University of Ireland, Galway.

How do values define human identity and the different activities through which this identity finds expression? *Values and Identities: Crossing Philosophical Borders* publishes research-led monographs and edited collections that face this problem head on. Titles in this series investigate specific forms of value and, in particular, how they interact across societal contexts to form more complex identities.

Titles in the Series:
Virtue as Identity: Emotions and the Moral Personality, Aleksandar Fati
Human Value, Environmental Ethics and Sustainability: The Precautionary Ecosystem Health Principle, Mark Ryan
Normative Identity, Per Bauhn
The Value of Money: The Metaphysics of Financial Value, Eyja M. Brynjarsdottir (forthcoming)
Incommensurability of Values and its Implications for Justice, Martijn Boot
Charles Taylor's Doctrine of Strong Evaluation: Ethics and Ontology in a Scientific Age, Michiel Meijer

Charles Taylor's Doctrine of Strong Evaluation

Ethics and Ontology in a Scientific Age

Michiel Meijer

London • New York

Published by Rowman & Littlefield International, Ltd.
6 Tinworth Street, London SE11 5AL
www.rowmaninternational.com

Rowman & Littlefield International Ltd. is an affiliate of Rowman & Littlefield
4501 Forbes Boulevard, Suite 200, Lanham, Maryland 20706, USA
With additional offices in Boulder, New York, Toronto (Canada), and Plymouth (UK)
www.rowman.com

Copyright © 2018 Michiel Meijer

All rights reserved. No part of this book may be reproduced in any form or by any electronic or mechanical means, including information storage and retrieval systems, without written permission from the publisher, except by a reviewer who may quote passages in a review

British Library Cataloguing in Publication Information Available
A catalogue record for this book is available from the British Library

ISBN: HB 978-1-78660-400-2
           PB 978-1-78660-401-9

Library of Congress Cataloging-in-Publication Data
Names: Meijer, Michiel, author.
Title: Charles Taylor's doctrine of strong evaluation : ethics and ontology in a scientific age / Michiel Meijer.
Description: Lanham : Rowman & Littlefield International, 2017. | Series: Values and identities: crossing philosophical borders | Includes bibliographical references and index.
Identifiers: LCCN 2017031689 (print) | LCCN 2017033781 (ebook) | ISBN 9781786604026 (electronic) | ISBN 9781786604002 (cloth : alk. paper) | ISBN 9781786604019 (pbk. : alk. paper)
Subjects: LCSH: Taylor, Charles, 1931–
Classification: LCC B995.T34 (ebook) | LCC B995.T34 M45 2017 (print) | DDC 191—dc23
LC record available at https://lccn.loc.gov/2017031689

∞™ The paper used in this publication meets the minimum requirements of American National Standard for Information Sciences—Permanence of Paper for Printed Library Materials, ANSI/NISO Z39.48-1992.

Printed in the United States of America

Contents

Acknowledgments		vii
Introduction: Ethics and Ontology in a Scientific Age		1
1	The Doctrine of Strong Evaluation	17
	1.1 Prologue	18
	1.2 Genesis and Development	22
	1.3 Strong Evaluation in Question	33
	1.4 Conclusion: How to Appreciate the Complex Nature of Strong Evaluation?	45
2	Interwoven Arguments	51
	2.1 Interweaving Anthropology, Ethics, Phenomenology, and Ontology	52
	2.2 Complicating the Doctrine of Strong Evaluation	61
	2.3 Unraveling the Doctrine of Strong Evaluation	72
	2.4 Conclusion: How to Understand Taylor's Interwoven Mode of Argumentation?	82
3	Philosophical Anthropology of Strong Evaluation	87
	3.1 What is Philosophical Anthropology?	88
	3.2 Interweaving Philosophical Anthropology and Ethics	93
	3.3 Transcendental Justification	101
	3.4 Conclusion: Philosophical Anthropology and Ontology	112
4	Ethics of Strong Evaluation	117
	4.1 The Broad and Deep Character of Morality	118
	4.2 Methods from Mandelbaum	126

	4.3 Ethics Beyond the Self	132
	4.4 Conclusion: Moral Phenomenology and Ontology	138
5	Ontology of Strong Evaluation	143
	5.1 Misunderstandings of Taylor's Ontology	145
	5.2 Taylor the Ontologist	152
	5.3 Articulations and Critiques	175
	5.4 Taylor the Hermeneutist	191

Conclusion: Ethics With or Without Ontology? 207

About the Author 214

Index 215

Acknowledgments

I am grateful to several persons who have supported me in writing this book, and, prior to this, the PhD dissertation on which it is based. I want to thank first of all Guy Vanheeswijck, my supervisor at the University of Antwerp. His enduring enthusiasm and guidance have been a great source of motivation. Also, I would like to thank John Linnegar for his critical remarks and constructive suggestions, which have contributed substantially to the quality of the writing. I am also indebted to Ruth Abbey, Nicholas Smith, and Arto Laitinen, who gave very stimulating feedback on the dissertation and suggested several useful improvements.

The most significant change resulting from their helpful comments is that I have dropped the periodization of Taylor's thought into an "early", "middle" and "late" period, while also revising the earlier suggestion of a non-anthropocentric "turn" in Taylor's more recent writings. The analysis developed in the present book is the same but now draws attention to certain shifts in emphasis in the different periods in which Taylor develops his views, rather than arguing for significant changes of mind. Furthermore, I have clarified in more detail where and how I depart from Abbey's, Smith's and Laitinen's interpretations of Taylor.

Some sections in this text have been published before, while others are due for publication. I thank the following journals for permission to use material from the following papers: "Strong Evaluation Down the Decades: Rearticulating Taylor's Central Concept," *Philosophy and Theology*, 2018 (forthcoming), used in sections 1.2 and 1.3; "A Phenomenological Approach With Ontological Implications? Charles Taylor and Maurice Mandelbaum on Explanation in Ethics," *Ethical Theory and Moral Practice*, 2017 (online first article, DOI: 10.1007/s10677-017-9837-7), used in section 4.2; "Human-Related, not Human-Controlled: Charles Taylor on Ethics and Ontology,"

International Philosophical Quarterly, 2017, 57 (3): 267–85, used in sections 4.3.1, 4.3.2, and 5.2.2; "Does Charles Taylor Have a Nietzsche Problem?" *Constellations: An International Journal of Critical and Democratic Theory*, 2017, 24 (3): 372–86, used in section 5.1.2; "Is Charles Taylor (Still) a Weak Ontologist?" *Dialogue: Canadian Philosophical Review*, 2017, 56 (1): 65–87, used in sections 5.3.2 and 5.3.3; and "Ontological Gaps. Retrieving Charles Taylor's Realism," *Philosophy Today*, 2019 (forthcoming), used in sections 5.2.1, 5.2.3, and 5.4.1.

Finally, I thank Fonds Wetenschappelijk Onderzoek – Vlaanderen (FWO) for the essential funding for the research; Thijmgenootschap for the young researcher's award; and the Department of Philosophy at the University of Antwerp for a supportive working environment. For their precious support throughout the years, I am extremely grateful to my friends and family, especially Aafke, Frank, Kim, and Manou. Last but not least, I am indebted to Hedwig, who has been an amazing partner, a helpful colleague, a persistent critic, and a loyal supporter all in one.

Michiel Meijer
Dordrecht, May 2016

Introduction

Ethics and Ontology in a Scientific Age

No human being can exist without values, yet with the rise of the modern scientific worldview it has become increasingly complicated to clarify their nature and relationship to the empirical sciences. Although human beings are inevitably part of nature as studied by science, no scientist has hitherto been able to clarify the full breadth of our ethical deliberations and actions exclusively in empirical terms. Given that values are essential to human identity because they allow us to define what is important to us, how, then, should we understand the connection between these moral self-understandings and empirical investigations of morality?

A common response to this question is that empirical science "debunks" common sense: many of our naïve intuitions about human life have been replaced by superior physical, biological, and psychological explanations. In this way, the empirical sciences have challenged a large part of our self-understanding as reflective moral beings. Within moral philosophy, this phenomenon has generated a host of "naturalistic" philosophical doctrines that take empirical science as our best guide to understanding reality—including ethics (in the spirit of Carnap and the logical positivists, thinkers such as Ayer, Hare, Mackie, Quine, and, more recently, Blackburn, Jackson, Railton, and Boyd all defend different brands of ethical naturalism). At the same time, common sense has continued to play an important role as a criterion in much "hermeneutical" philosophical inquiry, which argues that meaningful human action is an interpretative issue more than anything else, and that, therefore, the empirical sciences do not provide human beings with their most significant access to the world (exemplified in the writings of Husserl, Dilthey, Merleau-Ponty, Heidegger, and, more recently, Levinas, Gadamer, Ricoeur, and Taylor).

To this day, this climate reflects a deep divide between differing philosophical approaches to ethics and ontology and conflicting philosophical views on the significance of empirical explanations for understanding morality. In moral philosophy, then, this climate has cast doubt on the status and validity of moral claims in general and on the ontological implications of ethics in particular. It has proven difficult to specify accurately the differences between naturalistic and hermeneutical approaches to value. It seems clear, however, that at the heart of the disagreement is the issue of how to understand the relationship between ethics, ontology, and empirical science. This raises a more fundamental question: What—if anything—are we committed to ontologically by our ethical views?

Metaphysical and ontological discussions—discussions about what exists and the nature of reality—have long been among the most researched debates in philosophy. However, the many different approaches to ontology have grown so far apart over the last few decades that it has become highly debatable whether "ontology" still designates a single philosophical domain. For this very reason, many argue that ontological debates are nonsubstantive, pointless, or incoherent, thereby accepting that there is no objectively best language that accurately describes the structural features of reality. Within this climate, the very attempt to articulate the relationship between ethics and ontology is often contested. This predicament raises a crucial question: Does the peculiar status of metaphysics also demand the exclusion of ontological theorizing from ethics?

Reflecting on this question, some philosophers redefine moral knowledge as autonomous and discontinuous with nonmoral knowledge, resulting in intricate epistemological and ontological arguments which claim that moral truths—that is, those that do not "fit" into the world picture of science—do not need empirical evidence to be justified (Putnam, Taylor, Nussbaum). At first glance, such a view seems radically contrary to the dominant naturalistic Anglo-American debates in contemporary ethics. At the same time, many naturalistically oriented philosophers within these debates also seek to defend the autonomy of morality in the face of empirically informed reductions of the moral. They seek to do so either by arguing that morality is in some fundamental sense different from natural, empirically observable entities (Shafer-Landau, Wedgwood, Enoch, Parfit) or by arguing for broader, nonreductive types of naturalism (McDowell, Rorty, Hornsby, Price).

However, despite the tendency toward nonreductivism in Anglo-American ethics, the metaphilosophical assumptions underlying the debate concerning the relationship between ethics and ontology have remained naturalist. As a result, the defense of the autonomy of morality is now almost exclusively articulated from a naturalistic standpoint to the extent that the central question is this: How can morality *fit* in the natural world? From this perspective, the tasks of moral philosophy are, first, to assume the methodological superiority of the empirical sciences, and, second, to develop forms of ethics and ontology that can be aligned with the scientific worldview.[1] In this way, it is generally accepted that philosophical explanations of morality must be compatible with the view that our scientific understanding is the best story we now have about reality. Thus the problems of nonreductive naturalism arise: Where do moral properties (such as goodness and rightness) fit within such a reality, and how are we able to learn about them? These ontological and epistemological burdens continue to be subjects of intense debate in contemporary metaethics. However, the unexamined presupposition behind these burdens is that a reasonable form of nonreductivism must be elaborated from a naturalistic perspective. Moreover, the implicit conclusion that facts and values lie in different domains requires the additional assumption that ethical statements are not really "factual." This begs all the crucial questions about the relationship between ethics and ontology.

So while nonreductivism is gaining ground in contemporary moral philosophy, naturalism still seems to have won the all-important methodological war by dictating how metaethical questions should be addressed, namely by developing arguments that can be aligned with empirical science. In this regard, naturalism has indeed become "the only game in town" (Kitcher 1992; Stroud 1996). But even in the context of the more sophisticated nonreductive forms of naturalism, there is more at stake than an attempt to establish how ethical naturalism should be defined. An important issue that is rarely addressed in contemporary debates is how the various nonreductive forms of ethical naturalism may relate to hermeneutical proposals.

CHARLES TAYLOR'S UNUSUAL VOICE IN THE DEBATE

Against this background, what is striking about the philosophy of Charles Taylor is that it has been debunking naturalism in the human sciences since well before its recent popularity in philosophical ethics. In his view, it is commonplace in Western culture to think that humans as part of nature are in the end best understood in terms continuous with modern natural science. Refuting this approach, Taylor's concern is that crucial features of human life—especially moral ones—precisely disappear by adopting a scientific stance in general and by making the fact-value distinction a criterion of ethics in particular. In line with this, the leading notion of his central doctrine of "strong evaluation" is that moral agency essentially resists incorporation into the empirical sciences. Yet he sees a growing "naturalist temper" not just in the outlooks of "many students of the sciences of human behavior" but in our culture as such, "stopping short frequently of explicit espousal of full-blooded naturalism, but tending to be suspicious of the things that naturalism cannot accommodate" (1964, 3; 1995d, 137). This observation—that most people are reluctant to embrace naturalism fully and yet remain highly skeptical of all things that do not fit the naturalist model—is *the* underlying theme of Taylor's doctrine of strong evaluation.

By arguing mainly against the views of John Mackie and Simon Blackburn, Taylor generally uses the term "naturalism" in a rather restricted way, limiting the term to a scientistic form of philosophical position. Although he recognizes that "naturalism" is far from a straightforward position, his method involves not so much detailed engagements with naturalist approaches as the construction of a hermeneutical explanation about how naturalist thinking came to dominate our thinking about ethics and ontology. As a philosophical anthropologist, Taylor argues that the implicit agent in naturalist theory is a "monster" (1989, 32). As a moral philosopher, he criticizes much contemporary moral philosophy for annihilating our very sense of morality, that is, the sense that moral values are "in some way special, higher, or incommensurable with our other goals and desires" (2003, 308). As an ontological thinker, he seeks to convince us that moral reactions are best understood as "responses to some reality," as it lies in their nature to claim "truth, reality, or objective rightness" (2011b, 297–98).

In a major effort to link these issues together, Taylor proposes an outlook that not only stresses the difference between human nature and mere physical nature, but also draws attention to the connection between ethics and ontology in general and the close relationship between human identity and value in particular. His views are inspired, first, by an epistemological concern for the nature of human agency in dealing with the problem of knowledge; second, by an ethical concern for the central place of value in human life; and, third, by an ontological concern for the background conditions within which human thought and action take place. However, since Taylor's thinking is organized around an interpretation of the human subject that steers a course between Aristotelian and Murdochean ethics, Kantian epistemology, Merleau-Pontyan phenomenology, and Heideggerian ontology, his hermeneutical vocabulary is somewhat of a mismatch with the analytical discourse in which these issues are generally debated (e.g., in terms of moral facts and properties). This may have contributed to some neglect of Taylor's theories, at least within Anglo-American ethics. Yet it is precisely his unusual terminology that makes his views stand out from that of the others.

Difficulties arise, however, when considering the massive range of concerns raised and discussed in Taylor's oeuvre: he has engaged in such wide-ranging discussions that his thoughts have had to be collected in series of "philosophical papers," "philosophical arguments," and the "dilemmas and connections" with which he has been involved throughout his career.[2] His work covers "continental" subjects, such as philosophical anthropology, moral phenomenology, hermeneutics, the history of philosophy, political theory, and religion, and more "analytical" themes, such as epistemology, language theory, moral realism, philosophy of science, and philosophy of mind; it also invokes major topics debated in both continental and analytic traditions, such as ethics, ontology, and metaphysics. Complicating matters, Taylor's thinking cuts across these areas of interest as he explicitly combines philosophical methods that are usually seen as separate, noting that there is a kind of *unity* throughout his concerns despite the wide spectrum of themes.[3]

The tendency to connect rather than to separate philosophical questions is closely related to another characteristic of Taylor's work: his distinctive style of writing. Since the very beginning, he has been developing a terminology that challenges the more familiar terms used by philosophers. Some of Taylor's concepts, such as "moral phenomenology" and "moral ontology," explicitly straddle the boundaries of the philosophical domains he seeks to explore. This has led to the criticism that his thinking is too "idiosyncratic" (Kymlicka 1991, 159) or that he "blurs" basic distinctions (Johnston 1999, 101, 106), but these comments neglect the kind of strategy Taylor actually employs. His thinking typically thrives by providing a set of new concepts (categories, illustrations, metaphors) that he uses in a variety of ways and in pursuit of different, sometimes conflicting, ends. Driven by an ongoing dissatisfaction with the ways in which problems are formulated in dominant philosophical debates, his aim is to map a terrain and articulate issues left unexplored rather than to have the final word.

Given these observations, it should not surprise us that Taylor's thinking has allowed for multiple interpretations of his claims, both by his critics and by his interpreters. In these interpretations, Taylor's philosophical background has been traced back to Plato,[4] Aristotle,[5] Kant,[6] Hegel,[7] Merleau-Ponty,[8] Murdoch,[9] and Christianity,[10] while Taylor himself consistently emphasizes his indebtedness foremost to Heidegger.[11] Many commentators have also tried to uncover Taylor's own position. To mention only a few, his views have been presented as moving from a relativist position to a more realist view and vice versa (Bohman 1991; Rosa 1995); or as a slide into "Platonism" or some other "return" to moral realism (Olafson 1994, 194; Rosen 1991, 183–94). He has been characterized as a "teleologist" (Berlin 1994, 1–2), a "strong realist" (MacIntyre 1996, 523; cf. Laitinen 2008, 46), and a "weak ontologist" (White 2000, 43). Alongside Taylor "the critic of empiricism" stands Taylor "the hermeneutically oriented political philosopher," Taylor "the cultural historian," Taylor "the epistemologist of morality," Taylor "the moralist and critic of our contemporary age," and Taylor "the protagonist of theism" (Shapiro 1986, 312; Skinner 1991, 133). His arguments, then, have been criticized as "excessively moralistic" and "heavily intellectualist" (Flanagan 1996, 146, 157), whereas others have celebrated his "brilliant" analysis of our moral predicament (Rorty 1994, 199) and his "importantly true" claims about the nature of moral experience (Williams 1990, 48). More broadly, his work has been praised for "its remarkable consistency" (Weinstock 1994, 171), for "the challenge it poses to naturalistic conceptions of evaluation" (Anderson 1996, 35), and for taking on "the most delicate and exacting of philosophical questions, the question of who we are and how we should live" (Nussbaum 1990, 34).

STRONG EVALUATION AS AN INCLUSIVE DOCTRINE

In the face of the wide variety of interpretations, the present book centers on one single concept precisely to account for the complexity of Taylor's thought: *strong evaluation*. The concept of strong evaluation is vital to understanding many of his major positions. At one stroke, Taylor employs this notion to refute naturalism, to defend his philosophical-anthropological thesis about the self, to develop his phenomenological approach to ethics, and to raise ontological questions. In his most basic definition, "strong evaluation" depicts an ethical kind of reflection that involves "distinctions of worth" (1985a, 3). With this key concept, Taylor seeks to capture the sense that human beings understand themselves not by simply having certain desires but by *evaluating* their desires in terms of their worth. He describes this type of evaluation as "strong" because it recognizes not just plain desires but reaches beyond these to judge their value. In this way, he introduces the concept of strong evaluation to highlight that human beings experience some of their desires and goals as inherently more worthy than others.

Taylor has constant recourse to our experience of higher and lower values in his key publications, as it informs both his definition of human agency and his distinctive brand of morality. Moreover, he employs the concept of strong evaluation to criticize naturalistic views that discredit commonsense moral reactions for ethical theory and/or leave no room for the distinction between higher and lower values. Finally, strong evaluation is at the heart of Taylor's ontological thought, as he consistently appeals to this concept to discuss the metaphysical implications of ethics.

One way of mapping the terrain of strong evaluation is to see it as an inclusive doctrine that is divided between three large domains: philosophical anthropology, ethics, and ontology. First, Taylor argues that strong evaluation is to be understood as a universal feature of human agency. In this respect, the thesis of strong evaluation is part of his larger philosophical anthropology, which aims to describe those features of human action and experience that in his view are distinctively and universally human. Second, Taylor uses strong evaluation to endorse his moral phenomenology, which centers on the point that some goods, values, or goals strike us as being higher, more worthy, or more demanding than others. Third, this point only sets the stage for his highly contested ontological view that the source of value lies beyond human control. In this regard, Taylor employs strong evaluation to open up a distinctive "nonanthropocentric" perspective on the good, that is, to make room for the rather contentious *metaphysical* question of what it is that implicitly informs our experience of strong values.

Because of its inclusive nature, strong evaluation has been both understood and misunderstood in a variety of ways. Taylor recently explained his doctrine of strong evaluation as an attempt to develop what he calls "interwoven arguments."[12] In line with this, his views not only combine ethics with philosophical anthropology, but also have a way of interweaving phenomenological and ontological reflections with ethical inquiries. One example of Taylor's interwoven mode of thinking is that his anthropological and ethical views are intertwined in such a fundamental way that the two can hardly be separated. He believes that identity and value or, as he puts it, "selfhood" and "morality," are deeply interwoven because "our notion of the self is inextricably connected with our understanding of our moral predicament and moral agency" (1988, 298; 1989, 3). In elaborating on this, Taylor makes it clear that his concept of the self is linked to moral issues in a broad sense, having to do with how one ought to be and what is a good or worthwhile life (1989, 32). In this way, he strategically discusses human agency in connection with broad moral issues in developing his philosophical anthropology.

This picture of moral identity prepares the ground for Taylor's more applied "*ad hominem*" and "transcendental" arguments in criticizing ethical naturalism. In developing these arguments, Taylor has constant recourse to the close relationship between facts of human nature and ethical beliefs in order to expose and refute the imagined *agent* behind naturalistic moral theories. The "*ad hominem*" moment (Latin for "to the person"), then, is that Taylor's philosophical anthropology appeals to basic considerations of personal identity by invoking commonsense moral beliefs that no sane human person would be willing to give up. In this way, he defends what he calls an "*ad hominem* mode of practical reasoning" (1995a, 37) which states that we cannot make full sense of our late modern identities without recognizing strongly valued goods that we all share, such as respect and benevolence.

The main thrust of Taylor's *ad hominem* argument is to show the inadequacy of reductive naturalistic approaches to ethics that leave no room for strong evaluation. However, this critique is only the basis of a transcendental argument that seeks to convince us that strong evaluation is both a structural and inescapable feature of human agency. Put simply, Taylor's transcendental argument seeks to make clear that no other condition than strong evaluation makes our actions intelligible and that, therefore, any coherent understanding of human agency will include strong evaluation. Although he explicitly presents this argument as an exercise in "moral phenomenology" (1989, 68, 74, 81), he stresses that his view is "not only a phenomenological account" as it aims to establish something stronger, namely an account of the "transcendental conditions" of human life (1989, 32).

These points show that Taylor's *ad hominem* and transcendental perspectives include anthropological, ethical, and phenomenological points all in one. He then continues and extends his interwoven mode of argumentation by adding an ontological perspective, that is, by asking "what ontology can underpin our moral commitments," and by arguing—tentatively, yet boldly—that there is a tension between "the phenomenology of the incommensurably higher," on the one hand, and "a naturalist ontology which has difficulty finding a place for this," on the other (2003, 316; 2007, 607). In reply to this tension, Taylor defends his nonanthropocentric perspective as a middle position between "a 'Platonist' mode of moral realism," on the one hand, and "mere subjectivism," on the other (1994, 211). As this indicates, his thinking freely crosses the boundaries of different philosophical domains.

In an attempt to clarify the connections between Taylor's different arguments, I argue that a close examination of his use of the concept of strong evaluation brings out more clearly the continuing concerns in his writings as a whole. One of the most striking features of Taylor's employment of strong evaluation is that this concept straddles his different approaches, that is, his picture of the human agent, his account of morality, and his views on ontology. In trying to obtain clarity on his distinctive interwoven mode of argumentation, the focus therefore could not but be on "strong evaluation" as a binding theme, because Taylor typically employs this term to push the boundaries that separate his philosophical anthropology, his moral philosophy, and his ontological view. Moreover, because strong evaluation generates a variety of philosophical methods, a close examination of this concept in its different contexts is bound to clarify how Taylor's interwoven arguments fit together.

OBJECTIVES OF THE BOOK

The principal aim of this book is to unravel Taylor's hybrid position in crucial reference to both his concept of strong evaluation and his interwoven arguments. In so doing, this study puts forward an original argument regarding the interpretation of his work, as there exists somewhat of a gap in the literature on these issues. Given Taylor's status as one of the most important thinkers in the philosophy of the human sciences and contemporary ethical and political philosophy, it is surprising that so little attention has been paid to the unity of his writings as a whole.[13] The few monographs on Taylor stand in stark contrast to the countless reviews of and articles about his work. However, despite the numerous essays on Taylor's views on strong evaluation, human agency, ethics, and ontology, few attempts have been made at providing an overview of how these fit together. Furthermore, no one has explored the relationship between Taylor's interrelated yet separate methodologies.[14] Few of his interpreters ever raise the issues of how Taylor's profound and elaborate philosophical anthropology and moral phenomenology relate to his very tentative nonanthropocentric approaches to ethics and ontology, or of how his complex interweaving of *ad hominem* and transcendental argumentation inform and support his claims.

The major point of this book is to go some way toward filling this gap, as it not only addresses all of the above topics, but also explores the connections between them. While developing the focus on strong evaluation in a way that creates, as it were, one composition out of Taylor's different positions, this book explicitly builds further on Ruth Abbey's attempt to give guidance to the cohesion of Taylor's arguments as a whole (Abbey 2000). It does so, first, by carefully pursuing the development of Taylor's doctrine of strong evaluation from his very first philosophical papers (in 1958) until his most recent reflections (in 2016); second, by engaging with a wide expanse of the relevant secondary literature; and, third, by applying the standards of mainstream philosophy to Taylor's work, thereby seeking to extract maximum rigor and clarity from it.

The approach developed in this book brings to light that Taylor's strategy of interweaving different philosophical arguments is revealing but only partly successful. Most importantly, his doctrine of strong evaluation lacks an adequate ontological framework to sustain his nonanthropocentric perspective on the good. That is, whereas Taylor has no doubt that ontological reflections are vital for understanding ethics, he struggles until the very end of his career to clarify their meaning and importance. The identification of this issue in Taylor's early work, and the discussion of how the issue reappears in his more recent writings, presents a challenge to Taylor's doctrine of strong evaluation that has hitherto remained unnoticed.

It would seem, however, that the issue of what ontology can underpin our moral commitments is not simply *Taylor's* problem, as it crosses the boundaries of any one established academic discipline, arising as it does on the borderline between common sense, philosophy, and science. Moreover, the book also explores the idea that Taylor's interwoven mode of reasoning presents an interesting way of dealing with the problem of how to understand the relationship between ethics and ontology in a scientific age. Ultimately, Taylor's questions are these: Do we really believe that our moral responses need to be replaced by scientific explanations? And if not, how should we understand the relationship between moral experience, on the one hand, and naturalist ontology, on the other? Uncertainties about the status of philosophy and the aspiration to be "scientific" have led many philosophers to doubt the meaning or importance of such questions. Following Taylor's lead, this study seeks to show up the confusions such doubt involves and so to clarify the complex status of ethics and ontology within a science-dominated world. In this way, this book aims to unravel Taylor's interwoven arguments in between philosophical anthropology, ethics, and ontology in order to open up the broader question of the implicit ontological commitments behind our ethical beliefs.

More than anything else, this study is an investigation of the philosophical implications of strong evaluation. For this reason, it has been necessary to avoid Taylor's historical narratives and political views in order to make possible a thorough analysis of the way in which Taylor interweaves anthropological, ethical, and ontological arguments in developing his doctrine of strong evaluation. Furthermore, narrowing the focus to the concept of strong evaluation typically means neglecting a host of other issues. For reasons of clarity, my analysis starts from Taylor's first publication on strong evaluation: "Responsibility for Self" (1976), a paper that was reprinted as "What is Human Agency?" (1985f) almost a decade later. For the purposes of analysis, only those earlier writings that define the doctrine of strong evaluation or significantly add to it are included. In presenting Taylor's views about strong evaluation as an inclusive doctrine instead of an isolated issue, I have deliberately avoided writings in which the *term* "strong evaluation" does not occur (apart from some minor exceptions that nevertheless clarify the doctrine of strong evaluation). This means, for example, that Taylor's explanations of Hegel, as elaborated in *Hegel* (1975) and *Hegel and Modern Society* (1979), are excluded from this study, while also partly ignoring his more recent views on religion, secularism, and political theory as set out since the lecture "A Catholic Modernity?" (1999). Instead, this book investigates Taylor's attacks on naturalism, his *ad hominem* perspective and transcendental mode of argumentation in philosophical anthropology, his phenomenological and nonanthropocentric approaches to ethics, his distinctive ontological mode of reasoning, and, finally, the relationships between these views.

The first two chapters can be seen as a general introduction. Chapter 1 distributes Taylor's different uses of the concept of strong evaluation into three central domains: philosophical anthropology, ethics, and ontology. Chapter 2 then invokes his attempt to interweave his philosophical-anthropological, ethical, and ontological views, and discusses the reception of these views in the literature on Taylor's work. In chapters 3–5, the discussion turns from exegesis to critical questioning. Each chapter concentrates on one of the three levels of strong evaluation: philosophical anthropology (chapter 3), ethics (chapter 4), and ontology (chapter 5). Gradually moving toward the most problematic issue, it is shown how Taylor's investigations of strong evaluation ultimately evolve into one central question: *What are we committed to ontologically by our ethical views?* Pursuing the line of how this question enters into Taylor's thinking, each chapter concludes with an evaluation of the ontological implications of his views.

Chapter 1 begins with an overview of the different themes that revolve around strong evaluation, while also showing that Taylor's earliest writings (1958–1959) can be seen as an illuminating prologue to the doctrine of strong evaluation. The focus then shifts to the original account of strong evaluation in *Philosophical Papers* (1985) and the modifications in the original explanation of strong evaluation as Taylor employs it in more recent writings. The chapter concludes by discussing some misunderstandings of the concept of strong evaluation.

Chapter 2 starts with an examination of Taylor's attempts to establish the connections between the different levels of strong evaluation in *Sources of the Self* (1989). It addresses the link between his anthropological and ethical views and demonstrates how Taylor also seeks to fuse the subjects of ontology and phenomenology into his account of morality. I then put a spotlight on Taylor's characteristic nonanthropocentric mode of ontologizing by including his more recent writings (2003–2016), and continue to show that his nonanthropocentrism—while raising many important questions—has been pushed into the background in recent Taylor scholarship. In reply, I highlight a fundamental tension in Taylor's interwoven strategy that most studies tend to overlook, and suggest that a distinction should be drawn between the philosophical-anthropological, ethical, and ontological implications of strong evaluation to clarify the issues at stake.

Chapter 3 discusses Taylor's philosophical anthropology. It starts with an explanation of the context in which he elaborates his philosophical-anthropological approach, introducing Taylor's search for essential features of human agency against the background of his critique of contemporary moral theory. This discussion continues with an examination of Taylor's *ad hominem* perspective and concludes with an analysis of his use of transcendental argumentation in support of the doctrine of strong evaluation.

Chapter 4 investigates Taylor's moral philosophy. It shines a spotlight on his unusual moral-phenomenological method by comparing it with Maurice Mandelbaum's view on the scope of moral phenomenology, while also extending this comparison to the issue of how to locate the source of moral experience. The chapter concludes by highlighting the tension between Taylor's moral-phenomenological perspective and his attempt to reach beyond mere phenomenology by adopting a nonanthropocentric perspective on the good.

Chapter 5 explores Taylor's ontological view. It starts with the controversy that surrounds his work because of his commitment to Catholicism. It then locates some misunderstandings of Taylor's ontology and pursues the development of his ontological thought from his very first essay on ontology until his most recent writings on this topic. After this reconstruction, I continue to discuss several articulations and critiques of Taylor's ontology. Finally, I examine his latest views in *Retrieving Realism* (2015) and *The Language Animal* (2016) in the light of these discussions.

NOTES

1. The thrust of this debate is well described by Simon Blackburn, who argues that the central problem of contemporary ethics is one of "finding room for ethics, or placing ethics within the disenchanted, non-ethical order which we inhabit" (1998, 49).

2. See Taylor's *Philosophical Papers* (1985a), *Philosophical Arguments* (1995f), and *Dilemmas and Connections* (2011a).

3. As Taylor says in the introduction to *Philosophical Papers:* "Despite the appearance of variety in the papers published in this collection, they are the work of a monomaniac [. . .] If not a single idea, then at least a single rather tightly related agenda underlies all of them" (1985a, 1).

4. Olafson (1994, 193–94) and Smith (1997, 136).

5. Abbey (2000, 12), Beam (1997, 771), Laitinen (2008, 33), and Thiebaut (1993, 129).

6. Saurette (2005, 197–233) and Shapiro (1986, 315–17, 322).

7. Berlin (1994, 1).

8. Smith (2002, 1).

9. Kerr (2004, 84–85, 90).

10. Williams (1990, 45–48), Hittinger (1990, 125), Skinner (1991, 133, 147–50), Shklar (1991, 105–09), Lane (1992, 46–48), O'Hagan (1993, 74, 81), De Sousa (1994, 121), and Berlin (1994, 1). Taylor's Catholicism has worried some critics more than others. There is wide disagreement about the type of theism Taylor means to defend, varying from the observation that he is "wonderfully unpreachy" and "very unpretentious" (Williams 1990, 45) to caustic talk of "his reason for urging the Judaeo-Christian religion upon us" (Skinner 1991, 149).

11. References to Heidegger are numerous. The most crucial ones are (1985a, 3, 9, 11; 1985d, 45, 76; 1985c, 215; 1985e, 255; 1992, 133; 1989, 47, 50, 257, 481–82, 491, 524; 1995b, c, e; 2007, 3, 13, 95, 558–59; 2013; 2015, 23, 41, 45, 55, 57, 71, 93, 103, 106, 128, 140, 143, 151, 160–62; 2016).

12. Taylor used this expression to characterize his arguments about strong evaluation during a seminar at the University of Leuven, Belgium (June 2, 2015).

13. Ruth Abbey (2000), Nicholas Smith (2002), and Arto Laitinen (2008) are illuminating exceptions to this trend. See also Mark Redhead (2002) for a discussion of Taylor's political thoughts and affirmations.

14. The issue has been brought up, though, in an interview with Taylor by Rosa and Laitinen (2002, 183). Their question about the relationship between the three modes of reasoning Taylor employs in "Interpretation and the Sciences of Man"

(1985b), "Explanation and Practical Reason" (1995a), and "The Validity of Transcendental Arguments" (1995g) invokes the kind of issue I embark on investigating in this study.

REFERENCES

Abbey, Ruth. 2000. *Charles Taylor*. Teddington/Princeton: Acumen Press/Princeton University Press.

Anderson, Joel. 1996. "The Personal Lives of Strong Evaluators: Identity, Pluralism, and Ontology in Charles Taylor's Value Theory." *Constellations: An International Journal of Critical and Democratic Theory* 3(1): 17–38.

Beam, Craig. 1997. "The Clash of Paradigms: Taylor vs. Narveson on the Foundation of Ethics." *Dialogue* 36: 771–81.

Berlin, Isaiah. 1994. "Introduction." In *Philosophy in an Age of Pluralism: The Philosophy of Charles Taylor in Question*, edited by James Tully and Daniel Weinstock, 1–3. Cambridge: Cambridge University Press.

Blackburn, Simon. 1998. *Ruling Passions: A Theory of Practical Reasoning*. Oxford: Clarendon Press.

Bohman, James. 1991. *New Philosophy of Social Science: Problems of Indeterminacy*. Oxford: Polity Press.

De Sousa, Ronald. 1994. "Bashing the Enlightenment: A Discussion of Charles Taylor's Sources of the Self." *Dialogue* 33: 109–23.

Flanagan, Owen. 1996. *Self Expressions. Mind, Morals, and the Meaning of Life*. New York/Oxford: Oxford University Press.

Hittinger, Russell. 1990. "Critical Study: Charles Taylor, Sources of the Self." *Review of Metaphysics* 44 (September): 111–30.

Johnston, Paul. 1999. *The Contradictions of Modern Moral Philosophy. Ethics after Wittgenstein*. London/New York: Routledge.

Kerr, Fergus. 2004. "The Self and the Good. Taylor's Moral Ontology." In *Contemporary Philosophy in Focus: Charles Taylor*, edited by Ruth Abbey, 84–104. Cambridge, MA: Cambridge University Press.

Kitcher, Philip. 1992. "The Naturalists Return." *Philosophical Review* 101(1): 53–114.

Kymlicka, Will. 1991. "The Ethics of Inarticulacy." *Inquiry* 34: 155–82.

Laitinen, Arto. 2008. *Strong Evaluation Without Moral Sources*. Berlin: Walter de Gruyter.

Lane, Melissa. 1992. "God or Orienteering? A Critical Study of Taylor's Sources of the Self." *Ratio* 5: 46–56.

MacIntyre, Alasdair. 1996. "Review of Philosophy in an Age of Pluralism: the Philosophy of Charles Taylor in Question." *The Philosophical Quarterly* 46 (185): 522–24.

Nussbaum, Martha. 1990. "Our Pasts, Ourselves." *The New Republic* April 9th: 27–34.

O'Hagan, Timothy. 1993. "Charles Taylor's Hidden God." *Ratio* 6: 72–81.

Olafson, Frederick. 1994. "Comments on Sources of the Self by Charles Taylor." *Philosophy and Phenomenological Research* 54 (1): 191–96.
Redhead, Mark. 2002. *Charles Taylor: Thinking and Living Deep Diversity*. Lanham, MD: Rowman & Littlefield.
Rorty, Richard. 1994. "Taylor on Self-Celebration and Gratitude: Review of Sources of the Self." *Philosophy and Phenomenological Research* 54 (1): 197–201.
Rosa, Hartmut. 1995. "Goods and Life-Forms: Relativism in Charles Taylor's Political Philosophy." *Radical Philosophy* 71 (May/June): 20–26.
Rosa, Hartmut, and Arto Laitinen. 2002. "On Identity, Alienation and the Consequences of September 11th. An Interview with Charles Taylor." In *Acta Philosophica Fennica. Vol. 71. Perspectives on the Philosophy of Charles Taylor*, edited by Arto Laitinen and Nicholas Smith, 165–195. Helsinki: Philosophical Society of Finland.
Rosen, Michael. 1991. "Must We Return to Moral Realism?" *Inquiry* 34: 183–94.
Saurette, Paul. 2005. *The Kantian Imperative: Humiliation, Common Sense, Politics*. Toronto, OH: University of Toronto Press.
Shapiro, Michael. 1986. "Charles Taylor's Moral Subject: Philosophical Papers Volumes 1 and 2." *Political Theory* 14 (2): 311–24.
Shklar, Judith. 1991. "Review of Sources of the Self." *Political Theory* 19: 105–09.
Skinner, Quentin. 1991. "Who Are 'We'? Ambiguities of the Modern Self." *Inquiry* 34: 133–53.
Smith, Nicholas. 1997. "Reason after Meaning: Review of Philosophical Arguments." *Philosophy and Social Criticism* 23 (1): 131–40.
Smith, Nicholas. 2002. *Charles Taylor: Meaning, Morals and Modernity*. Cambridge, MA: Polity.
Stroud, Barry. 1996. "The Charm of Naturalism." *Proceedings and Address of the American Philosophical Society* 70: 43–55.
Taylor, Charles. 1964. *The Explanation of Behaviour*. London: Routledge and Kegan Paul.
Taylor, Charles. 1975. *Hegel*. Cambridge, MA: Cambridge University Press.
Taylor, Charles. 1976. "Responsibility for Self." In *The Identities of Persons*, edited by Amélie Rorty, 281–299. London: University of California Press.
Taylor, Charles. 1979. *Hegel and Modern Society*. Cambridge: Cambridge University Press.
Taylor, Charles. 1985a. *Human Agency and Language: Philosophical Papers vol. 1*. Cambridge, MA: Cambridge University Press.
Taylor, Charles. 1985b. "Interpretation and the Sciences of Man." In *Philosophy and the Human Sciences: Philosophical Papers vol. 2*, 15–57. Cambridge: Cambridge University Press.
Taylor, Charles. 1985c. "Language and Human Nature." In *Human Agency and Language: Philosophical Papers vol. 1*, 215–47. Cambridge: Cambridge University Press.
Taylor, Charles. 1985d. "Self-Interpreting Animals." In *Human Agency and Language: Philosophical Papers vol. 1*, 45–76. Cambridge, MA: Cambridge University Press.
Taylor, Charles. 1985e. "Theories of Meaning." In *Human Agency and Language: Philosophical Papers vol. 1*, 248–92. Cambridge, MA: Cambridge University Press.

Taylor, Charles. 1985f. "What is Human Agency?" In *Human Agency and Language: Philosophical Papers vol. 1*, 15–44. Cambridge, MA: Cambridge University Press.

Taylor, Charles. 1988. "The Moral Topography of the Self." In *Hermeneutics and Psychological Theory*, edited by Stanly Messer, Louis Sass and Robert Woolfolk, 298–320. New Brunswick, NJ: Rutgers University Press.

Taylor, Charles. 1989. *Sources of the Self. The Making of the Modern Identity*. Cambridge, MA: Cambridge University Press.

Taylor, Charles. 1992. *The Ethics of Authenticity*. Cambridge, MA: Harvard University Press.

Taylor, Charles. 1994. "Reply to Commentators." *Philosophy and Phenomenological Research* 54 (1): 203–13.

Taylor, Charles. 1995a. "Explanation and Practical Reason." In *Philosophical Arguments*, 34–60. Cambridge, MA/London: Harvard University Press.

Taylor, Charles. 1995b. "Heidegger, Language, and Ecology." In *Philosophical Arguments*, 100–26. Cambridge, MA/London: Harvard University Press.

Taylor, Charles. 1995c. "Lichtung or Lebensform: Parallels between Heidegger and Wittgenstein." In *Philosophical Arguments*, 61–78. Cambridge, MA/London: Harvard University Press.

Taylor, Charles. 1995d. "A Most Peculiar Institution." In *World, Mind, and Ethics. Essays on the Ethical Philosophy of Bernard Williams*, edited by J. Altham and R. Harrison, 132–55. Cambridge, MA: Cambridge University Press.

Taylor, Charles. 1995e. "Overcoming Epistemology." In *Philosophical Arguments*, 1–19. Cambridge, MA/London: Harvard University Press.

Taylor, Charles. 1995f. *Philosophical Arguments*. Cambridge/London: Harvard University Press.

Taylor, Charles. 1995g. "The Validity of Transcendental Arguments." In *Philosophical Arguments*, 20–33. Cambridge, MA/London: Harvard University Press.

Taylor, Charles. 1999. *A Catholic Modernity? Charles Taylor's Marianist Award Lecture*. Edited by James L Heft. New York, NY: Oxford University Press.

Taylor, Charles. 2003. "Ethics and Ontology." *The Journal of Philosophy* 100(6): 305–20.

Taylor, Charles. 2007. *A Secular Age*. Cambridge/London: Belknap Press of Harvard University Press.

Taylor, Charles. 2011a. *Dilemmas and Connections*. Cambridge/London: The Belknap Press of Harvard University Press.

Taylor, Charles. 2011b. "Disenchantment-Reenchantment." In *Dilemmas and Connections*, 287–302. Cambridge, MA/London: Belknap Press of Harvard University Press.

Taylor, Charles. 2013. "Retrieving Realism." In *Mind, Reason, and Being-in-the-World. The McDowell-Dreyfus Debate*, edited by Joseph Schear, 61–90. New York, NY: Routledge.

Taylor, Charles. 2016. *The Language Animal: The Full Shape of the Human Linguistic Capacity*. Cambridge: The Belknap Press of Harvard University Press.

Taylor, Charles (with Dreyfus, Hubert). 2015. *Retrieving Realism*. Cambridge, MA: Harvard University Press.

Thiebaut, Carlos. 1993. "Charles Taylor: On the Improvement of Our Moral Portrait: Moral Realism, History of Subjectivity and Expressivist Language." *Praxis International* 13: 126–53.
Weinstock, Daniel. 1994. "The Political Theory of Strong Evaluation." In *Philosophy in an Age of Pluralism: the Philosophy of Charles Taylor in Question*, edited by James Tully and Daniel Weinstock, 171–93. Cambridge, MA: Cambridge University Press.
White, Stephen. 2000. *Sustaining Affirmation: the Strengths of Weak Ontology in Political Theory*. Princeton, NJ: Princeton University Press.
Williams, Bernard. 1990. "Republican and Galilean: Review of *Sources of the Self*." *The New York Review of Books* 37(November 8): 45–48.

Chapter 1

The Doctrine of Strong Evaluation

This chapter pursues the development of Taylor's employment of the concept of strong evaluation from his first philosophical papers until his most recent writings. The term "strong evaluation" first appears in "Responsibility for Self" (Taylor 1976), a paper that was revised and republished in *Philosophical Papers* as "What is Human Agency?" (1985e). This is the first and only text that is exclusively about strong evaluation. However, Taylor has constant recourse to the term in his key articles and books, and takes it up most recently in *The Language Animal* (2016, 63, 192, 199).[1] In Taylor's most basic definition, "strong evaluation" depicts an ethical kind of reflection that involves "distinctions of worth" (1985b, 3). As noted in the Introduction, this term refers to the reality that human beings understand themselves not by simply having certain desires but by *evaluating* them in terms of worthiness, and so rank some of their desires, inclinations, and choices as higher or more important than others.

Although strong evaluation is introduced in *Philosophical Papers*, it occurs most frequently in part I of *Sources of the Self*, a section that, as Taylor explains, draws attention to the "relation between self and morals" by having recourse to "moral phenomenology," and sets out to explore the "moral ontology" behind our moral and spiritual intuitions (1989, x, 8–10, 68, 74, 81). As will emerge, it is not just that strong evaluation straddles Taylor's various approaches; more importantly, he uses this concept to *connect* his positions on topics that have been on his mind across the full range of his diverse writings: philosophical anthropology, ethics, and ontology.

This chapter begins with an overview of the different themes that revolve around strong evaluation, while also showing that Taylor's earliest writings can be seen as an illuminating prologue to it (section 1.1). I then examine the genesis of strong evaluation in *Philosophical Papers* and *Sources of the Self* and the modifications in the original explanation of strong evaluation as Taylor employs it in more recent writings (section 1.2). I continue to discuss basic criticisms and misunderstandings that have resulted from certain changes of emphasis in Taylor's employment of the concept of strong evaluation, and finally conclude by criticizing one interpretation that fundamentally misreads Taylor's intentions (section 1.3).[2]

1.1 PROLOGUE

1.1.1 Debunking Naturalism

Thematically, the following subjects revolve around strong evaluation: Taylor's overall critique of reductionist modes of thinking, his philosophical anthropology, his moral phenomenology, and his views on ontology. The first component is an ongoing critique of (moral, social, epistemological, ontological) theories that, on Taylor's reading, reduce, deny, suppress, or repudiate altogether the phenomenon of strong evaluation. It is not just that he is not satisfied with reductive approaches to human action and experience. Rather, Taylor is not even sure that his opponents see the issue that he is trying to delineate about strong evaluation. He has, therefore, invested a great deal of effort in developing two distinct—yet closely related—arguments against the reductionist outlook that he believes is thriving: a philosophical anthropology and a moral phenomenology.

Although these arguments lay separate claims, they are entangled in such a fundamental way that the two can hardly be separated. Taylor believes that selfhood and morality are "inextricably intertwined" themes, because "our notion of the self is inextricably connected with our understanding of our moral predicament and moral agency" (1989, 3; 1988, 298). From an argumentative viewpoint, the fusion of philosophical anthropology and ethics provides Taylor with an argument that poses a double challenge to reductionism. Reductionist theories have been wrong on both counts, Taylor maintains, arguing that they make sense neither of the ways in which human beings live their lives nor of moral experience. In this way, he argues that the imagined agents of utilitarian and naturalist theory would be an "impossibly shallow character" and a "monster," respectively, whereas what we need to clarify in ethics is precisely how basic human lives are lived (1985e, 26; 1989, 32, 58). He also criticizes much modern and contemporary moral philosophy for having a "cramped" and "truncated" view of morality (1989, 3), unable to come to grips with the very ways in which people "think, reason, argue, and question ourselves about morality" (1989, 7).

As these claims indicate, the context in which Taylor introduces strong evaluation is first and foremost a polemical one. Strong evaluation may therefore best be understood by contrasting it with what it denies. In a reflection on his major writings, Taylor summarizes *Philosophical Papers* as a collection of "mostly critiques of mechanistic, and/or reductive, and/or atomistic approaches to human sciences" that depend on "faulty philosophical thinking and/or obviously over-simplified views of human life" in their attempts to model human on natural science (2007a). In particular, as he explains in the introduction to *Philosophical Papers*, Taylor's target is the commitment to "naturalism" that in his view is shared by all reductive theories (1985b, 2). The attack on naturalism is a central motivation of Taylor's thought. Like the argument against psychological behaviorism in *The Explanation of Behaviour* (1964), it can generally be seen as a critique of a certain type of understanding of human agency. Strong evaluation comes in at the heart of this critique as a positive, counterthesis about the self. Taylor calls his rival account "philosophical anthropology"—perhaps because of, rather than despite, his impression that this term seems to make English-speaking philosophers "uneasy" (1985b, 1).

Taylor has been quite consistent in his multiple descriptions of naturalism. His most basic definition depicts naturalism as a particular view about "science and human nature" (1989, 531, note 47), that is, the view that human nature is to be understood "according to the canons which emerged in the seventeenth-century revolution in natural science" (1985b, 2). After *Philosophical Papers*, naturalism is described as "the belief that we ought to understand human beings in terms continuous with the sciences of extra-human nature" (1989, 80) and as "the belief that humans as part of nature are in the end best understood by sciences continuous in their methods and ontology with modern natural science" (1995b, 137). In a more recent paper, Taylor adds the notion of "ethical" naturalism, that is, "the view that arises among thinkers for whom seeing humans as part of nature means seeing their behavior and life form as ultimately explicable in terms that are consonant with modern natural science" (2003, 306). In another recent work, he also writes about "scientific" naturalism, which aims to "account for the actions, feelings, intentions, etc. of persons from the 'objective, third-personal perspective' that natural scientists adopt" (2013, 88, note 15; 2015, 15, note 16).

Refuting all these naturalisms, Taylor's main concern is that crucial features of human life precisely disappear by adopting a scientific stance. Yet he sees a broader "naturalist temper" not just in the outlooks of "many students of the sciences of human behavior" but in our Western culture as such, "stopping short frequently of explicit espousal of full-blooded naturalism, but tending to be suspicious of the things that naturalism cannot accommodate" (1964, 3; 1995b, 137). This observation—that most people are reluctant to fully embrace naturalism and yet remain highly skeptical of all things that do not fit the naturalist model—I want to argue, is *the* underlying theme of Taylor's doctrine of strong evaluation.

Taylor's distinctive brand of morality can be considered as the entry point through which his thinking moves from philosophical anthropology to ethics. Yet it also provides access to another branch of his thoughts on strong evaluation: ontology. Moving beyond mere philosophical-anthropological and moral-phenomenological claims, Taylor has been developing a third counterargument to naturalism. Compared with his philosophical anthropology and moral phenomenology, what is striking about Taylor's ontological perspective is that it challenges his opponents, as it were, from the opposite direction. That is, rather than argue (both anthropologically and phenomenologically) that naturalist theories paint a false picture of human *subjectivity* in general and moral experience in particular, he now criticizes them for neglecting the *objectivity* of the good over the moral agent. In this respect, Taylor warns us that moral thinking can easily slide into a "celebration of our creative powers," whereas ethics "at its best" is precisely an attempt to "surmount subjectivism" (1989, 510). The explicit nonanthropocentric nature of Taylor's ontological thought seems to indicate a different line of argumentation, allowing it to be discussed on top of his anthropological and phenomenological arguments. As these points suggest, his arguments stop neither at philosophical-anthropological levels nor at moral-phenomenological ones, as Taylor's distinctive nonanthropocentric viewpoint steers a middle course between a Platonic type of moral realism and ethical subjectivism.

At this early stage, though, all this remains to be argued out by examining in more detail the specific ways in which Taylor connects strong evaluation with issues of philosophical anthropology, ethics, and ontology. For now, it suffices to note that (1) strong evaluation is rooted in a critique of naturalist approaches to human agency; (2) it informs both Taylor's philosophical-anthropological counterthesis about the self and his phenomenological approach to ethics; and (3) the issue further raises questions of ontology that reach beyond philosophical anthropology and moral phenomenology.

1.1.2 The Early Writings

The polemical thrust of strong evaluation can be traced back a bit further. In this respect, Nicholas Smith points out that Taylor is skeptical of reductive analysis already at the beginning of his academic career, inspired by the linguistic philosophy that flourished at Oxford in the 1950s.[3] Yet, Taylor also emphasizes the limits of linguistic analysis when he asserts that "most philosophical problems can't be solved simply by the study of ordinary language," arising as they do in "such bodies of doctrine as theology, metaphysics or science or on the borderline between these and ordinary fact" (1959b, 107). In fact, he explains in another early paper that some issues are better understood as "ontological" rather than as "linguistic" in that some strata of our language "presuppose a 'world' in which the things and happenings we speak about in the other strata cannot find a place" (1959a, 136). What is both intriguing and extremely puzzling about this text is that Taylor at once connects naturalism, philosophical anthropology, language, and ontology when he says:

> The problems are posed by the advance of science, or at least by a greater awareness of the nature of the world around us. Once we begin to talk about nature in terms that are not animistic, we begin to wonder about persons, for they, after all, are parts of nature, are material objects also. But we want to say that they are something "more" as well. (1959a, 138)

This brings us back to the above observation that despite the inclination to make sense of our world in naturalist terms, we are equally inclined to think that human behavior is in some way fundamentally different from the processes studied by natural scientists. It is this problem, it would seem, that has led the young Taylor to the terrain of philosophical anthropology, the opening theme of his doctoral dissertation, published as *The Explanation of Behaviour* (1964). As will emerge, it is in this philosophical-anthropological context that he initiates his concept of strong evaluation.

There is, however, a third early text in which Taylor explores an additional philosophical area. Evoked perhaps by the drawbacks of linguistic philosophy, the young Taylor also shows an interest in Merleau-Ponty's attempt to describe the "pre-objective" world preceding the (limited) world of reductive, scientific discourse.[4] Yet, on Taylor's reading, the method of phenomenological reduction that is supposed to open up the content of "original" experience and to make possible a "pure" description simply cannot succeed. As he says, suspending one concept for reexamination fundamentally requires that "others are taken for granted in order to carry out this examination," which shows that reflection on our concepts is "much too sophisticated an activity to be undertaken without the use of concepts" (1959b, 102–103). In this respect, Taylor adds elsewhere, "the very attempt to describe the pre-predicative seems to destroy it. This confusion in method is nowhere clarified by Merleau-Ponty" (1958, 113).

I will not discuss Taylor's engagement with Merleau-Ponty's phenomenology here.[5] For present purposes, it suffices to illustrate how Taylor's attack on naturalism and his early writings set the stage for his "official" account of strong evaluation. Three points can be made here. First, Taylor's thought is triggered by a kind of frustration or dissatisfaction with views that were dominant at the beginning of his career, both with naturalist types of understanding of human agency and with the philosophical methods of linguistic analysis and phenomenology. He chides naturalism for having an oversimplified view of human action, criticizes linguistic philosophers for their conviction that "all philosophical problems arise from mistakes about language," and rejects Merleau-Ponty's phenomenology because of its underlying notion that "we can do without our concepts" (1959b, 109). Second, Taylor seems to be convinced right at the outset that all naturalist explanations are necessarily reductive, and that all reductive explanations of human behavior are insufficient.[6] Third, although the young Taylor's multiple investigations of linguistic philosophy, ontology, and phenomenology ultimately orient him around philosophical anthropology, he does not want to stick to the principles of a specific philosophical method in approaching these issues. Nonetheless, the seemingly unrelated early writings raise a central question about the nature of agency to which Taylor's more mature answer is, as we will see, strong evaluation. I will examine this question in more detail in the next section by discussing the most informative text about strong evaluation: "What is Human Agency?"

1.2 GENESIS AND DEVELOPMENT

1.2.1 Philosophical Anthropology of Strong Evaluation

Against the naturalist trend in contemporary philosophy, Taylor has been proposing a philosophical-anthropological outlook that stresses the difference between human nature and mere physical nature. He develops this view in the paper "What is Human Agency?" (1985e) by invoking Harry Frankfurt's concept of "second-order" desires, that is, a desire to "want to have (or not to have) certain desires and motives" (Frankfurt 1971, 5). For example, when I am asked how I will act when faced with a drowning child while I am eating an ice cream at the beach, I will most likely reply that I would be inclined to save the child rather than to continue to enjoy my ice cream. The preference for having a desire to save the child rather than to identify with the desire for ice cream is a desire of the second order. Obviously, I do not care about having a desire for ice cream or not, but I do care about my desire to save a human life if the occasion arises. In the case of arbitrating between different desires, I am concerned with what my will *should* be. According to both Frankfurt and Taylor, this reflective act of caring about my will refers to something distinctively human, namely "the capacity for reflective self-evaluation" or, in Taylor's terms, "the power to *evaluate* our desires" (Frankfurt 1971, 11; Taylor 1985e, 16, original emphasis).

Yet Taylor also believes that the nature of human agency allows for a further distinction between "two broad kinds of evaluation of desire," that is, between "weak" and "strong" evaluation (1985e, 16). His most significant modification of Frankfurt's theory is that he speaks of the worthiness of desires rather than their desirability, as Taylor's leading notion is that being a human agent not only involves a basic understanding of oneself as the locus of one's desires and choices, but also seeing oneself against a background of qualitative distinctions, that is, "a background of distinctions between things which are recognized as of categoric or unconditioned or higher importance or worth, and things which lack this or are of lesser value" (1985b, 3).

From this perspective, I am engaged in "weak" evaluation when the worth of my desires is left outside my reflection on them. In this way, I could weigh desired actions simply to determine the most attractive option (1985e, 16). For example, during my stay at the beach, I might be hesitating between buying a vanilla or a strawberry ice cream. If I ultimately opt for vanilla, I do so not because there is something more worthy about eating vanilla ice cream, but just because I feel like it. By contrast, the central feature of "strong" evaluations is that they involve distinctions of worth and the *classification* of desires in such terms as higher and lower, admirable and contemptible, and noble and base (1985e, 16). In the case of the drowning child, it is because I see saving a human life as more worthy than enjoying ice cream that I ultimately decide to ignore the ice cream's appeal. Again, I would rather be someone who wants to save a human life than someone who prefers enjoying ice cream to saving a drowning child.

The paper "What is Human Agency?" has set the basis of the doctrine of strong evaluation. Most of the other essays in *Philosophical Papers* in which the notion of strong evaluation is brought up are alternative formulations of earlier points, apart from some minor additions.[7] However, Taylor does not stop at simply drawing a distinction between weak and strong evaluation. His next step is to argue that strong evaluation is "inescapable" in our self-understanding and experience and that strong evaluations are "inseparable" from our nature as agents (1985e, 33–34). Put differently, as Taylor envisages it, strong evaluation is essential to being human, that is, it is one of "the basic categories in which man and his behavior is to be described and explained" (1964, 4). His aim is, therefore, to demonstrate that strong evaluation cannot be rejected without losing the very concept of a human agent, and to show that human action *must* involve a background of distinctions of worth. At this early stage, however, Taylor admits not to having made a sound philosophical anthropology out of his central concept of strong evaluation just yet (1985e, 27–28).

As we shall see (in chapter 3), it is not until *Sources of the Self* that Taylor will advance the discussion of "What is Human Agency?" by developing a transcendental argument concerning strong evaluation, defending the picture of a strong evaluator as an account of the transcendental conditions of human life (1989, 32). For now, however, I would first like to highlight the characteristic way in which Taylor continues to employ the concept of strong evaluation after *Philosophical Papers* both as a philosophical-anthropological term and as a moral-phenomenological concept. That is, he will be expanding his understanding of strong evaluation by clarifying it as central to human agency and morality alike.

1.2.2 Ethics of Strong Evaluation

After setting the stage in *Philosophical Papers*, the doctrine of strong evaluation is continued in *Sources of the Self*, most centrally in the first part of this book (1989, 3–107). Taylor opens with the claim that a large part of contemporary moral philosophy has accredited a too "narrow" view of morality by focusing on the definition of moral obligation rather than the nature of the good life (1989, 3). Against this background, he announces to develop a much broader conception of morality in order to retrieve the "richer background languages" behind our everyday moral practice (1989, 3–4). For this project, Taylor thus needs a wider concept than what is usually labeled with the term "moral." This is where the notion of strong evaluation comes in, as he uses it to cover both moral issues in a narrow sense and other questions beyond the moral. What these "nonmoral" questions have in common with moral issues (in a narrow sense) is that they all involve distinctions of worth or "strong evaluation." That is,

> they involve discriminations of right or wrong, better or worse, higher or lower, which are not rendered valid by our own desires, inclinations, or choices, but rather stand independent of these and offer standards by which they can be judged. (1989, 4)

In part I of *Sources of the Self*, Taylor mainly uses strong evaluation to endorse his broad conception of morality. In this respect, he acknowledges that he is following Bernard Williams' distinction between morality and ethics, by which "morality" is used for the narrower domain of obligatory action as a subcategory of the ethical, and "ethics" for the wider domain of strong evaluation, including issues of dignity and what is a good or worthwhile life (1989, 53). However, in the larger, historical part of the book (parts II–V), Taylor starts employing the concept of strong evaluation in a more critical way. A great deal of effort is invested into showing how and why modern and contemporary moral theories cannot find a conceptual place for strong evaluation. The main target is the naturalist ethics of classical utilitarianism, which he criticizes for excluding strong evaluation altogether by constructing ethics exclusively out of simple de facto desires, thereby leaving no room for our commonsense recognition of higher and lower values (1989, 249).

Taylor then argues that, despite its intention to do so, utilitarian theory does not abandon strong evaluation at all. On the one hand, he explains, the utilitarian reduction of human motivation to mere pleasure seems to eliminate all strong evaluative motivations; that is, it eliminates the commonsense recognition that "certain goals or ends make a claim on us, are incommensurable with our other desires and purposes" (1989, 332). Yet, on the other hand, the utilitarian himself engages in strong evaluation by stressing the moral importance of ordinary human happiness and universal benevolence (1989, 336). In other words, utilitarianism would not be an ethical theory without adhering to a moral ideal, that is, without an object of strong evaluation, something higher that commands our allegiance. This is why, as Taylor explains, the utilitarian sees sympathy not as a simple motivation but as a "strongly valued" one, that is, something you "ought" to feel because it is part of a "higher" way of being (1989, 337). The problem with a utilitarian, naturalist ethics of this kind thus is that it is incomprehensible as an *ethical* theory. As a *naturalist* ethics, it makes a point of rejecting the distinction between higher and lower goods, whereas as a naturalist *ethics*, it endorses this distinction itself.

Central to Taylor's criticism of utilitarianism is the notion of "incommensurability" or "incomparability."[8] Both terms invoke an experience that he claims to be indubitable and beyond cavil, namely that we recognize that there is a "higher" way of acting or living, as opposed to a more debased one. This sense, however, is precisely what the utilitarian agent lacks. As a utilitarian, I respond only to quantitative differences between desires and goals.[9] When I hesitate between vanilla and strawberry ice cream, my reflection is of the weak, utilitarian type to the extent that I do not feel constrained at all to choose either one. I can literally do as I "please." I might even choose to buy a drink instead or decide to neither eat nor drink, and to take a nap. However, in the case of strong evaluations, a declared lack of interest is such that it shows you up as being "blind" or "insensitive" to issues of fundamental importance (1985a, 239). When faced with the drowning child, I could not abstain from trying to save the child by insisting that I have other goals and desires too, say, that I prefer enjoying an ice cream or feel like taking a nap. Clearly, I would hate myself if I had ignored the child, or if I stopped caring about people being murdered, or tortured, or raped. Incommensurability here thus means that I class my goals and desires in a way that some of them simply become irrelevant. The desire for ice cream just does not "weigh" at all in the face of a drowning child. Yet the imagined agent of utilitarian theory is far from being an agent in the above sense as the "complete" utilitarian would be an "impossibly shallow character," seeking to fulfill desires without even considering the qualitative distinctions that normal, sane human beings find basic and important (1985e, 26).

In terms of strong and weak evaluation, the utilitarian agent can be seen as a paradigmatic weak evaluator, a "simple weigher of alternatives" (1985e, 23).[10] For Taylor, this person would be hard to view as human, because it is precisely the capacity for second-order desires that captures the distinctively human. In fact, the whole point of Taylor's picture of a weak evaluator is to prove its implausibility, that is, to make the case that no one actually acts as utilitarian theory would have us do, nor wants to do so: as human beings, we are not concerned with mere outcomes, but with what our will is to be in terms of higher and lower goals. Taylor explains the notion of incommensurably higher value in crucial reference to Kant, who clarified this issue in terms of the distinction between the categorical and the hypothetical. As Taylor argues, to recognize higher and lower value is to recognize "the distinction that Kant drew between hypothetical and categorical imperatives" (1985a, 238). Furthermore, he continues, Kant tried to capture the sense of the incommensurably higher with his notion of "Achtung" that we feel before the moral law (1985a, 240).

At the same time, however, Taylor also criticizes Kant for developing a too narrow definition of ethics as consisting of a single set of considerations or calculations (1985a, 233). This means, in other words, that Taylor both endorses and opposes Kant's approach to ethics. On the one hand, he explicitly takes his cue from Kant's notion of ethics as involving higher goods that command our respect beyond mere desirability. On the other hand, he proposes to "extend a Kantian analysis beyond the case of the unambiguously moral" (1985a, 240), that is, to sustain the central place of the incommensurably higher in moral thought while also extending the definition of morality beyond a narrow understanding.[11] Whereas Kant's boundary between the categorical and the hypothetical is meant to distinguish the moral from the nonmoral, Taylor employs a broad definition of morality precisely to capture the *diversity* of goods behind our languages of strong evaluation, that is, to include not just those we call "moral," but also, for example, goods in the aesthetic domain (1985a, 238).

Taylor then continues the initial argument of "The Diversity of Goods" (1985a) in *Sources of the Self* (1989) by arguing that much contemporary moral theorizing is reductive in that it has room neither for strong value nor for qualitative contrasts, the incommensurability higher, and the diversity of goods. However, in this book, Taylor seems to have dropped the philosophical-anthropological terminology of the original context of strong evaluation in "What is Human Agency?" (1985e). Instead, he uses strong evaluation increasingly to endorse his moral philosophy, which he now calls exploring "moral phenomenology" (1989, 68, 74, 81). The emphasis in the doctrine of strong evaluation thus shifts from an initial philosophical-anthropological concern for the distinctively human toward a phenomenological account of moral experience that centers on strong evaluation in subsequent writings.

What is involved in this particular type of phenomenology is explained in the paper "Explanation and Practical Reason" (1995a), the only text of *Philosophical Arguments* that takes note of the concept of strong evaluation. In this paper, Taylor seeks to undermine the naturalist conception of morality as a human projection on a neutral world by defending our commonsense moral reactions. He explains:

> The attempt is to show, in one way or another, that the vocabularies we need to explain human thought, action, feeling, or to explicate, analyze, justify ourselves or each other, or to deliberate on what to do, all inescapably rely on strong evaluation. [. . .] It tries to show us that in all lucidity we cannot understand ourselves, or each other, cannot make sense of our lives or determine what to do, without accepting a richer ontology than naturalism allows, without thinking in terms of strong evaluation. (1995a, 38–39)

He calls the appeal to moral common sense the "*ad hominem* mode of practical reasoning," a logic that in Taylor's view is "central to the whole enterprise of moral clarification" (1995a, 37). As mentioned earlier (in the Introduction), Taylor argues for the connection between philosophical anthropology and ethics by developing an *ad hominem* perspective that strategically appeals to widely shared moral beliefs and values, such as respect for human life. Yet, he continues, it is precisely the inclination of "the naturalist temper, with its hostility to the very notion of strong evaluation [. . .] to make the *ad hominem* argument seem irrelevant to ethical dispute" (1995a, 59). Here we see Taylor expressing his central concern from yet another angle: while most people remain quite unattracted by the naturalist attempt to invalidate basic moral responses, because on the contrary their moral reactions strike them as being right in a fundamental way, they can anxiously doubt whether, say, a strong sense of disgust with killing innocent people can really be justified. The naturalist, then, typically encourages this sense of doubt by arguing that merely the *experience* of moral demands such as respect and benevolence proves nothing about what we *ought* to do. To put it in classical philosophical terms, to invoke our moral experience to decide issues of practical reason is to commit the notorious "naturalistic fallacy," falsely deriving an "ought" from an "is."

In Taylor's view, however, this charge is flawed, because it is based on a crucial misunderstanding about the nature of moral goals. Obviously, the fact that I have a strong desire, for example, for vanilla ice cream, does by itself nothing to show that I ought to desire it. But in Taylor's view this is-ought objection is simply beside the point, as it applies only to our weakly evaluated goals, not the ones we recognize as moral. Let me flesh this out.

The crucial point of strong evaluation is that we experience some of our desires and goals as more significant than others. It is these goods that really "matter" to us as agents, that is, they determine the degree of fulfillment in our lives. Because of this, we identify with these strong commitments in such a fundamental way—and this is the main thrust of the argument—that we cannot really reject them entirely. If, for some strange reason, I suddenly stopped caring about people drowning, I cannot just shrug my shoulders and say that I do not "feel like" caring about drowning victims today. To do so would seem both terribly strange and terribly frightening. In contrast, I do not think of my desire for vanilla ice cream in these terms. If, for example, I feel more like strawberry ice cream today, yesterday's preference for vanilla ice cream would simply no longer have a claim on me. In the case of strong evaluations, however, the fact that we identify with a diversity of strong goods does nothing to reduce their respective claims. In fact, as Taylor puts it, "*we* would be shown up as insensitive or brutish or morally perverse" if we no longer felt the demand that strongly valued goods such as respect and benevolence make on us (1995a, 37, original emphasis).

In Taylor's view, this gives us an anchor for practical reason without committing the naturalistic fallacy because it shows that we "can't be lucid about ourselves without acknowledging that we value this end" (1995a, 37). In other words, in the case of strongly valued goals our deep commitments indeed show that we *ought* to desire these goods because without them we would lose the very possibility of being human agents in the full sense. It comes as no surprise, however, that this cannot be made intelligible from within a naturalist perspective that takes only our weaker, de facto desires as the ultimate justification for our actions.

Taylor's argument here against naturalism strongly resembles his *ad hominem* critique of utilitarianism, in that both critiques are directed against the imagined *agent* behind the "official" theory. These arguments are "interwoven" in the sense that they show, first, at the ethical level, that utilitarianism and naturalism paint a false picture of moral experience, and, second, at the philosophical-anthropological level, that the imagined agent behind these theories would be either an "impossibly shallow" one or a "monster" (1985e, 26; 1989, 32). In this way, Taylor counters the objection of the naturalistic fallacy by convincing us that the charge can be made only on a highly distorted picture of a human being, one that insists that human agents cannot be motivated by anything stronger than mere impulse. By contrast, in the light of Taylor's rivaling portrait of a strong evaluator, it is not a fallacious but an essential feature of human beings that they are able to derive "oughts" from their experience. From this perspective, a life that lacks such oughts will be lacking in humanness.

1.2.3 Ontology of Strong Evaluation

In the remaining writings about strong evaluation in the 1980s, Taylor mostly rearticulates one or more of the above anthropological or moral issues. After this period, Taylor uses the concept of strong evaluation far less often, and almost all occurrences are repetitions of points made earlier. In fact, when reading *A Secular Age* (2007b), one easily gets the impression that he has settled the issue of "strong evaluation." In this book—Taylor's most voluminous work—he abandons the term almost completely, as he refers to strong evaluation only twice, on both occasions in relatively insignificant ways (2007b, 544, 595). Considered against this background, it seems rather unlikely that the writings after *A Secular Age* will reraise the issue of strong evaluation. Surprisingly, though, Taylor does just that in the paper "Disenchantment-Reenchantment" (2011). Furthermore, it is not just that this text simply refers to strong evaluation, but rather embarks on a dimension that remained unexplored in Taylor's previous uses of the concept.

In "Disenchantment-Reenchantment," Taylor examines the contrast between what he calls the premodern "enchanted world," that is, "one filled with spirits and moral forces, and one moreover in which these forces impinged on human beings" and the modern "disenchanted" or "mind-centered" world in which (Taylor thinks) we live today: "A world in which the only locus of thoughts, feelings, and spiritual élan is what we call minds" (2011, 287, 288). More particularly, he wants to discuss the different status these contrasting worldviews give to typically human responses, and the perceptions, beliefs, and propositions humans have about the world that surrounds them. Labeling this cluster of thoughts and feelings with the term "human meaning," he then argues that it is peculiarly characteristic of the disenchanted view to locate human meanings exclusively "in" the mind, that is, that we are "explaining the meaning of things by *our* responses, and these responses are 'within' us, in the sense that they depend on the way we have been 'programmed' or 'wired up' inside" (2011, 289, 292, italics mine).

On this account, meaning appears as a function of how we as minds operate, and is projected on the outside world from our minds. Yet, if we look at the enchanted world, Taylor continues, we see a perplexing absence of the inner-outer boundary that seems to us so basic and commonsensical. This is mainly because, as he explains, the enchanted view placed meaning "within the cosmos," that is, the cosmos reflected a "Great Chain of Being," in which "meaning is already there in the object/agent; it is there quite independently of us; it would be there if we didn't exist" (2011, 291). What has all this got to do with strong evaluation? As it turns out in the rest of the text, Taylor uses the comparison enchantment-disenchantment to argue once more against the naturalist view that sees human meanings as arbitrary projections. His central concern comes down to this:

> When we have left the "enchanted" world of spirits, and no longer believe in the Great Chain, what sense can we make of the notion that nature or the universe which surrounds us is the locus of human meanings which are "objective," in the sense that they are not just arbitrarily projected through choice or contingent desire? (2011, 294)

Taylor's next step is to argue that it does not follow from the collapse of the enchanted worldview that we only arbitrarily confer human meanings today. To make this point, Taylor notes not only that "the attribution of these meanings counts for us as strong evaluations," but also that "underlying strong evaluations there is supposed to be *a truth of the matter*" (2011, 294, 297, italics mine). In fact, Taylor is now trying to bring out an issue that was only implicit in his former account of strong evaluation:

> The understanding behind strong evaluations is that they track some reality. [. . .] Put simply, our moral reactions suppose that they are responses to some reality, and can be criticized for misapprehension of this reality. [. . .] We can't just say that explanations of why we experience these meanings are irrelevant to their validity; that they stand on their own, because we *feel* them strongly. Our attributing these meanings makes a stronger claim. It lies in their nature as strong evaluations to claim truth, reality, or objective rightness. (2011, 297–98, original emphasis)

To be sure, these points closely resemble Taylor's reply to the naturalistic fallacy: the charge of falsely deriving normative claims from our experience is off the mark, because moral reactions make a claim beyond our de facto desires and instinctive reactions. As strong evaluations, they make assertions about the worthiness of goods rather than their desirability. Following the terminology of "Disenchantment-Reenchantment," we can now look into this by reflecting on the different types of human meaning involved in strong and weak evaluation. In weak evaluations, something is experienced as meaningful simply because we desire it, whereas in strong evaluation there is a use of "meaning" for which being desired is not sufficient. Indeed, some desires can be judged as unworthy or base. Therefore, the meaning that is manifested in our strongly evaluated motivations must in some way be different from the appeal coming from our desires. This raises a crucial question: If our experience shows that strong evaluations cannot be traced back to contingent desire, then how do we account for the moral meanings things have for us? Where does *that* appeal come from? More than anything else, however, this question is metaphysical.

The crux of the matter is that the issue of worthiness can arise only when our desires are related to some reality beyond these desires themselves that enables us to judge them. As we have seen in the preceding sections, this is the whole point of Taylor's doctrine of strong evaluation: to convince us that human agency cannot be understood without recognizing goods that are independent of our behaviors, wants, and needs. In Taylor's view, in other words, "disenchantment" does not in any way undermine the way we are motivated by such independent goods, yet he sees a strong tendency to reductive explanations of human life that aim to rule these out. More importantly, his claim that strong evaluations appeal to objective moral demands rather than subjective preferences shows the issue of strong evaluation in a rather different light. Thematically speaking, the portrait of strong evaluations as crucial responses to some independent reality enables him to draw attention to the *ontological* implications of strong evaluation.

Taylor makes this issue more explicit in the paper "Ethics and Ontology" by arguing that there is a lack of fit between our commonsense experience of strong evaluation, on the one hand, and "the ontology we allow ourselves as post-Galilean naturalists," on the other (2003, 319). In developing this critique, Taylor consistently has recourse to his image of morality as involving higher values by insisting that "ethics involves a range of 'values' that are essentially understood to be on a different level, to be in some way special, higher, or incommensurable with our other goals and desires," and that "we would not have a category like the ethical or the moral, unless this were so" (2003, 308). This moral phenomenology feeds into a full-out attack on naturalist ontology, which he criticizes for being reductive in general and for making the fact-value distinction a criterion of ethics in particular. He argues:

> Returning to the issue of naturalism, it is clear that this qualitative status of the ethical is a deep source of trouble. [. . .] it cannot see how values of an incommensurably higher range can have a place in post-Galilean nature. [. . .] the higher in this sense is one of the things expunged from the cosmos by post-Galilean science. It had its place in the great "chain of being," but not in the "mechanized" world picture. (2003, 309)

This raises a crucial question: If our strong evaluations cannot be made transparent to post-Galilean science, then how—if at all—can a disenchanted model, defining ontology in naturalistic terms, allow for our actual moral deliberation as strong evaluators? Taylor continues this discussion in his latest defense of "robust realism" by reraising the broader question of whether an account of "physical nature as meaningless" can be reconciled with an account of the cosmos as "having a meaning and human beings having a privileged place in it," while concluding that this seems an "unpromising strategy" since the basis of our science is to invoke "a universe whose causal laws take no account of us and our human meanings" (2015, 158–59). Regrettably, Taylor does not remark on how this metaphysical perspective relates to his earlier views, but I want to venture that his explicit rejection of "post-Galilean ontology" is an important change of emphasis as it deviates from both the philosophical-anthropological analysis in *Philosophical Papers* and the moral-phenomenological investigations in *Sources of the Self*.

We find Taylor's final articulation of strong evaluation in *The Language Animal* (2016). In this book, he only briefly mentions strong evaluation in developing his Romanticist "constitutive" theory of language, which states that language enables us (among other things) to be "responsive to issues of strong value" (2016, 37). In elaborating on this, Taylor explains that "certain crucial metabiological meanings" incorporate in human life a sense of "strong evaluation," here explained as arising in cases "where what is valued comes across to us as not depending on our desires or decisions" (2016, 192).

Taking the above points together—that is, after having pursued Taylor's use of strong evaluation from his very first writings up to his most recent publication—we can identify the following central features of the doctrine of strong evaluation:

1. The concept of strong evaluation finds its roots in Frankfurt's theory of second-order desires, and is introduced by Taylor to describe a structural feature of human agency.
2. Strong evaluation depicts a type of essentially human reflection based on qualitative distinctions concerning the worth of goods, and is contrasted with weak evaluation, in which a desire-based concept of evaluation is presupposed.
3. Strong evaluation informs both Taylor's philosophical-anthropological definition of human agency and his moral-phenomenological conception of moral experience.
4. As an ethical term, Taylor employs the concept of strong evaluation not only to elaborate his broad account of morality, but also to defend his understanding of ethics as involving incommensurably higher values and to criticize ethical theories that leave no room for strong evaluation.
5. Furthermore, strong evaluation is at the heart of Taylor's *ad hominem* account of practical reason, defending his moral phenomenology against naturalist views that tend to discredit our commonsense moral reactions for practical reason.
6. Finally, Taylor also uses the concept of strong evaluation in a more metaphysical sense by throwing a spotlight on the issues of truth, reality, and ontology that revolve around it.

Against this background, it seems a truism to say that such a comprehensive notion has evoked a wide variety of interpretations and critiques. I will consider some of these in the next sections.

1.3 STRONG EVALUATION IN QUESTION

1.3.1 Criticisms and Misunderstandings

As we have seen, the concept of strong evaluation is mostly fleshed out in the 1980s. Yet in a reply to his commentators five years after the publication of *Sources of the Self*, Taylor admits that he is still struggling to find the right term. In fact, he suggests that the whole concept of strong evaluation was a mistake: "My mistake was in using the word 'evaluation' [. . .] I should really find another term" (1994a, 249). Intriguingly, Taylor seems to be showing a similar doubt in his introduction of strong evaluation in "What is Human Agency?" As he explains, it is not just that the verb "evaluate" misleadingly suggests that our evaluations emerge only from *our* activity of evaluation, but also that the "Nietzschean" term "value" (implied by "evaluation") further suggests that values are mere "creations," which are not grounding in any reasons since they "ultimately repose on our espousing them" (1985e, 28–29). We sense immediately how far this is from Taylor's own conception of evaluation. His assertion that strong evaluations invoke "objective rightness" makes a more compelling claim than that we just want some things very strongly (2011, 298). Quite to the contrary, he defends the view that our strong responses involve truth claims rather than basic dispositions.

This explains why Taylor keeps on hesitating over the word "evaluation" to make this very point: while he wants to show that some of our evaluations are not rendered valid by our own desires or choices but by something stronger, he is acutely aware of how our modern vocabulary easily allows for misinterpretations of the concept of strong evaluation as something that emerges exclusively from us, as a function of our activity as "minds." I would like to look at some of these misinterpretations to bring out Taylor's rather paradoxical predicament, namely that some critiques of strong evaluation are symptomatic of the naturalistic, mind-centered view that Taylor seeks to undermine with this very concept.

To understand strong evaluation from within a naturalistic perspective is to understand it as a human-internal capacity, that is, to relate it to the functioning of the mind and the way that this affects one's behavior. This is the starting point of Owen Flanagan's discussion of the concept of strong evaluation: "Charles Taylor argues that the capacity for what he calls strong evaluation is a necessary feature of persons" (Flanagan 1996, 142). Flanagan then reconstructs Taylor's distinction between strong and weak evaluation as one between two ideal types of actual, living persons. I want to highlight how distortive this way of representing the doctrine of strong evaluation is.

Because, as Flanagan argues, Taylor "wants there to be a distinction between weak and strong evaluators" (1996, 146), we cannot be both: persons are *either* strong evaluators, who overrule their own desires "on the basis of some sort of ethical assessment," *or* they are weak evaluators, who do so "on the basis of other kinds of assessment" (1996, 144). Against this background, Flanagan seeks to show that "the distinction between weak and strong evaluators will be hard to draw in any unequivocal terms" (1996, 146). In so doing, he notes that Taylor has "no characterization of weak evaluation" because of his belief that "there are no persons who fit the description" (Flanagan 1996, 167, note 11). Moreover, when we observe that "there simply is no such thing as a pure strong evaluator" either, then it should be clear, Flanagan argues, that the whole contrast between strong and weak evaluation is rather useless:

> Normal persons sometimes behave wantonly; for example, we scratch where it itches. And even when we assess and evaluate our motives, we often do so in nonethical terms. Persons who go in for strong ethical evaluation often make vacation plans on the same basis as savvy weak evaluators. It would be unrealistic as well as excessively moralistic to think that they should do otherwise. (1996, 146)

Three points can be made here. First, Taylor gives a rather compelling description of a weak evaluator in his characterization of the impossibly shallow character of the classical utilitarian agent (1985e, 26). Put simply, this shows that the picture of a weak evaluator is not meant as a psychological profile, as Flanagan's reading suggests, but has a distinctively metaphoric function. That is, in order to show what human agency would be like without strong evaluation, Taylor argues that a "complete" utilitarian would no longer be recognized as human. Ruth Abbey makes the second point. As she clarifies, "Taylor is not suggesting that each and every choice an individual makes is the subject of strong evaluation. Some choices do not imply or invoke any sense of higher or lower value" (2000, 18). This explains that people might behave "wantonly" and "nonethical" in some cases, while in other cases making qualitative distinctions by adopting a second-order stance. The third point concerns Taylor's broad conception of morality, and it is made by Nicholas Smith when he explains that Flanagan's objection rests on a "too narrow construal of a moral concern" because "moral principles are only one way of characterizing one of the dimensions of strong value" (2002, 95). Taylor himself makes this explicit by emphasizing that languages of strong evaluation can also be "aesthetic and of other kinds as well" (1985e, 24, note 27).

All of the above points fly in the face of Flanagan's critique. But there is more. It is not just that his characterization of strong evaluation is based on an overly moralistic reading of Taylor's claims. More importantly, his psychologized understanding of a strong evaluator as "one who has well-developed capacities for specifically ethical evaluation" blocks out Taylor's crucial distinction between higher and lower goods (Flanagan 1996, 154). We can illustrate this by looking at another of Flanagan's doubts: "If we understand the ethical so broadly that anyone who evaluates her desires in terms of 'better' and 'worse' is a strong evaluator, then the person convinced of the superiority of her style, fashion, or social class will turn out to be a strong evaluator" (1996, 147).

Ironically, this is Taylor's point indeed, but he endorses it in a way that cannot be made intelligible on Flanagan's account. This is because Flanagan's criticism glosses over what Taylor calls the "very basis" for strong evaluation, that is, for there being desires or goals that are "intrinsically *worth* fulfilling" (1989, 383, original emphasis). Surely the point that qualitative distinctions are central to strong evaluation does not mean that "anything goes," in the sense that a strong evaluator arbitrarily chooses any good he or she likes. As the present analysis makes clear, strong evaluation involves goods that are seen as having incommensurably higher worth, goods that we ought to desire, even if we do not. Yet on Flanagan's characterization of the ethical as "notoriously observer-relative," all goals are weakly evaluated.[12] In this way, his critique betrays an understanding of the moral life that echoes the naturalistic approach Taylor opposes. In fact, the whole point of the distinction between strong and weak evaluation is precisely to contest a truncated view of morality as Flanagan's. The irony is that the challenge is not felt at all. In this respect, Flanagan's critique is a good example of how a reductive reading of strong evaluation hinders understanding.

Ultimately, it would seem that this is mainly due to Flanagan's reduction of strong evaluation to "the ability to condemn and override some of [one's] own desires as unworthy" (1996, 144). To see why this distorts the doctrine of strong evaluation is to understand Taylor's reservations about using the term "evaluation." To understand strong evaluation as an internal capacity implies that we can choose either to use or not to use this capability. This is particularly explicit when Flanagan remarks that persons who "don't *go in for* strong evaluation" simply do not act out of strong evaluation (1996, 154, italics mine). This way of putting the matter suggests that strong evaluation is ultimately our doing and thus optional, but it completely ignores the deeply social embeddedness of strong evaluations. As Mark Redhead aptly puts it, "given our dependence on language of qualitative contrast, we cannot simply choose to be an atheist one day and a Catholic the next" (2002, 162).

We can see, though, how the image of strong evaluations as simply our creations fits in with Flanagan's characterization of strong evaluation as a psychological feature of human beings: we are free to develop this particular capacity for ethical assessment or not. This picture brings us back to Taylor's suspicion that the term "evaluation" might easily encourage the idea that our strongly valued goods ultimately repose on our de facto commitment to them. Flanagan's reading of strong evaluation as an optional moralistic feature of human beings shows this to be a reasonable suspicion indeed.

Again, this interpretation cannot accommodate Taylor's point that some goods are seen as norms that exist independently of one's capacity for recognizing such goods. Against this background, the image of a weak evaluator is of very little use as a psychological profile because it is purely hypothetical, meant to support the imperative claim that strong evaluation is essential to full, ordinary human agency (1985b, 3). In other words, Taylor makes all these caricatures of human selves—the simple weigher of alternatives, the impossibly shallow utilitarian, the monster of naturalist theory—simply to show what would happen if strong evaluation were to be left out (simple weigher), disrupted (utilitarianism), or eliminated altogether (naturalism). If anything, he hopes to make one thing crystal clear: that we are not in any of these cases imagining a class of human beings.

There is another reason why Taylor hesitates over the word "evaluation": because of its overtones of critical reflection and contemplation. He explains:

> I don't consider it a condition of acting out of a strong evaluation that one has articulated and critically reflected on one's framework. Clearly this would be to set too narrow entry conditions. I mean simply that one is operating with a sense that some desires, goals, aspirations are qualitatively higher than others. [. . .] My mistake was in using the word "evaluation," with its overtones of reflection and deliberate opting for one alternative rather than another. I should really find another term. (1994a, 249)

One of the implications of understanding strong evaluation as an internal capacity is that there can be no strong evaluation without reflection and articulation. Yet Taylor rejects this rationalistic reading by speaking of a "sense" of qualitative distinction, thereby emphasizing that strong evaluation also has an *affective* dimension. Because of this double reflective-affective nature, the concept of strong evaluation has been criticized both for being too rationalistic and for having too strong an emotive connotation. Flanagan advocates the first type of critique. In his view, strong evaluation involves an overly rationalistic understanding of human beings. Paul Saurette seems to utter the opposing criticism when highlighting "the central role of commonsense recognition in Taylor's philosophy" (2005, 208). In the remainder of this section, I discuss both interpretations in an examination of the relationship between the reflective and the affective underpinnings of strong evaluation.

Flanagan argues that Taylor's distinction between strong and weak evaluation "does not usefully capture many types of persons," because "for one thing, it is too intellectualist" (1996, 152). He elaborates on this by referring to Taylor's view in *Philosophical Papers* that "strong evaluation is essentially linked to articulateness" as articulateness is "necessary" for strong evaluation (Flanagan 1996, 154–55). One of the drawbacks of "Taylor's heavily intellectualist picture" is that it cannot allow for "identity in people whose lives are guided by cares, concerns, imports, and commitments, but who are, for whatever reason and to whatever degree, inarticulate about them" (1996, 157–58). Yet Flanagan also observes that Taylor starts to write about strong evaluation rather differently in *Sources of the Self* by speaking of a "sense" of a qualitative distinction, and by arguing that one's framework does not necessarily need to be articulated "theoretically" (1989, 20). However, as Flanagan rightly emphasizes, this change in emphasis in *Sources of the Self* is in tension with the articulacy requirement in *Philosophical Papers*.

How should we understand this tension? Clearly, the importance of the notion of articulation in Taylor's oeuvre cannot be overstated. It is not just that articulation is central to *Philosophical Papers*, but also that Taylor keeps on emphasizing the importance of articulation on several locations in *Sources of the Self*. For example, he writes that we can discover the meaning of life "through articulating" it (1989, 18). Furthermore, the third chapter, titled "Ethics of Inarticulacy" (1989, 53–90), is exclusively about the importance of articulacy for ethics, and how modern moral philosophy, as Taylor understands it, fails to articulate the goods on which its theories are based. He continues to underline the importance of articulation in the fourth chapter by arguing that articulation can bring us "closer" to the good; that there seem to be "very strong reasons in favor of articulacy" wherever goods serve as moral sources; and, moreover, that without any articulation whatsoever, we would "lose contact with the good" (1989, 92, 96, 97). In a move that parallels his broad definition of morality, Taylor has explained elsewhere to be using also the notions of "language" and "articulation" in an "unusually broad" sense, because this enables us to see more lucidly in this area (1989, 91; 1991, 253):

> Of course, when I speak of "articulation" here, I mean more than formulation in what might be recognized as theoretical terms, in some philosophical or theological doctrine. Our sense of [. . .] goods is fleshed out, and passed on, in a whole range of media: stories, legends, portraits of exemplary figures and their actions and passions, as well as in artistic works, music, dance, ritual, modes of worship, and so on. (1997, 179)

Against this background, the central point of Taylor's emphasis on articulation seems clear enough: only articulated goods can be truly motivating, expressed either in linguistic descriptions and philosophical prose or in expressions beyond the bounds of language as normally conceived.

But what about the emotive aspect? What is this "sense" of qualitative distinction that is also distinctive of strong evaluation? We can illustrate the affective dimension by looking at Saurette's interpretation, who argues that it is not so much the appeal to our powers of expression, but to our "affective moral common sense" that characterizes Taylor's doctrine of strong evaluation (2005, 214). He explains, "while sometimes using overly rationalist language to describe our 'moral responses' (e.g., he calls strong evaluations 'assessments')," Taylor nonetheless asserts that such responses are "more accurately described as 'anchored in feelings, emotions, aspirations and could not motivate us unless they were'" (Saurette 2005, 215).[13] When we further acknowledge Taylor's statement in *Sources of the Self* that the "most reliable" moral view must be "grounded on our strongest intuitions" (1989, 75), it should be clear, Saurette argues, that "Taylor's account explicitly rests on an articulation of the visceral and affective intuitions of our commonsense moral recognition" (2005, 214). He then makes an insightful connection between this appeal to common sense and Taylor's image of morality as involving higher goods. As Saurette observes,

> How are we sure that we all experience and rely on strong evaluation? Because we all *feel* admiration and respect or contempt and disgust in certain circumstances, and these emotions are inseparable from a framework of strong evaluation. [. . .] According to Taylor, "these emotions are bound up with our sense that there are higher and lower goals and activities. I would like to claim that if we did not mark these contrasts, if we did not have a sense of the incommensurably higher, then these emotions would have no place in our lives." Since we all have these emotions, we all must share an imperative image of morality as strong evaluation. (2005, 214)[14]

In other words, Taylor does not stop at discussing basic moral feelings but adds that we can only have these strong reactions if—and only if—we understand morality as involving goods that are in some way higher than, or incommensurable with, our other goals and desires. This point—that Taylor invokes moral common sense to authorize and empower his conception of morality as involving higher goods—is well taken when we recall Taylor's strategic appeal to Kant's notion of *Achtung* in developing his views on ethics (1985a, 240).

1.3.2 Reflective or Affective?

In the above section, we have seen how the double reflective-affective nature of strong evaluation has triggered criticisms from opposite directions. On the one hand, Taylor's emphasis on articulacy about the good has allowed a rationalistic interpretation of strong evaluation. On the other hand, the analysis of how strong evaluation is rooted in moral feelings made it clear that this is a rather one-sided interpretation. Moreover, it was noted that Taylor's appeal to moral common sense does not simply stand on its own, as it also informs and validates his understanding of morality as involving higher goods.

Smith provides a more radical interpretation. For him, the fact that articulation is neither necessary nor sufficient for strong evaluation is enough to abandon the term "strong evaluation," and to replace it with "strong value." As he argues, "the notion of strong value [. . .] is more fundamental than the notion of strong evaluation," considering, first, that strong evaluations "make explicit the sense of worth the evaluator has in his pre-reflective life," and, second, that "we do not have to be engaged in deliberation to have a sense that things differ in quality or worth" (Smith 2002, 91). Yet on closer inspection, Smith's reconceptualization not only overstates the affective aspect of strong evaluation, but also overlooks Taylor's insistence on the importance of articulation. Let me flesh this out.

On the one hand, Smith rightfully stresses that "strong value is logically and ontologically prior to strong evaluation" (2002, 94–95) in that in most contexts the meaning of strong evaluation is, as Abbey puts it, "closer to an intuitive judgment or response than to the outcome of a reasoned, reflective process" (2000, 19). We can easily imagine a host of situations in which this is so. But such "instant" responses are no small feats. Consider what is involved in the example of the drowning child. To begin with, I have to recall my belief that human life is of ultimate value, incommensurable with my desire for ice cream. Then I have to resist the temptation of the ice cream, throw the ice cream away, and hurry toward the water in an attempt to save the child. To act at all, I thus have to have recourse to an implicit hierarchy of goals and desires in a way that some of these become irrelevant. The point here is not just that moral goods make a demand on us, but that in many situations the demand is so strong that our considerations remain completely implicit. We just know right off. In these cases—and this seems a very persuasive reason in favor of the notion of strong value—it is therefore rather deceptive to speak of strong "evaluation," because the sense of qualitative contrast is so strong that we simply do not *need* to reflect.

On the other hand, Smith's insistence on the notion of strong value leaves out something crucial about the phenomenon of strong evaluation, because it neglects the immense potential Taylor ascribes to the human capacity for articulation. To be sure, Taylor's description of moral intuitions as so deeply engraved that they are "almost like instincts" (1989, 5) does encourage the idea that the strong value they convey is more fundamental than the evaluations we engage in on account of them. But Taylor makes a crucial *distinction* between instinctive and moral reactions precisely to stress that only our moral reactions "involve *claims*, implicit or explicit, about the nature and status of human beings" (1989, 5, italics mine). In this regard, moral reactions differ from other "gut" responses, such as our nausea at certain smells, because, unlike the moral case, we generally do not think that there is something more to articulate beyond our instinctive feeling of disgust. Thus while a reaction such as nausea is just a brute fact, we "*argue and reason* over what and who is a fit object of moral respect" (1989, 6, italics mine). The very distinction between strong and weak evaluation makes the same point. While it is true that weak evaluators can be articulate to some extent (they can express whether they really feel like A or B), they cannot explain their preferences but for the fact that they are preferences. They lack the language to articulate the deeper issues of what these desires express "in the way of modes of life" (1985e, 26). However, we lose sight of this distinction between a poor and a richer language when we opt for strong value—with its overtones of sensibility, emotion, and instinct—instead of strong evaluation.

Against this background, the concept of strong evaluation appears more fundamental than the concept of strong value, for although the process of strong evaluation often is pre-reflective or inarticulate, people make sense of their lives only by giving *reasons* for their feelings and responses. That is, without an explanation of why certain feelings and responses reflect a stronger sense of value than others, these experiences would be just as unintelligible and empty as our instinctive, gut responses. Such a picture of strong evaluation is clearly at odds with Taylor's view that our strong responses capture goods that we *ought* to feel, and that someone who fails to sense these goods is missing something essential.

Strong evaluation thus constitutes and structures our moral-evaluative lives in the broadest sense; that is, it focuses our perception of qualitative distinctions reflectively, while also orienting us affectively on account of these assessments. As a result, strong evaluations not only imply claims about the nature and status of human beings, but also exert genuine influence on a person's motivations. In the end, this means that strong evaluations straddle the boundary between the reflective and the affective. As *implicit* assessments of higher and lower worth they are part of the intuitive, tacit mode of understanding, but the more *explicit*, articulated strong evaluations participate in the level of deliberated judgment and belief.

1.3.3 How Not To Read Taylor

A large body of literature about Taylor ignores or rejects his interwoven mode of argumentation and reduces the doctrine of strong evaluation to one of its components (either philosophical-anthropological or ethical or ontological).[15]

In recent years, however, some counterinterpretations have emerged in reply to the drawbacks of these analyses. These accounts want to restore the wider focus by providing a more holistic reading of Taylor's claims.[16] Two points can be made here. On the one hand, reductionist readings of strong evaluation are partly right to criticize Taylor for not separating the different levels of strong evaluation as sharply as a clear grasp of his interwoven tactic would require. On the other hand, since the difficulty emerges from a deliberate strategy to *connect* different arguments, it becomes compelling to those who criticize Taylor for blurring basic distinctions to do more than just observe that he uses unconventional methods. Instead, they should address Taylor's underlying assumption that there is much to be gained from exploring the relationships between the different levels of strong evaluation by pushing the boundaries of distinct philosophical domains. Yet this seems to be an aspect that some of Taylor's critics have missed.

The determination to drive a wedge between the very issues that Taylor seeks to bring together is perhaps most strongly expressed in Paul Johnston's discussion of *Sources of the Self*, for his main goal is to make clear how Taylor's substantive positions are mixed up with conceptual confusions. The conceptual approach is evident right at the start of Johnston's account, for he begins by noting that Taylor "blurs the distinction between evaluation and strong evaluation" and continues by laying out how Taylor also fails to distinguish between "having an understanding of the world and having an ethical understanding of the world" (1999, 101, 106). I want to consider both criticisms, because these clearly illustrate the limitations of reconstructing Taylor's views in terms of mainstream analytical distinctions.

Johnston takes his cue from the concept of strong evaluation as defined in the opening pages of *Sources of the Self*: "What exactly does Taylor mean by discriminations that are not rendered valid by our own desires but stand independently of them and offer standards by which they can be judged?" (Johnston 1999, 101) He then argues that a goal like becoming famous does provide a standard for other desires (as they can either promote or obstruct becoming famous) without being independent of them. That is, it depends on the person's preferences whether he or she sees the goal of becoming famous as an independent standard or as "simply the expression of dispositions that happened to have been inculcated into her" (Johnston 1999, 101). Taylor, however, "blurs the distinction between evaluation and strong evaluation and this enables him to argue that anyone who evaluates must believe in ethics" (1999, 101).

In Johnston's view, what Taylor fails to recognize is that although "most people want to make moral judgments," the individual may also hold that "commitment to any goal is simply an expression of an individual's preferences or dispositions" (1999, 101). This means that strong evaluation is not essential to human agency as "someone who rejects ethics still has preferences and so can have intentions and make choices" (Johnston 1999, 102). Then, without any further ado—without looking at the diverse ways in which Taylor uses the concept of strong evaluation to characterize morality[17] and without asking how he understands ethics—Johnston concludes that "strong evaluation is avoidable and anyone who rejects the idea that there are correct judgments on human action is committed to avoiding it" (1999, 101).

This understanding of strong evaluation is defective in at least three respects. First, it fails to take into account the basic distinction between strong and weak evaluation and the different types of articulation involved in them. As we have seen, although weak evaluators can be articulate about their preferences to the extent that they can express their basic needs, they lack the richer vocabulary of worth that is distinctive of strong evaluations. Johnston seems to lose sight of this point, though, because from the beginning he understands "ethics" as involving only weakly evaluated ends. It is not just that his discussion overlooks that strong evaluation involves goods that are experienced as having incommensurably higher worth. More importantly, Johnston misses the point that Taylor seeks to undercut his very understanding of evaluation and ethics. On Taylor's definition of morality as involving higher goods, individual preferences or dispositions are simply irrelevant for moral argument. Yet because Johnston does not elaborate on this and simply posits that "it is quite possible to deny that there is a correct way of assessing actions" and that we may hold that "all evaluations are on a par" (1999, 101), the issue of how to define morality cannot even be raised. Like Flanagan, who states that the domain of the ethical just *is* "observer-relative" (1996, 146), Johnston explains right at the outset that "the most appropriate starting point for our discussion is not a definition of ethics but the fundamental logical point that any judgment about human actions will inevitably be from one perspective among the countless number that are logically possible" (1999, 3). As a result, the aim of discussing strong evaluation while explicitly avoiding a definition of ethics both obscures Johnston's own moral commitments and stifles the debate of what morality consists in.

Second, because Johnston implicitly relies on a subjectivist understanding of human evaluation,[18] his account of strong evaluation can address neither Taylor's claim that we experience some of our goals as intrinsically more significant than others nor that the issue of worthiness can only arise independently of our preferences. In this regard, Johnston argues that the possibility of an alternative characterization of evaluation shows Taylor's concept of strong evaluation to be "avoidable," but this does not prove his point. It may be true that most people tend to favor subjectivist models of evaluation, but this merely shows the omnipresence of reductionist thinking, not that strong evaluative self-interpretations are avoidable.

Third, Johnston's critique would have been far more interesting if he had considered the way in which Taylor uses the concept of strong evaluation as an *ad hominem* argument against subjectivist notions of evaluation, that is, to illustrate that we understand ourselves in terms of strong evaluations that generally refuse to be treated as relative. As Taylor puts it: "In the case that the preference is for ice cream you may not care about losing it, but what if it is for caring about people being tortured? Would you want to degenerate that point?" (in: Rosa and Laitinen 2002, 188) Instead of discussing this argument, Johnston simply insists that "*pace* Taylor, it is a logically possible position [to] hold that all evaluations are relative to a goal" (1999, 101). The only kind of answer that Johnston can conceive of offering with regard to Taylor's question above is one in strictly analytical terms. He wants to show that it is *conceptually* possible to reduce moral claims to the status of preferences. Within this reductionist account, the *ad hominem* point articulated by Taylor cannot be addressed at all.

Johnston's second point of critique concerns Taylor's distinction between instinctive and moral reactions. He first notes that for Taylor "there is no path from a scientific description of the world to ethics" (Johnston 1999, 106). He then argues that Taylor "confuses the real issues by trying to assimilate moral judgments and empirical claims" (Johnston 1999, 106) by highlighting Taylor's claim that we should treat our moral instincts as "our mode of access to a world in which ontological claims are discernible" (Taylor 1989, 8; quoted in Johnston 1999, 106). In Johnston's view, this last point is particularly revealing, because it shows the crucial misunderstanding that morality provides access to the world like sensory experience. At one stroke, Taylor thus "leaves empirical and moral claims looking misleadingly similar" and "confuses our need to make sense of the world with the possibility of making sense of it in moral terms" (Johnston 1999, 107, 102–103).

However, if we consider more closely the context in which Taylor speaks about gaining "access" to the world via our moral intuitions, we can see that he does not so much argue that "claims of science cannot disprove ethics" (Johnston 1999, 107), but, rather, that taking the neutral stance of science cuts us off from the very background that constitutes our moral reactions. That is, whereas natural science requires that we neutralize our responses, moral reasoning is possible only within a world that is "shaped by our deepest moral responses" (1989, 8). This point is crucial because it enables us to see what Taylor is actually doing here: to lose the boundary between ethics and ontology by making explicit the ontological claims underlying our moral reactions.

In other words, his view is that a clear distinction must be drawn between scientific explorations, on the one hand, and investigations of moral ontology, on the other, since these are radically different approaches to reality. Regrettably, Johnston sees no need to discuss Taylor's concept of moral ontology, because it is here, I think, that he should focus his critique of "blurring the distinction between having an understanding of the world and having an ethical understanding of the world" (Johnston 1999, 106). In this respect, it is worth noting that Johnston not simply eschews an elaboration of his rather one-dimensional picture of ethics,[19] but that it lies in the very nature of his rigorous conceptual approach to keep its most basic assumptions inarticulate. When he asserts that "ethics is not a mode of access to anything nor is there evidence for moral claims" (Johnston 1999, 107), his critique turns out to depend on a strict division of facts and values. But because this separation remains completely unarticulated, Johnston cannot make sense of Taylor's attempt to connect these two domains, that is, to make clear that facts and values are intrinsically related via the ontological claims behind our moral reactions.

Johnston's case is particularly interesting because this type of inarticulateness exemplifies one of the central issues Taylor is fighting against. So much of Johnston's effort goes into showing how conceptual confusions seductively prevent us from seeing Taylor's failure to understand "ethics," that he completely misses the ontological concern that the doctrine of strong evaluation is all about. This is partly due to the fact that Johnston sees himself in a strictly conceptual role, narrowly concerning himself with the use of moral concepts rather than substantive moral claims. This perspective leaves no room for Taylor's idea that moral thought should concern itself with the claims behind the demands we acknowledge, with ontological views. We can see, though, how Johnston's method fits his recommendation to replace "the lofty ambition of resolving the great questions of life" with "the humbler, but achievable goal of conceptual clarification" (1999, xii). On this view, awareness of the moral space that our strong evaluations seek to define has been so deeply suppressed that Taylor's very attempt to bring it to the fore goes completely unnoticed.

On the whole, the criticisms of Johnston and Flanagan are archetypes of the paradox encountered earlier, that some critiques of strong evaluation indicate the reductionist mode of thought that Taylor's doctrine of strong evaluation seeks to attack head on. It would seem, therefore (in the above two cases at least), that Taylor is not just unsuccessful in convincing his readers of his claims, but that he even fails to pass on his most basic insights. However, this acknowledgment should not make his views seem any less significant; unless, that is, we are prisoners of the reductionist mind-set ourselves, which takes only those ideas to be clear and convincing which can be argued in the formulations of mainstream philosophy. Reductionism, then, proves to be quite a tenacious (and in the cases of Flanagan and Johnston mostly implicit) feature of contemporary thought, so that it creeps back in even where it is exposed and refuted. In this respect, it is telling that Taylor says to be "fighting uphill" in *Sources of the Self* (1989, 90), while announcing in *Retrieving Realism* to be proposing a position that is "going to be difficult to defend," that is, "in the context of today's culture" (2015, 154).

1.4 CONCLUSION: HOW TO APPRECIATE THE COMPLEX NATURE OF STRONG EVALUATION?

This chapter has given an overview of Taylor's use of strong evaluation as it is developed from his earliest writings up to his most recent publications. Ultimately, strong evaluation originates from a three-layered attack on reductive explanations of human life. As the central concept of all three axes of this critique, strong evaluation at once informs Taylor's philosophical anthropology, his moral phenomenology, and his views on ontology. Although the above reconstruction of the three levels of strong evaluation does not provide an answer to the important question of how Taylor's philosophical anthropology, his moral phenomenology, and his ontology are related, it does demonstrate the unconventional way in which he operates. Therefore, the main result so far is the modest one that Taylor uses the concept of strong evaluation in a *variety* of ways (descriptive, normative, diagnostic, critical), moving from one domain to another (philosophical anthropology, ethics, phenomenology, ontology). Having identified the three-leveled nature and potential of the doctrine of strong evaluation, we can now focus on the questions this approach invokes along these three axes. How does Taylor justify his philosophical-anthropological, moral-phenomenological, and ontological claims? This is the subject of the following chapters. The next chapter, then, discusses the ways in which Taylor's commentators have explained his interwoven arguments by way of introduction to the more problematic aspects of the doctrine of strong evaluation.

NOTES

1. See Taylor (1985c, 265; 1985d, 65–68, 73–74; 1985f, 220–22, 226; 1989, 4, 14, 20, 29–30, 42, 60, 63, 122, 249, 332–33, 336, 337, 383, 514; 1991, 242; 1994a, 249; 1994b, 209; 1995a, 37–39, 59; 1995b, 134; 2003, 312; 2007b, 544, 595; 2011, 294–95, 297–302; 2016, 63, 192, 199).

2. Parts of the discussion in sections 1.2 and 1.3 also appear in Meijer (2018).

3. As Smith explains: "The main lesson to be learned from the linguistic movement, he thinks, is the need for caution in adopting *reductive* modes of analysis. [. . .] By revealing the complexities of ordinary language, the linguistic philosophers helped to uncover deep problems facing reductionist theories of meaning [. . .] Taylor would deploy the same strategy when dealing with reductionist analyses of human action put forward by behaviourism" (2002, 22, original emphasis).

4. See his papers "The Pre-Objective World" (1958) and "Phenomenology and Linguistic Analysis" (1959b).

5. Although the young Taylor is critical of Merleau-Ponty's project of a pure phenomenology, there is no doubt that Merleau-Ponty is also a source of inspiration for Taylor. I discuss Taylor's ambiguous relationship to phenomenology in section 2.3. For a more elaborate account of the young Taylor's engagement with linguistic philosophy and phenomenology, see Smith (2002, 18–34).

6. In this respect, Rorty has criticized Taylor for making "little attempt to explore the possibility of a *non*-reductive naturalism" (1994, 197, original emphasis). I elaborate on this in section 5.3.4.

7. See, for example, the papers "Self-Interpreting Animals" (1985d, 66–67) and "What's Wrong With Negative Liberty" (1985f, 220).

8. Taylor uses these two notions interchangeably. For example, he uses the term "incommensurability" in "The Diversity of Goods" (1985a, 237–40), whereas in *Sources of the Self* (1989, 62–65) "incomparability" is more central. However, as Ruth Chang notes, there is a subtle difference. "Incommensurability" means that different items "cannot be precisely measured by some common scale of units of value," whereas "incomparability" is simply "the idea that items cannot be compared" (Chang 1997, 2). In the context of strong evaluation in which Taylor uses these terms, the favored term seems to be "incommensurability." For although you can *compare* "enjoying ice cream" with "saving a human life," the crucial point is that they cannot be equally *measured* because of the sense that the preservation of life is on a different—that is, higher—level than the lust for ice cream, which makes the former incommensurably (not: incomparably) higher than the latter.

9. See also Taylor's reply to the objection that utilitarians too make use of a qualitative contrast by distinguishing pleasure from pain in "What is Human Agency?" (1985e, 20, note 5).

10. Mark Redhead makes this point: "The paradigmatic weak evaluator is a utilitarian. He eschews languages of qualitative contrast and makes decisions instead on the basis of quantitative differences between desires that, due to a given contingent set of circumstances, happen to be incompatible" (2002, 159).

11. See Paul Saurette (2005) for a different interpretation of the Kantian roots in Taylor's moral philosophy. According to Saurette, Taylor is highly influenced by Kant's "'imperative image of morality' which views moral thought as necessarily following universal and necessary laws" (2005, 16). I discuss Saurette's reading of Taylor in sections 1.3.1 and 2.2.2.

12. As he argues: "The domain of the ethical and thus what counts as ethical assessment is notoriously observer-relative. What looks like non-ethical assessment from an outsider's perspective may be ethical from an insider's perspective" (Flanagan 1996, 146).

13. The quotations are from Taylor's "Self-Interpreting Animals" (1985d, 65, 67).

14. The quotation is from Taylor's "The Diversity of Goods" (1985a, 239).

15. Next to countless critical reviews of *Sources of the Self*, Flanagan (1996) and Johnston (1999) are good examples of this narrow approach.

16. Most notably, Abbey (2000), Smith (2002), and Laitinen (2008).

17. As we have seen, these include: to explain morality in terms of higher goods, to discredit naturalist views that rule out commonsense moral reactions for practical reason, to endorse a phenomenological account of morality (broadly conceived) in critical opposition to rivaling ethical theories that focus exclusively on duty and obligation, and to show the inadequacy of reductive anthropologies that leave no room for qualitative distinctions.

18. Throughout his discussion, Johnston consistently has recourse to the view that evaluations simply reflect how "people are disposed rather than some intrinsic merit of the evaluations themselves" (1999, 101).

19. As he says: "The important point is that ethics is not about the individual finding a way of understanding the world with which she can live; rather it is about trying to understand the world correctly. Similarly, it is not about finding the most appropriate terms to define one's self-identity, but about reaching a conclusion on what is right and wrong. [. . .] Holding moral views involves claiming that anyone who understands the world correctly will accept that certain standards of behaviour are correct and should be followed by everyone" (Johnston 1999, 105).

REFERENCES

Abbey, Ruth. 2000. *Charles Taylor*. Teddington/Princeton: Acumen Press/Princeton University Press.

Chang, Ruth, ed. 1997. *Incommensurability, Incomparability and Practical Reason*. Cambridge, MA: Harvard University Press.

Flanagan, Owen. 1996. *Self Expressions. Mind, Morals, and the Meaning of Life*. New York/Oxford: Oxford University Press.

Frankfurt, Harry. 1971. "Freedom of the Will and the Concept of a Person." *Journal of Philosophy* 67 (1): 5–20.

Johnston, Paul. 1999. *The Contradictions of Modern Moral Philosophy. Ethics after Wittgenstein*. London/New York: Routledge.

Laitinen, Arto. 2008. *Strong Evaluation Without Moral Sources*. Berlin: Walter de Gruyter.

Meijer, Michiel. 2018. "Strong Evaluation Down the Decades: Rearticulating Taylor's Central Concept." *Philosophy and Theology* (forthcoming).

Redhead, Mark. 2002. *Charles Taylor: Thinking and Living Deep Diversity*. Lanham, MD: Rowman & Littlefield.

Rorty, Richard. 1994. "Taylor on Self-Celebration and Gratitude: Review of Sources of the Self." *Philosophy and Phenomenological Research* 54 (1): 197–201.

Rosa, Hartmut, and Arto Laitinen. 2002. "On Identity, Alienation and the Consequences of September 11th. An Interview with Charles Taylor." In *Acta Philosophica Fennica. Vol. 71. Perspectives on the Philosophy of Charles Taylor*, edited by Arto Laitinen and Nicholas Smith, 165–95. Helsinki: Philosophical Society of Finland.

Saurette, Paul. 2005. *The Kantian Imperative: Humiliation, Common Sense, Politics*. Toronto, OH: University of Toronto Press.

Smith, Nicholas. 2002. *Charles Taylor: Meaning, Morals and Modernity.* Cambridge, MA: Polity.
Taylor, Charles. 1959a. "Ontology." *Philosophy* 34: 125–41.
Taylor, Charles. 1964. *The Explanation of Behaviour.* London: Routledge and Kegan Paul.
Taylor, Charles. 1976. "Responsibility for Self." In *The Identities of Persons*, edited by Amélie Rorty, 281–99. London, OH: University of California Press.
Taylor, Charles. 1985a. "The Diversity of Goods." In *Philosophy and the Human Sciences: Philosophical Papers vol. 2*, 230–47. Cambridge, MA: Cambridge University Press.
Taylor, Charles. 1985b. *Human Agency and Language: Philosophical Papers vol. 1.* Cambridge, MA: Cambridge University Press.
Taylor, Charles. 1985c. "Legitimation Crisis?" In *Philosophy and the Human Sciences: Philosophical Papers vol. 2*, 248–88. Cambridge, MA: Cambridge University Press.
Taylor, Charles. 1985d. "Self-Interpreting Animals." In *Human Agency and Language: Philosophical Papers vol. 1*, 45–76. Cambridge, MA: Cambridge University Press.
Taylor, Charles. 1985e. "What is Human Agency?" In *Human Agency and Language: Philosophical Papers vol. 1*, 15–44. Cambridge, MA: Cambridge University Press.
Taylor, Charles. 1985f. "What's Wrong With Negative Liberty." In *Philosophy and the Human Sciences: Philosophical Papers vol. 2*, 211–29. Cambridge, MA: Cambridge University Press.
Taylor, Charles. 1988. "The Moral Topography of the Self." In *Hermeneutics and Psychological Theory*, edited by Stanly Messer, Louis Sass and Robert Woolfolk, 298–320. New Brunswick, NJ: Rutgers University Press.
Taylor, Charles. 1989. *Sources of the Self. The Making of the Modern Identity.* Cambridge, MA: Cambridge University Press.
Taylor, Charles. 1991. "Comments and Replies." *Inquiry* 34: 237–54.
Taylor, Charles. 1994a. "Reply and re-articulation." In *Philosophy in an Age of Pluralism: The Philosophy of Charles Taylor in Question*, edited by James Tully and Daniel Weinstock, 213–57. Cambridge, MA: Cambridge University Press.
Taylor, Charles. 1994b. "Reply to Commentators." *Philosophy and Phenomenological Research* 54 (1): 203–13.
Taylor, Charles. 1995a. "Explanation and Practical Reason." In *Philosophical Arguments*, 34–60. Cambridge, MA/London: Harvard University Press.
Taylor, Charles. 1995b. "A Most Peculiar Institution." In *World, Mind, and Ethics. Essays on the Ethical Philosophy of Bernard Williams*, edited by J. Altham and R. Harrison, 132–55. Cambridge, MA: Cambridge University Press.
Taylor, Charles. 1997. "Leading a Life." In *Incommensurability, Incomparability and Practical Reason*, edited by Ruth Chang, 170–83. Cambridge, MA: Harvard University Press.
Taylor, Charles. 2003. "Ethics and Ontology." *The Journal of Philosophy* 100 (6): 305–20.

Taylor, Charles. 2007a. "Reflections on Key Articles and Books." Accessed June 25 2014. http://www.templetonprize.org/ct_reflections.html.

Taylor, Charles. 2007b. *A Secular Age*. Cambridge/London: Belknap Press of Harvard University Press.

Taylor, Charles. 2011. "Disenchantment-Reenchantment." In *Dilemmas and Connections*, 287–302. Cambridge, MA/London: Belknap Press of Harvard University Press.

Taylor, Charles. 2013. "Retrieving Realism." In *Mind, Reason, and Being-in-the-World. The McDowell-Dreyfus Debate*, edited by Joseph Schear, 61–90. New York, NY: Routledge.

Taylor, Charles. 2016. *The Language Animal: The Full Shape of the Human Linguistic Capacity*. Cambridge, MA: The Belknap Press of Harvard University Press.

Taylor, Charles (with Ayer, A.J.). 1959b. "Phenomenology and Linguistic Analysis." *Proceedings of the Aristotelian Society, supplementary volume* 33: 93–124.

Taylor, Charles (with Dreyfus, Hubert). 2015. *Retrieving Realism*. Cambridge, MA: Harvard University Press.

Taylor, Charles (with Kullman, Michael). 1958. "The Pre-Objective World." *The Review of Metaphysics* 12 (1): 108–32.

Chapter 2

Interwoven Arguments

The present analysis shows that the concept of strong evaluation covers three central domains: philosophical anthropology, ethics, and ontology. The aim of this chapter is to make clear why we cannot just stop at this point, that is, at the mere recognition that Taylor uses the concept of strong evaluation in different ways. This is because the most distinctive element of Taylor's thought is that he seeks to connect his various positions, in an attempt to develop what he calls "interwoven arguments."[1]

Taylor's interwoven mode of argumentation has come a long way in the last decades. He first argues for the close relationship between philosophical anthropology and ethics in the paper "The Moral Topography of the Self" (1988), and then continues to develop this idea by explicitly connecting selfhood and morality in the first part of *Sources of the Self*. However, in this book, Taylor extends his understanding of the ethical even further by introducing the notions of "moral ontology" and "moral phenomenology" (1989, 8, 68). It would seem, therefore, that in Taylor's view, ethics is closely intertwined with philosophical anthropology, ontology, and phenomenology alike.

In addition to these modifications in his view on ethics, Taylor's most recent writings also show a change in emphasis in his approach to ontology. Although a preoccupation with an "ontology of the human" is central to *Sources of the Self* (1989, 5), Taylor increasingly takes up ontological questions from a distinctive nonanthropocentric perspective in the course of his writing.[2] That is, while he initially presses ontological questions to elaborate a philosophical-anthropological critique of reductionist understandings of human agency, he consistently expands his ontological view beyond anthropological concerns to investigate the *metaphysical* reality that best explains our strong evaluations. How to understand these distinctive tactics, both of

Taylor's aim to interweave his different arguments and of his expanded nonanthropocentric approach to ontology?

This chapter seeks to answer this question in an ongoing discussion with Taylor's commentators. I first examine Taylor's attempts to establish the connections between the different levels of strong evaluation in the period directly after the publication of *Philosophical Papers*. My central claim is that the first part of *Sources of the Self* tries to say too much at one stroke, which blurs the distinctions between Taylor's different methods in general, and the relationships between his anthropological, ethical, phenomenological, and ontological claims in particular (section 2.1). In order to illustrate how the three levels of strong evaluation (philosophical-anthropological, ethical, and ontological) have been discussed in the literature on Taylor's work, I continue to examine the ways in which several commentators have responded to Taylor's interwoven arguments. I argue that the common trend in Taylor scholarship to endorse his loose or relaxed employment of the concept of ontology not only distorts Taylor's arguments but also reduces his nonanthropocentric viewpoint to an anthropological one (section 2.2). In reply, I highlight a fundamental tension in Taylor's interwoven strategy that most studies tend to overlook, and suggest that a distinction should be drawn between the philosophical-anthropological, moral-phenomenological, and ontological implications of strong evaluation to clarify the issues at stake (section 2.3). The benefits of this approach are twofold. On the one hand, the continuing focus on the concept of strong evaluation ensures acknowledgment of the inner cohesion of its different levels. On the other hand, differentiating Taylor's interwoven claims in recognition of their interaction clearly highlights the elusive nature of his nonanthropocentric ontologizing, opening up the question of the metaphysical status of his ontological view.

2.1 INTERWEAVING ANTHROPOLOGY, ETHICS, PHENOMENOLOGY, AND ONTOLOGY

In this section, I first look into Taylor's explanations of the connection between philosophical anthropology and ethics (section 2.1.1), while also demonstrating how he seeks to link the subjects of ontology and phenomenology to his account of morality (section 2.1.2). I continue to examine Taylor's unusual employment of the concept of ontology by putting a spotlight on his mixed use of anthropological and nonanthropocentric conceptions in the course of his writing (section 2.1.3).

2.1.1 Philosophical Anthropology and Ethics

Taylor refers to the relationship between philosophical anthropology and ethics already in *The Explanation of Behaviour*. As he says in reference to Aristotle, there is a type of ethical reflection that "attempts to discover what men should do and how they should behave by a study of human nature and its fundamental goals" (1964, 4). In fact, Taylor sees this type of reflection as being not just "of fundamental and perennial importance for what is often called philosophical anthropology" but "also central to ethics" (1964, 3–4). For Taylor, then, the issue is this: Can we understand human agency adequately just as any other process in nature, or does a satisfactory explanation of human life require the premise that "there is a form of life which is higher or more properly human than others" and that "a purpose or a set of purposes which are intrinsically human can be identified?" (1964, 4). Although Taylor does not allude to this question in the rest of *The Explanation of Behaviour*, he clearly opts for the second answer in "The Moral Topography of the Self," arguing that "our description of ourselves as selves is inseparable from our existing in a space of moral aspiration and assessment" (1988, 302, 298).

In line with this, the connection between selfhood and morality is put forward as the opening theme of *Sources of the Self* (1989, 3). Taylor thus not only criticizes contemporary moral philosophy for providing a one-sided account of morality (1989, 3–4), but also offers a positive account of how our notion of human agency is "inextricably connected with our understanding of our moral predicament and moral agency" (1988, 298). Strong evaluation, then, turns out to be *the* central concept of our understanding both of human agency (selfhood, personhood, identity) and of morality. By throwing a spotlight on the tight relationship between selfhood and morality Taylor thus explicitly reaches beyond common conceptions that treat them simply as discrete issues. This means that having recourse to familiar philosophical categories, that is, to *separate* philosophical anthropology and ethics, is to change the subject.[3] What is particularly distinctive of Taylor's approach is his use of a "spatial metaphor" to establish the connection between selfhood and morality. He introduces this image as follows:

> My main thesis is: that the self exists essentially in moral space by means of a master image, a spatial one. And this is what I invoke as well in speaking of a "moral topography" of the self. This manner of speaking might seem fanciful or arbitrary, but it is not. At least, the image is not mine, but is anchored in moral consciousness itself. I mean by this [. . .] that our most basic and inescapable languages of the self incorporate spatial terms, most centrally within/without and above/below. (1988, 300)

Sources of the Self continues this picture. In this book, Taylor restates that his use of a spatial metaphor is "more than personal predilection," because there are signs also in psychology that the link between moral and spatial orientation lies "very deep in the human psyche" (1989, 28). He then defines the concept of identity in a way that not only reaffirms the union of selfhood and morality, but also sanctions the crucial role of the incommensurably higher for human action. Taylor understands human identity as that which allows us to "define what is important to us and what is not" and which, as it makes possible these qualitative distinctions, could never be completely devoid of such strong evaluations (1989, 30).

Taylor makes two claims here. The first claim seems clear enough: the philosophical-anthropological concern of what we are and what matters to us is essentially linked to our sense of morality (in a broad sense). However, the premise underlying this point is not that we are human agents simply because certain issues "matter" for us (1989, 34), but because—and this is the second, implicit claim—some goods matter *more* than others and strike us as imperative. If all values mattered to us in the same way, Taylor maintains, we would not have a category like the ethical or the moral to distinguish between good and bad, admirable and contemptible, virtuous and vicious, and so on. Therefore, Taylor's general claim that a human agent is always at the same time a moral agent simultaneously authorizes the picture of the moral as involving higher goods. Taylor thus connects philosophical anthropology and ethics to sustain a certain definition of morality, defending the "interwoven" argument that being a human agent necessarily involves the recognition of higher goods.

2.1.2 Moral Ontology and Moral Phenomenology

Given these observations—that Taylor employs a spatial metaphor both to demonstrate the link between philosophical anthropology and ethics and to support his picture of morality—I will move on to another way in which Taylor advances his spatial image: via the notion of "moral space." While the idea of a moral space is first explored in the paper "The Moral Topography of the Self," it is elaborated most clearly in the second chapter of *Sources of the Self,* titled "The Self in Moral Space" (1989, 25–52). As we have seen, Taylor initially introduces a spatial image to make the case for the connection between selfhood and morality. Yet, adding metaphors like "contact" with the good, or how we are "placed" in relation to it, and to speak of the self as something that can exist only in a "space" of moral issues, brings out the connection between ethics and ontology (1989, 44, 49).

In brief, moral space is the realm in which our strong evaluations make sense. That is, since we are living in a "space" in which we cannot but face questions about what good human action consists in and what goals are worth pursuing, strong evaluation provides the kind of orientation we need in face of these questions (1989, 28). Because of this, Taylor argues, defining myself or knowing who I am is "a species of knowing where I stand," that is, in the space of human meaning in which we think, feel, and judge (1989, 27). Not knowing where you stand or who you are means that you lack a framework within which things have a "stable significance," that is, a standpoint from which to judge some actions as important or worthwhile and others as unimportant or empty (1989, 27–28). Conversely, to know where you stand is to be oriented. If we accept this picture of human agency in terms of moral orientation, Taylor continues, then we must also accept that we orient ourselves in a space of questions that *must* be answered, in the sense that these questions exist "independently" of our success or failure in finding the answers (1989, 30). Thematically speaking, this means that morality is not just related to selfhood, but also to ontology. In this way, Taylor consistently develops his interwoven mode of argumentation: just as his definition of human agency involves the acknowledgment of higher values, there must also be recognition of the moral ontology without which our strong evaluations would not make sense (1989, 5–8).

Taylor employs the concept of moral ontology mainly to substantiate his nonanthropocentric view that value does not simply flow from what we de facto want. As we have seen (in section 1.3.2), he tries to show that we make sense of our lives by giving *reasons* for our moral reactions beyond desirability, invoking truths rather than preferences. What Taylor calls "ontological accounts," then, are explanations of such truth claims (1989, 6). If, for example, we believe that human life has to be respected, an ontological account is what gives rational articulation of what respect-for-life means in terms of the ontological status of human beings, for instance, by depicting human beings as "creatures of God," as "immortal souls," or as "rational agents," or whatever other characterization that shows *why* we ought to treat human beings with respect (1989, 5). For Taylor, ethics is thus related to ontology in that our moral reactions cannot be made intelligible without such explanatory views about the ontology that defines humanity's place in the world. In this sense, moral reactions are "affirmations of a given ontology of the human" (1989, 5).

There still remains one topic that revolves around Taylor's spatial metaphor: the link between ethics and phenomenology. As he says, moral ontologies are not just handed down by tradition, but can also be rooted in "moral phenomenology, that is, our experience of our moral predicament"; indeed, Taylor adds, "they must be so rooted somewhere if they are to have any credence" (1988, 302). In one way, we have already encountered this point in the discussion of the reflective-affective nature of strong evaluation (in section

1.3.2): moral ideals can only motivate us if they are anchored in human experience. Yet, things start to look rather different in *Sources of the Self*, where Taylor systematically has recourse to moral phenomenology in refuting reductionist (naturalist, subjectivist, relativist, projectivist) understandings of morality (1989, 68, 74, 81). Although Taylor presents his approaches to ethics as exercises in both ontology and phenomenology, he explains neither the procedures of these approaches nor the relationships between them. On the one hand, his notions of moral ontology and moral phenomenology clearly indicate that Taylor's reasoning steers a course between ethical, ontological, and phenomenological inquiries. On the other hand, it is not so clear what can actually be achieved, ontologically, by a phenomenological approach to ethics. As we will see (in section 2.2.3), one of the limitations of Taylor's method is that phenomenological description alone is not yet an argument against reductive views.

For now, however, it suffices to take note of Taylor's central strategy to interweave different philosophical arguments in order to strike a blow at reductionism from all of these perspectives. Taking the above points together, we can see the fourfold function of Taylor's spatial metaphor. He employs it (1) to demonstrate the connection between selfhood and morality; (2) to support his conception of morality as involving higher goods; (3) to insist on the ontological underpinnings of our strong evaluations; and (4) to make the phenomenological point that moral theory must be grounded on human experience in order to be credible. To get a better hold on Taylor's massive ambition to link all of these views together, it is insightful to go back to *Philosophical Papers*; more particularly, to the introduction of this book. Here, Taylor gives an instructive overview of his philosophical agenda at that time. As one would expect, the introduction to *Philosophical Papers* already contains most of Taylor's key themes, but what is especially interesting is that some points are made with much more certainty than others. On the one hand, Taylor is quite confident about his thesis about the self and the inadequacy of rivaling naturalistic views, as he declares to give an account of "what tempts naturalists to adopt their thin theory of the self in terms of our richer theory" (1985, 4). Yet, on the other hand, he is quite hesitant when he speaks about the background itself that makes possible our moral self-understanding:

> I do not know how clear I can be about this at the present stage, but perhaps I can gesture towards the question in this way: If one of the fundamental uses of language is to articulate or make manifest the background of distinctions of worth we define ourselves by, how should we understand *what* is being manifested here? Is what we are articulating ultimately to be understood as our human response to our condition? Or is our articulation striving rather to be faithful to something beyond us, not explicable simply in terms of human response? [. . .]

I would dearly like to be able to cut through the clutter and confusion that we all labor under so as to be able to explore this question, but I have to admit that I am far away from this at present. (1985, 11–12, original emphasis)

Put simply, whereas Taylor seems assured that his arguments will clearly and convincingly establish that naturalism turns out to be parasitic on certain anthropological and moral beliefs,[4] he is most uncertain about how this relates to ontology. This is revealing for understanding Taylor's interwoven arguments in that it enables us to see more clearly how his tentative nonanthropocentric approaches to ethics and ontology tend to be obscured by his more profound claims about selfhood.

In fact, some of Taylor's conceptualizations tend to distort rather than clarify. As noted, he seeks to entwine ontological reflections with his views on selfhood and morality in *Sources of the Self* by adding the concept of "moral ontology." However, Taylor employs this term in such a loose and undecided way that he fails to clarify the relationship between his views on ontology, philosophical anthropology, and ethics.[5] Further adding to the confusion, Taylor uses ontology and anthropology interchangeably when he speaks about an "ontology of the human" to depict the different philosophical anthropologies (concepts of man) involved in the explanatory accounts that try to make sense of our moral reactions (1989, 5–6). On top of this, he further complicates this already-complex position by occasionally referring to it as a "moral phenomenology" (1989, 68, 74, 81). Yet, since Taylor does not differentiate between his different approaches, the key problem is not just that his hybrid position is notoriously difficult to follow, but, as we will see later on (in section 2.3), that it obscures the metaphysical implications of the doctrine of strong evaluation.

At this point, it is worth noting that most of Taylor's interpreters follow his example by using the terms "philosophical anthropology" and "ontology" as substitutes. Stephen White, for example, approves of this routine when he assures that his own concept of "weak ontology" is "largely appropriate" for the kind of reflection Taylor has in mind when addressing "philosophical-anthropological" issues, because in so doing, White continues, Taylor speaks of the "ontology of human life" (White 2000, 43; Taylor 1990, 261). Others similarly uphold Taylor's broad notion of ontology. Abbey, for example, describes Taylor's philosophical anthropology as an account of the "ontological features of the self" (2000, 56). Saurette sketches strong evaluation as an "inescapable ontological element constitutive of human agency," while Smith, Kerr, and Laitinen literally follow Taylor in depicting his philosophical anthropology as an "ontology of the human," a "moral ontology of the human," or an "ontology of human persons."[6]

It therefore seems clear that his interpreters, like Taylor himself, do not take a great interest in differentiating philosophical anthropology from ontology. At the same time, however, most of Taylor's commentators recognize a kind of tension implicit in this terminology. Abbey notes that not all of Taylor's interpreters have appreciated his approach to the self (2000, 56), referring to the critiques of Olafson (1994, 192–193), Rosa (1995, 25), and Flanagan (1996, 154). Saurette ensures that Taylor's "definition of human agency is not guaranteed by the authority of an ontology" (2005, 208). Analogously, Smith observes that "Taylor runs the risk of 'anthropologizing' or 'ontologizing' historically contingent features of subjectivity" (2002, 8), while Kerr insists that we "want to hear much more about the ambiguities inherent in this version of a 'moral ontology of the human,'" stressing the uncertain and tentative character of Taylor's ontological view (2004, 101). Surprisingly though, despite their awareness of certain tensions in Taylor's interwoven mode of thinking, none of these authors take the opportunity to challenge his vocabulary at this point. In my view, however, it is a source of great confusion that Taylor does not clearly separate his different approaches, for it leaves unexplained how his positions in philosophical anthropology, ethics, and ontology relate to one another. In fact, given his central aim to develop *interwoven* arguments, it is most peculiar that both Taylor and his interpreters invest so little in explaining the cohesion of his major positions.

2.1.3 Taylor's Nonanthropocentric Ontologizing

As the above sections make clear, Taylor uses the concept of ontology in a loose and relaxed way. It is also clear that he does not see contradiction in synchronizing some of his concerns. As Taylor says in a reflection on White's *Sustaining Affirmation*:

> My term "philosophical anthropology" is meant to cover much the same matters as White does with "ontology": it tries to define certain fundamental features about human beings, their place in nature, their defining capacities (language is obviously central to these), and their most powerful or basic motivations, goals, needs, and aspirations. (2005, 35)

Taylor's explicit remark that he sees philosophical anthropology and ontology as interchangeable notions has incited some of his readers to conclude that the central focus of Taylor's work has been "the formulation of a philosophical anthropology" (Rosa and Laitinen 2002, 183). Yet, one of the limitations of this characterization is that it leaves no room for the important observation that Taylor "wants to open up a non anthropocentric perspective on the good" already in *Sources of the Self* (Kerr 2004, 84). Given that his writings after *Sources of the Self* continue to make room for nonhuman sources of value, it would seem Kerr is on to something important here.

In these writings, Taylor goes beyond a mere anthropological use of ontology, in a crucial attempt to transcend anthropocentrism in moral thinking. In so doing, he explicitly praises the work of Iris Murdoch for criticizing the "narrowness" of contemporary moral philosophy, and for urging us to abandon the narrow question of "a good and satisfying life" to the consideration of the good as something that "cannot be entirely or exhaustively explained in terms of its contributing to a fuller, better, richer, more satisfying human life" (1996/2011, 4–5).[7] In other words, as Taylor understands her, Murdoch rightly criticizes contemporary moral philosophy for being overly anthropocentric, as its central focus on human flourishing leaves no room for goods of *intrinsic* value, that is, value in their own right independent of any use they have for human beings. However, Taylor's endorsement of this Murdochian conception of a good beyond the self gets lost from view by synchronizing his "anthropocentric" philosophical anthropology and his "nonanthropocentric" ontology—an inconsistency with which, as we have seen above, Taylor himself has no difficulty.

Taylor's nonanthropocentrism takes center stage in his more recent writings, in which he poses the questions of what we are "committed to ontologically by our ethical views and commitments," and "what ontology can underpin our moral commitments" (2003, 305; 2007, 607). Reflecting on this issue, his diagnosis is that we must respond to the following challenge: *either* we correct our (implicit) naturalist ontology *or* we must revise the most striking features of our moral experience. As has been noted (in section 1.1.1), Taylor's central claim is that a naturalist perspective cannot accommodate (what he sees as) the most striking features of human reality: the contrast between first-order and second-order desires, the distinction between strong and weak evaluation, and the appeal of incommensurably higher goods. As he says, there is no room for such ordinary moral experiences within "the ontology we allow ourselves as post-Galilean naturalists" in the sense that the latter, when presented as a *philosophical* thesis, cannot explain "how values of an incommensurably higher range can have a place in post-Galilean nature" (2003, 309, 319).

Taylor elaborates on this in *Retrieving Realism* by separating what he calls "life meanings, which we share as biological creatures" from "human meanings," that is, "meanings on a moral, or an ethical, or a spiritual level, having to do with what are seen as the highest goals or the best way of life" (2015, 108). Against this background, Taylor makes two claims: a positive yet hesitant one, and a negative yet confident one. The positive claim states that the attribution of human meanings is not arbitrary, but "in response to something" (2015, 129). However, Taylor emphasizes, we can see this only when we abandon post-Galilean models and reflect on human life on its own terms, since moral meanings are essentially understood to be different from basic natural desires. The negative claim, then, argues that the attempt to reduce human meanings to basic life meanings in an all-inclusive scientific theory seems an "unpromising strategy" since "the basis of our science is the discovery of a universe whose causal laws take no account of us and our human meanings" (2015, 158–59). In this respect, Taylor has moved from a modest view to a bolder one. Whereas he leaves open the possibility of such a superseding theory in "Ethics and Ontology" by concluding that the "hoped-for-reconciliation" between moral phenomenology and naturalist ontology is "somewhat premature" (2003, 320), he later suggests that the studies of physical and human nature invoke incompatible ontological realities, now arguing for "two independent accounts of reality, one describing those aspects of nature as it is in itself revealed to detached observers, and another account of reality as it is revealed to involved human beings" (2015, 153).

Seen in this light, it is clear that Taylor's nonanthropocentric understanding of strong evaluation deviates from the initial philosophical-anthropological question of what characterizes a human agent. Regrettably, Taylor himself does not remark on what is behind the changes of emphasis in his different writings. However, even when there is no significant change of mind, it remains striking that this full-out attack on naturalist ontology makes a much bolder claim than Taylor's critique of the "motivated suppression of moral ontology" in *Sources of the Self* (1989, 10), as he now seeks to undercut naturalistic *metaphysical* beliefs and not just anthropological ones. As will emerge in the following sections, it is precisely this nonanthropocentric attack on naturalist metaphysics that gets obscured from view in the way some of Taylor's commentators have reconstructed his ontology.

Against this background, *the central aim of the analysis developed in this book is to obtain a clearer picture of how Taylor's firm claims about selfhood and morality relate to his highly tentative nonanthropocentric positions in ethics and ontology.* I believe this question is crucial, because Taylor will have to be honest about his own metaphysical view in criticizing naturalist ontologies, for these cannot be rejected without reaching out to some ontological contraposition beyond philosophical anthropology and moral phenomenology. Following Kerr, I suspect that this type of concern revolves neither around philosophical anthropology nor around moral phenomenology, but around a nonanthropocentric ontological perspective on the good.

I will elaborate on this in the remainder of this chapter, arguing that Taylor's strategy to encapsulate different philosophical domains in order to strike several blows at naturalism runs into a number of problems. At the same time, I hold that he is on to something very important, exploring the interstitial[8] spaces between philosophical areas that intramural debates can make no sense of. Most crucially, what Taylor leaves unexplained is the relationship between the different *methods* behind his philosophical-anthropological, moral-phenomenological, and ontological claims. Does the doctrine of strong evaluation distinguish between genuinely different modes of reasoning and understanding or is Taylor simply saying the same thing in different ways? And if they are different, should they not also be confined to different areas: arguments in philosophical anthropology, phenomenological explanation in ethics, and reasoning in ontological debates. But what, then, one might ask, is the relationship between the different arguments?

2.2 COMPLICATING THE DOCTRINE OF STRONG EVALUATION

The above discussion raises the following question: How should we understand Taylor's interwoven mode of argumentation in between philosophical anthropology, ethics, phenomenology, and ontology? Reflecting on this question, several interpreters acknowledge Taylor's tendency to link philosophical issues together.[9] Rather than to insist on mainstream analytical distinctions, these commentators adhere to Taylor's characteristic language in elaborating his views. At least two reasons support this approach. First, anyone who attempts to distinguish Taylor's various concerns is in fact "trying to sever themes that resist separation" (Abbey 2000, 3–4), because Taylor not only combines philosophical anthropology and ethics (section 2.1.1), but also has a way of entwining ontological and phenomenological reflections with his account of morality (section 2.1.2), while also exploring a distinctive nonanthropocentric approach to both ethics and ontology (section 2.1.3). Second, we also saw that Taylor himself does not see the need to separate his claims, since all these claims are relevant for his central topic of strong evaluation. Although these considerations suggest that segregating Taylor's views can only be distorting, I think that doing so will not only clarify Taylor's different modes of reasoning, but will also uncover certain difficulties in his methods.

Moreover, as I will try to show in the following sections, in their efforts to make Taylor's account plausible within the limits of his own language, his interpreters themselves are often lacking in clarity to such an extent that the need to differentiate Taylor's claims is reinforced rather than weakened. I first examine the closely related readings of Nicholas Smith and Ruth Abbey, focusing on the philosophical-anthropological levels of Taylor's project (section 2.2.1). Subsequently, I emphasize the elusive nature of Taylor's ontological claims by discussing the views of Hartmut Rosa, Paul Saurette, and Stephen White (section 2.2.2). Finally, I invoke the phenomenological aspect of Taylor's views by adding the critiques of Arto Laitinen and Frederick Olafson (section 2.2.3).

2.2.1 A Two-Dimensional Approach

Put simply, my claim is that Taylor's doctrine of strong evaluation is in need of conceptual clarification. It became clear in the previous chapter (section 1.3) that this is no easy task as taking a too-*narrow* approach to Taylor's arguments, such as Flanagan's and Johnston's, easily misconstrues his views. In this section, however, I want to make the opposing point and highlight how the endorsement of an overly *broad* approach by Taylor's major interpreters, Smith and Abbey, has limited their clarifications of Taylor's ontological project.

As argued (in section 2.1.3), one major drawback of Taylor's relaxed notion of ontology is that it leaves unexplained the relationships between his anthropological and phenomenological arguments, on the one hand, and his nonanthropocentric perspectives in ethics and ontology, on the other. Interestingly, Smith seems to acknowledge this tension when he discusses the young Taylor's engagement with the phenomenology of Merleau-Ponty. As Smith explains, while "phenomenology may be well-suited to clarifying the structure of lived experience [. . .] it is not clear what *ontological* conclusions can be established by such argument" (2002, 33, original emphasis). What seems even more striking for understanding Taylor's interwoven arguments is Smith's conclusion that "some of Taylor's ontological claims are insufficiently backed up by his arguments" (2002, 240). As we will see, however, since Smith understands ontological claims essentially as philosophical-anthropological ones, his analysis does not allow us access to Taylor's nonanthropocentric perspective.

We need to consider two points to appreciate Smith's claims about ontology: his understanding of Taylor's project as a whole and his explanation of the scope of Taylor's arguments. In Smith's view, Taylor's critique of naturalism feeds into a philosophical-anthropological project that includes both a "transcendental" and a "historical" task (2002, 7). While the first involves showing "*that* meaning is a constitutive component of human reality" via transcendental argumentation, the second addresses the issue of "*how* it is," that is, to show "the *historicity* of the meanings that inescapably structure human reality," requiring a historical approach (Smith 2002, 7, original emphases). Smith then continues to show that the transcendental and historical levels of Taylor's project correspond with two different types of argument. As he says, "the nature and extent of a philosophical anthropology based on transcendental argument becomes clearer in view of a distinction Taylor draws between two kinds of dialectical movement," that is, one "ontological," and another "interpretative" (Smith 2002, 63–64).

For present purposes, it suffices to illustrate how Smith's endorsement of Taylor's terminology tends to limit the picture he draws of Taylor's arguments as a whole. In this regard, it is crucial that Smith follows Taylor's anthropological use of the concept of ontology, upholding his phrase of an "ontology of the human." As he explains, "one of Taylor's chief aims is to rehabilitate the idea of an ontology of the human," that is, "an account of the distinctive, essential features of human reality" (Smith 2002, 237). Smith's reading of Taylor can be further characterized by focusing on two of his most central claims. The first is the assertion that Taylor's "transcendental-ontological" argument is, by its very nature, fairly limited in its scope: "We have not learnt anything about how things are 'in themselves,' that is, how things are independent of our experience. We have not arrived at any metaphysical truths" (Smith 2002, 63). Put simply, Taylor's mode of reflection is "unlikely to countenance anything but a thin or minimal ontology of the human" (2002, 101). However "thin" its ontological results may be, Smith continues, it is clear that Taylor's transcendental argument contains far more ontological substance than the second, "interpretative" type of argument, because "in Taylor's view, interpretative dialectics does not entitle us to ontological claims," that is, "it does not inform us about the essence of human subjectivity" (2002, 64). However, Smith continues, the interpretative approach still has a role to play in the historical aspect of Taylor's project, because "it is a useful tool for understanding changes in the way human subjectivity is conceived and actualized" (2002, 64). As a result, Smith's study indicates that the ontological import of Taylor's positions is necessarily limited. On the one hand, only a thin or minimal philosophical anthropology (or "ontology of the human") can be established by Taylor's transcendental argument. On the other, the historical account that gives substance to Taylor's philosophical anthropology does not entitle him to ontological claims at all.

Related to these limitations, Smith sees a more general tension in Taylor's work. As Taylor at once tries to identify "universal features of human subjectivity" along the transcendental axis of his project and aims at describing the "contingent cultural manifestations" of these universal features along the historical axis, he "runs the risk of 'anthropologizing' or 'ontologizing' historically contingent features of subjectivity" (Smith 2002, 101, 107). In this respect, Smith criticizes Taylor for not having clearly separated his two principal approaches, as it is "not always clear where Taylor's philosophical anthropology ends and where his philosophic history begins" (2002, 8). Other critics express similar concerns. Olafson, for example, finds it "extremely difficult to see what kind of balance Taylor thinks he has struck between a common and universal selfhood and the historically quite diverse versions of what selfhood involves" (1994, 193), whereas Flanagan finds it "extremely puzzling that such a historicist as Taylor is tempted to make such essentialist claims at all" (1996, 154).

In her explanation of Taylor's work, Abbey has elaborated a similar characterization of Taylor's ontological project prior to Smith. In fact, she was the first to suggest that "a useful way of understanding Taylor's approach to selfhood is to distinguish two different, but complementary aspects: its historicist and its ontological dimensions" (Abbey 2000, 56). Smith's analysis is largely based on Abbey's original distinction, as both accounts defend Taylor against reductionist readings by attributing a "two-dimensional" approach to him, arguing that Taylor's philosophy draws either on ontological and historicist aspects (Abbey) or on transcendental-ontological and historical-interpretative aspects (Smith). Abbey further summarizes Taylor's approach to selfhood as an attempt to "both acknowledge the features that are common to all humans while also allowing for the great variety of ways in which these same features are experienced" (2000, 71). On the whole, she argues, we can come to grips with Taylor's philosophical-anthropological, historical, and ontological claims all at once by drawing a distinction between "things that change and those that stay the same" (2000, 9).

This two-dimensional clarification of Taylor's thought is revealing in two respects. On the one hand, Abbey and Smith have persuasively shown the inadequacy of reductionist approaches to Taylor's writings. On the other hand, however, I believe that neither Abbey's nor Smith's two-dimensional interpretation fully captures the complexity of Taylor's doctrine of strong evaluation. This is mainly because their endorsement of a broad conception of ontology in explaining issues that Taylor labels both as philosophical-anthropological and ontological limits their accounts of Taylor's project as a whole. One major disadvantage of equating ontology with philosophical anthropology is that it reduces ontological inquiry in general and makes invisible Taylor's nonanthropocentric view in particular. That is, by explaining Taylor's claims exclusively in terms of human experience and self-understanding, Abbey's and Smith's readings cannot accommodate Taylor's concern for the metaphysical underpinnings of strong evaluation, nor do they bring us closer to his nonanthropocentric approaches to ethics and ontology.

This issue is further complicated in *Retrieving Realism*, in which Taylor seems to refute Smith's idea that a theory about human agency does not reveal anything about "how things are 'in themselves,' that is, how things are independent of our experience" (Smith 2002, 63). As Taylor says, "the idea is deeply wrong that you can give a state description of the agent without any reference to his or her world (or a description of the world qua world without saying a lot about the agent)" (2015, 94). In making this claim, he seems to extend his picture of the human agent (philosophical anthropology) by including certain issues about "the world qua world" (metaphysics), but this move cannot be made intelligible on a reading that recognizes only the philosophical-anthropological and historical aspects of Taylor's thought. That is, when Smith invokes Taylor's "ontological" claims, he does not appeal to the metaphysical implications of strong evaluation but discusses claims about "the essence of human subjectivity" or features "without which an agent would not be recognizably human" (2002, 64, 88). He further insists that Taylor's transcendental argument specifically lends validity to an account of human *subjectivity*, as Taylor wants to show "how justified claims about the limits of subjectivity are possible" in order to "identify essential features of human reality" (Smith 2002, 239). Metaphysics is just not relevant here.

At first glance, the same type of human-centeredness seems to characterize Abbey's book, as she argues that Taylor's claims can generally be raised under "the rubric of human nature" or "investigations of philosophical anthropology," since most of his concerns relate to "the wider question of what it is to be human" (2000, 57). Although this way of explaining Taylor's ontology leaves little room for his allusions about the metaphysical reality underlying our human nature, Abbey nonetheless recognizes features of Taylor's thought that reach beyond philosophical anthropology. In this way, she mentions Taylor's belief that "human beings experience the goods that command their respect in a nonanthropocentric way, as not deriving solely from human will or choice nor depending only on the fact of individual affirmation for their value" (2000, 31). In later work, Abbey also refers to "Taylor's method of defending a non-subjectivist account of morality" and stresses "Taylor's attempt to transcend subjectivism or anthropocentrism in ethical thinking by adumbrating a moral ontology that makes room for sources of moral motivation and allegiance that are non-or extrahuman" (2004, 9–10).

Intriguingly, she further suggests that Taylor's nonanthropocentric view on moral sources is rather incomplete when she adds that it is "not so clear whether these sources are *necessarily* non anthropocentric" (2000, 29, italics mine). This point is spot on because to this day, there is no consensus on the metaphysical implications of Taylor's nonanthropocentric view, as it remains unclear what metaethical position he means to defend in support of his nonanthropocentrism. In fact, Abbey explains that Taylor's continued nonanthropocentric affirmations after *Sources of the Self* put him in a rather peculiar philosophical position:

> in previous writings his claim has been that humans feel their strongly valued goods to be grounded in something more than individual choice. But this is presented as part of his "best account" of moral experience, and as something that could be disproved. The suggestion that humans need to surpass anthropocentrism does not enjoy the ontological status it seems to acquire in these later works. (2000, 212)

In the face of this crucial observation—that the later Taylor seems to modify his ontological view beyond philosophical anthropology and moral phenomenology—it is somewhat of a letdown that neither Abbey nor Smith elaborates on the important question of how Taylor's tentative nonanthropocentric ontologizing relates to his more developed views on selfhood and morality. Instead—without looking at the different ways in which Taylor uses the concept of ontology and without considering the tensions between these different uses—Abbey and Smith continue to uphold Taylor's broad employment of the concept of ontology in explaining his views. That is, although Abbey writes in detail about the "ontological dimensions of selfhood" (2000, 55–72), she leaves unexplained—her own keen observation—that Taylor's nonanthropocentric approach to ontology explicitly reaches *beyond* the self. In the same way, Smith emphasizes that Taylor's thesis of strong evaluation is both an "ontological thesis" and "a matter of anthropological necessity" (2002, 88, 93), yet without asking supplementary questions about the relationship between the anthropological and ontological dimensions of this intricate view. The problem with Abbey's and Smith's broad explanations, then, is that they restate rather than resolve the issue of how to understand the connections between Taylor's interwoven arguments; arguments that push the boundaries of philosophical anthropology, ethics, ontology, phenomenology, and metaphysics. Surprisingly, Smith even invokes the very idea that there is "something conceptually misplaced about the idea of an ontology of the human," yet he himself does not seem hindered by the ambiguity of this concept in explaining Taylor's views (2002, 239).

On the whole, the holistic analyses of Abbey and Smith are illuminating correctives of the many distorting reductionist readings of Taylor's writings, drawing attention to the philosophical-anthropological and the historical dimensions of Taylor's thought. They are also right to point out that Taylor is entering dangerous ground because of this two-dimensional approach. Yet at the same time, their accounts tend to block from view that this is not Taylor's only concern. It is not just that we do not *need* the notion of ontology to explain anthropological issues, but more that there is no conceptual place left for Taylor's more metaphysical concerns in Abbey's and Smith's anthropological interpretations of Taylor's ontology. More particularly, their views cannot explain how and where the issue of nonanthropocentrism enters in Taylor's thought. In this respect, falsely equating philosophical anthropology and ontology is as if a category that Taylor needs for his nonanthropocentric urges is being illegitimately credited with a philosophical-anthropological grounding.

2.2.2 Weak Anthropology Versus Strong Ontology?

The difficulty of recognizing the full scope of Taylor's ontology seems partly due to his ambiguous formulations. For although he already adopts a nonanthropocentric perspective in *Sources of the Self*, this was visible at that stage only between the lines because of his unclear concepts of a "moral ontology" and an "ontology of the human." Because of these terms, Taylor's ontological claims have been interpreted as merely depicting features of human self-understanding, while he is also trying to open up the more metaphysically sensitive question of what it is that implicitly informs and directs these self-understandings. By adding this extra question, Taylor moves—tentatively, yet boldly—beyond the bounds of philosophical anthropology.

My hypothesis is that we can only come to grips with this nonanthropocentric tactic if we (1) draw a clear distinction between philosophical anthropology and ontology; (2) focus our attention on the metaethical context in which Taylor makes his nonanthropocentric ontological claims; and (3) trace Taylor's nonanthropocentrism back to the concept of strong evaluation. The previous section makes the case for the first point: if we want to account for the full breadth of Taylor's ontological views, then we should stop treating his human-focused anthropological claims as identical to his nonanthropocentric metaphysical concerns. The second point is related to Taylor's engagement with the moral philosophy of Murdoch and to the way in which he explicitly applies his nonanthropocentric ontological perspective to ethical (not philosophical-anthropological) questions in the papers "Iris Murdoch and Moral Philosophy," "Ethics and Ontology," and "Disenchantment-Reenchantment." The third point stages Taylor's view that it lies in the nature of strong evaluations to "claim truth, reality, or objective rightness," while also elevating his questions of what we are "committed to ontologically by our ethical views and commitments" and "what ontology can underpin our moral commitments" (2011b, 298; 2003, 305; 2007, 607). The advantage of this novel interpretation of Taylor's views is that it shifts the level of debate. That is, instead of arguing about whether Taylor's claims are best understood as transcendental, historical, philosophical-anthropological, or ontological, the present interpretation draws attention to a central background assumption of Taylor's thinking as a whole, namely *that there is a genuine connection between ethics and ontology that is best explained by a non anthropocentric understanding of strong evaluation.*

However, the connection between ethics, ontology, and strong evaluation must be explored with caution. This is because although we may no longer run the risk of confusing Taylor's anthropological and ontological claims, we can still fall into the same trap by blurring the distinction between ethical and ontological claims, that is, to misapprehend Taylor's account of ethics as an ontological theory. Rosa seems to make a mistake of this kind when he argues that we can evaluate in a strong sense only "if we take some intrinsically valuable goods (which direct these strong evaluations) as *ontological givens*," which commits him to the rather puzzling conclusion that "we are forced by transcendental necessity *to give an ontological grounding* to what we see as the fundamental goods" (Rosa 1995, 22, 24, italics mine). Saurette, to take another example, goes one step further. In his view, Taylor is "laying out a philosophical anthropology that appears to function similarly to an incontestable ontology replete with moral implications" (Saurette 2005, 198). The problem with this way of lumping Taylor's arguments together is not merely that it is beyond comprehension, but that it blunts the force of each of Taylor's separate positions.

This is where the need to differentiate Taylor's claims emerges in full force. For example, it may be helpful to separate Taylor's understanding of morality as involving higher goods from the more metaphysical concern with where the appeal of such independent goods comes from. Put differently, to say that human beings tend to derive ontological imperatives from their moral experience is one thing, but to ask what brings about this phenomenon is yet another. Even though Taylor's nonanthropocentrism indeed seems to leave room for the possibility of an "ontological foundation" of moral goods (whatever this might mean), it seems clear enough, *pace* Rosa, that human beings cannot simply give this ontological grounding *themselves*. For this reason, or so it would seem, Saurette emphasizes that "Taylor follows Kant in avoiding strong ontological claims about the nature of the world, instead making only weaker transcendental claims about the nature of our embodied subjectivity" (2005, 206), thereby echoing Smith's point about the limited ontological scope of Taylor's arguments.

Against the background of Smith's and Saurette's distinction between Taylor's "weak" anthropological claims and the "strong" ontological claims that he seems to have been deliberately avoiding, it is particularly interesting to look into White's characterization of Taylor as a "weak ontologist." White's weak ontological approach responds to two concerns: it accepts that all fundamental conceptualizations of self, other, and world are "contestable" and yet insists that such conceptualizations are "necessary" and "unavoidable" for an adequately reflective ethical and political life (White 2000, 8). A key element of weak ontology is the rejection of traditional modes of "strong" ontologizing that involve "too much 'metaphysics'" (1997, 505). White therefore seeks to sustain affirmation of our ethical-political commitments in a way that acknowledges their contingent and nonmetaphysical character at the same time. White's portrait of Taylor as a weak ontologist, then, is motivated by two main concerns. First, he wants to rehabilitate Taylor as a genuine ontological thinker, since "no thinker today has done more to press broad ontological questions than Charles Taylor" (White 2000, 42). Second, in so doing, White wants to defend Taylor against critics that wrongly assume that he is "offering a return to what I have called strong ontology; that is, some foundationalist, determinate truth about the shape and direction of self and world" (2000, 43).

At this stage of the discussion, it is still too early to give White's analysis the treatment it deserves.[10] However, the idea of weak ontology is helpful for raising the question of Taylor's ontology in at least two respects. First, even without getting into the details, White's approach to ontological theory seems far more fruitful than reductionist attempts that rest on the destructive logic that, as Abbey aptly puts it, "one is either a Platonic moral realist or a projectivist" (2000, 31). Second, however, it also would seem right at the outset that Taylor does not fit well into White's picture of a weak ontologist. For one thing, it is doubtful whether White's explicit nonmetaphysical stance is compatible with the nonanthropocentric elements in Taylor's thought. In this regard, it remains to be argued out in more detail whether Taylor's attack on naturalist ontology is still consonant with the basic weak ontological assumption that "all fundamental conceptualizations of self, other, and world are contestable" (White 2000, 8). Moreover, many commentators point out that Taylor's philosophical anthropology and his moral phenomenology insist on *universal*—rather than contestable—features of both selfhood and morality. As a philosophical anthropologist, he seeks to define "those timeless features of human agency that hold across cultures whenever we try to define the historically specific sense of self of a given age" (1988, 299). As a moral philosopher, he sets out to delineate structural features of moral experience that exist in "every" culture (1989, 16).

These points indicate a fairly strong stand (realist, essentialist, or some sort) on Taylor's part; at least on what human nature and morality consist in, but maybe even on the issue of "the way the world is," to put it in strong ontological terms. However, because Taylor also believes that "what we are as human agents is profoundly interpretation-dependent" (1988, 299), and, moreover, because his interwoven arguments steer a course between various philosophical domains, it still remains to be seen what types of argument—weak, strong, or other—stand in support of Taylor's nonanthropocentric viewpoint.

2.2.3 Phenomenological *Fiat*

Given the above observations, I believe that the first step to fully appreciate the strong elements of Taylor's thought is to detach ontology from philosophical anthropology in order to keep track of his nonanthropocentric perspective—which, as we have seen (in section 2.2.1) becomes invisible by equating philosophical anthropology with ontology—and to connect Taylor's ontological concerns to his ethical views instead. The advantage of doing so is that it draws attention to the relationship between Taylor's deeply interwoven nonanthropocentric views on ethics and ontology.

Unfortunately, though, there is a catch in his approach to ethics. This has to do with the fact that Taylor's account of morality is, as we have seen, phenomenological. We can start illustrating why this is problematic for the ontological dimension of strong evaluation by looking at Laitinen's understanding and critique of Taylor. Laitinen radically separates strong evaluation from what he calls "ontological sources of morality," and makes a distinction between Taylor's phenomenological claims, which he supports, while rejecting Taylor's interweaving of ethical and ontological claims altogether. As Laitinen explains his approach, this means separating "two layers" in Taylor's doctrine of strong evaluation: on the one hand, there is "the real engaged, cultural, lifeworldly layer of strong evaluations"; on the other, there is "the layer of ontological sources of morality, which is an ultimately superfluous theoretical construction or fiction" (Laitinen 2008, 6).

In fact, being able to drive a wedge between strong evaluation and ontological sources of morality is a crucial point in Laitinen's argument. At the same time, he argues that the elimination of such sources does not mean that we should no longer accept "Taylor's value-based pluralistic realism" (Laitinen 2008, 6). In one stroke, Laitinen thus wants to defend Taylor's moral phenomenology and moral realism while yet resist Taylor's distinctive justification of these positions in between ethics and ontology. He then repeats Smith's point that Taylor's argument for the inescapability of strong evaluation "can be argued for transcendentally" as strong evaluation is "a condition of specifically human agency" (Laitinen 2008, 6). Unlike Smith, however, Laitinen cannot just stop at this philosophical-anthropological level, as he also wants to endorse Taylor's realism. Yet Laitinen's explicit rejection of the *ontological* dimension of Taylor's ethics (i.e., the rejection of "ontological sources of morality") commits him to the peculiar statement that Taylor's "pluralist realist conception of strong evaluation" must be favored because of the "phenomenological priority it enjoys"—even in spite of the recognition that Taylor's view is "supported '*merely*' by phenomenology and comparative arguments" (Laitinen 2008, 6–7, italics mine).

Interestingly, this is precisely the kind of language for which Olafson criticizes Taylor, arguing that he tries to settle his rejection of antirealism in ethics by "a species of *phenomenological fiat*" (Olafson 1994, 194, italics mine). In Olafson's view, difficulties arise not only from Taylor's conception of higher goods but also from his nonanthropocentric notion of "a 'demand' that is made on us by the world—a demand that 'emanates from the world' and not just from ourselves" (Olafson 1994, 194).[11] Olafson's problem with these formulations, then, is that "the language of 'demands' and 'emanation' is nowhere shown to have a more secure basis in moral phenomenology than does that of 'projection'" (Olafson 1994, 194). In other words, as Olafson understands him, Taylor criticizes antirealism on behalf of a nonanthropocentric understanding of ethics that mandates him to do so, but he offers no real explanation or argument for the superiority of this phenomenological approach. In defense of Taylor, Abbey clarifies *why* Taylor thinks his moral phenomenology is best. As she says:

> It would make no sense to him to try to explain moral life in abstraction from one of its central forces; that is, humans. Beginning with humans and the way they experience morality, he claims that the most plausible explanation of morality is one that takes seriously humans' perception of the independence of the goods. He believes, therefore, that his moral theory is superior to all forms of projectivism, which explain morality away as meaning imposed by humans on a morally neutral world. (Abbey 2000, 29)

However, it is not just that Taylor is walking into very uncertain territory here, but more that his aim to describe the way humans experience morality begs the question. This is because although Taylor "*posits* that the best account of moral life does include reference to transcendent moral sources," it is not so clear "whether these sources are *necessarily* non anthropocentric" (Abbey 2000, 29, italics mine). As Taylor himself explains, it all comes down to what the "most illusion-free moral sources" are, but, he admits, all this "remains to be argued out" (1989, 342).

Against this background, I think Olafson is on to something important, namely a tension between Taylor's "weak" phenomenological approach to ethics on the one hand, and his "strong" nonanthropocentric ontological claims, on the other. In this respect, Laitinen points out that "mere phenomenological description is not yet an argument against reductivists" (2008, 80). In fact, he continues, "this is the reason why Taylor takes up the idea of transcendental arguments, indeed to back up phenomenological insights he draws from Merleau-Ponty, and also to back up some common sense views" (2008, 80). Given these clarifications, the imperative question seems to be this: If Taylor's transcendental argument merely stands in support of his philosophically *weaker* claims (either philosophical-anthropological or moral-phenomenological), then how does he validate his *stronger* ontological claims? Unfortunately, Laitinen's approval of Taylor's "minimal realism about morality" or "phenomenological moral realism" because of its "phenomenological priority" (2008, 7, 161, 167) is talking around the issue rather than addressing it, for it does not make clear how a transcendental phenomenological description of moral experience simultaneously allows for moral-realist claims. In this regard, Olafson's observation of a "phenomenological *fiat*" is spot on. Since it seems highly unlikely that ontological claims can be authorized by having recourse to transcendental argumentation, I suspect that either Taylor himself or some of his interpreters are overplaying their hand. I will elaborate on this in the next section.

2.3 UNRAVELING THE DOCTRINE OF STRONG EVALUATION

Olafson's critique of a phenomenological fiat has important implications for the doctrine of strong evaluation. As we have seen (in section 2.1.3), one of the issues that emerge from Taylor's nonanthropocentric ontologizing is that our strong evaluations cannot be explained solely in anthropological and phenomenological terms because they lay claims beyond human self-understanding. At the same time, however, the moral-phenomenological level of Taylor's thought nonetheless *begins* with human experience, describing how human beings experience the "higher" call of moral demands independently of their respective desires. This raises the crucial question whether strong evaluation exists solely at phenomenological and anthropological levels, that is, as a truth of human subjectivity without further support in nonhuman reality (as Abbey, Smith, and Laitinen seem to argue); or that it also provides access to metaphysical facts beyond the human. Further investigations are needed to answer this question, because the dominant interpretations of Taylor's ontology tend to gloss over his nonanthropocentric claims, either by explaining his ontology in philosophical-anthropological terms (Abbey, Smith) or by rejecting his ontological explanation of moral sources (Laitinen). This indicates that we not only need a better understanding of Taylor's ontological claims, but that we also need a different methodological focus.

Against this background, my purpose in this section is to highlight a central problem in Taylor's thought and to explore what type of inquiry might solve this problem. I first argue for a tension between Taylor's phenomenological approach to ethics and his claims about ontology (section 2.3.1), while also laying out how this tension affects his attack on naturalist ontology (section 2.3.2). Finally, I explore the possibility that Taylor's interwoven mode of argumentation might prove to be an effective way of dealing with the problems at hand (section 2.3.3).

2.3.1 A Phenomenological Approach to Ethics with Ontological Implications?

The fact that strong evaluations are rooted in human experience while also raising nonanthropocentric issues brings us to the question of how ethics and ontology are related in Taylor's work. Throughout different writings, Taylor touches the issue of what we are committed to ontologically by our ethical views and commitments, but there is always something tentative in his adhesion. The problem of how ethics and ontology are related is evoked in all the key publications on strong evaluation, but it is not extensively explored in any of these works. On the one hand, it thus seems clear that Taylor sees this question as a valuable one. On the other, he never omits to insist that it is not all that clear how we should go about answering it. Ironically, even at the very end of "Ethics and Ontology"—the paper in which he puts the connection between ethics and ontology forward as a central theme—Taylor is still becoming more aware of how far he is from finding a proper formulation of the issue. He raises the same problem in *A Secular Age* by asserting that one of the greatest challenges for ethics is "the issue of how to align our best phenomenology with an adequate ontology" (2007, 609). Also worth noting is the closing section of *Retrieving Realism,* which states that "there remain deep differences of basic ontology" despite Taylor's insistence on there being at least some "partial convergences" between our ethical views (2015, 164, 167).

Although the tension between "weak" claims—of philosophical anthropology and moral phenomenology—and "strong" claims—of moral realism and metaphysics—is only really put to work in these late, highly tentative writings, it is implicit in Taylor's oeuvre as a whole. This is because he understands morality as requiring a double approach: both human focused and nonanthropocentric. Whereas Taylor's philosophical-anthropological and moral-phenomenological explanations clarify the structural features of human reality, the metaphysical dimension of the good turns on something different, something stronger, and therefore necessitates a nonanthropocentric viewpoint.

Although Taylor's principal aim is to connect his different arguments and to "resolve the opposition itself by arguing that subjectivity and objectivity are essentially intertwined in the realm of value" (Anderson 1996, 17), there is a real tension from the outset with regard to his methodology. As Abbey and Smith have clarified, Taylor is fully aware this—that is, insofar as the tension is explained in terms of the philosophical-anthropological and the historical levels of his project. In this way, Taylor explicitly acknowledges the risks involved in his project of separating the "human universals" from the "historical constellations" (1989, 112). However, shining a spotlight on Taylor's nonanthropocentric ontologizing (section 2.1.3) has altered this two-dimensional picture. In fact, his interwoven arguments look surprisingly different when we consider his claims from a novel methodological perspective. In my view, the difficulties of Taylor's strategies do not reside in the tense relationship between his philosophical-anthropological and historical approaches, but in his method of moral phenomenology on the one hand, and his nonanthropocentric approaches to ethics and ontology on the other. This means that the present interpretation of Taylor's ontology differs from the readings of Abbey and Smith in that it advances their two-dimensional picture by adding a *third*, nonanthropocentric dimension. In so doing, I also depart from Laitinen's approach: instead of rejecting Taylor's tendency toward nonanthropocentrism in ethics and ontology, I argue that we should take it far more seriously than has been done before in Taylor scholarship.

The crucial point is this: Taylor wants to reject reductive conceptions of morality and to refute naturalist ontology *at one stroke*. We can illustrate this problem by looking at the beginning of *Sources of the Self*. In trying to understand our moral predicament, Taylor informs us, we must not let ourselves be influenced by mainstream contemporary ethics because it employs such a "narrow" definition of morality (1989, 3). In order to retrieve the moral and spiritual background of our ordinary reactions and responses, we should rather put contemporary moral theorizing "in brackets," or "suspend" its relevance, to put it in traditional phenomenological terms.[12] For only if we succeed in doing so, Taylor maintains, will we be able to "uncover buried goods through rearticulation" (1989, 520). Here, then, is the reason why Taylor incites his readers to go through a kind of "moral-phenomenological reduction" with respect to their knowledge of what morality is, and to follow him in his disclosure of our "original" moral experience, without assuming the truth or validity of any moral theory. As a result, Taylor's alternative to the reductionist mind-set in contemporary ethics is in fact another kind of reduction, namely a *methodological* reduction that aims to expose the "background picture of our spiritual nature" that implicitly informs the central moral intuitions of our age (1989, 3–4).

What is essential to the paradigmatic phenomenological method in Husserl's sense, however, is that we consider any statement about the external world as void of ontological implications. But this is a step Taylor does not want to take. Quite to the contrary, the question that emerges from his views is precisely "how to *align* our best phenomenology with an adequate ontology" (2007, 609, italics mine). It would seem, therefore, unlike Husserl's phenomenology, that Taylor's moral-phenomenological investigations indeed have certain ontological implications.

Both Smith (2002, 31–32) and Laitinen (2008, 79–80) have emphasized Taylor's ambivalent relation to phenomenology. On the one hand, Taylor is clearly indebted to the phenomenologies of Heidegger and Merleau-Ponty for his critique of the subject/object ontology introduced by Descartes.[13] On the other hand, he has been skeptical from the outset of the very objective of a pure self-authenticating vocabulary of phenomenological description. As noted (in section 1.1.2), the young Taylor explicitly criticizes Merleau-Ponty in this regard, arguing that "we must always take some concepts for granted in examining others, accept some assumptions in order to call others into question" (1959, 103). In line with his early view, the later Taylor continues to insist on the fundamental embeddedness of human language and knowledge:

> Our particular awareness, our grasp on particular things, are embedded in a more general framework take, which gives them their sense. This take is holistic: you can't break it down into a heap of particular grasps. And—what is the same thing from another side—it is inescapable: all particulate grasps suppose it, lean on it. (2015, 23)

However, Taylor explains, the fact that we are "always and inevitably thinking within such taken-as-there frameworks" does not mean that phenomenology's attempt to attain *contact* with reality is vain, but it does necessitate "a reembedding of thought and knowledge in the bodily and social-cultural contexts in which it takes place" (2013, 73, 75; 2015, 20, 18). This means that after having rejected modern phenomenology's ideal of pure, presuppositionless description at the start of his career, the later Taylor moves on to show that human beings are inescapably "in unmediated touch with everyday reality" (2015, 131). As he explains in reference to what he calls the "contact theories" of Heidegger, Merleau-Ponty, and Wittgenstein:

> The attempt is to articulate the framework or context within which our explicit depictions of reality make sense, and to show how this is inseparable from our activity as the kind of embodied, social, and cultural beings we are. The contact here is [. . .] something primordial, something we never escape. It is the contact of living, active beings, whose life form involves acting in and on a world which also acts on them. (2013, 73; 2015, 18)

This means that, unlike Husserl, who proposed that in practicing phenomenology we ought to bracket the question of the existence of the world around us, Taylor insists that his moral phenomenology puts the question of "what ontology can underpin our moral commitments" right back on the agenda (2007, 607). In fact—and this point is essential—he argues that his phenomenology of moral experience is allied with a *realist* ontology. Although Taylor nowhere explicitly presents himself as an advocate of moral realism in his key publications, he has admitted, as he puts it, to be "thinking of myself as a moral realist," arguing for "a kind of moral realism" (1991, 246, 242).

Methodologically speaking, however, Taylor wants to have it both ways by adopting this hybrid position. His moral-phenomenological critique of contemporary moral philosophy is based on—and therefore limited to—our own experience of being in the world; yet he also seeks to transcend human experience by raising the issue of what we are committed to ontologically by our ethical intuitions. As noted (in section 2.2.3), Olafson has made plain that there is a real tension here, and, moreover, one that can neither be solved by drawing a distinction between "things that change and those that stay the same" (Abbey 2000, 10) nor between "ontological" and "interpretative" dialectics (Smith 2002, 63–64). But if we do not want to eliminate altogether Taylor's interwoven tactic by opting for just one of the two poles (phenomenology or ontology)—as Laitinen urges us to do by arguing for *Strong Evaluation Without Moral Sources* (2008)—then a central problem arises in what is perhaps best described as Taylor's "moral-realist phenomenology": How to align his initial *phenomenological* starting point, which focuses on the human point of view, with his *nonanthropocentric* realism about a world that also acts *on* us, "independently of one's success or failure in finding one's bearings" (1989, 30)? Put differently, what, if anything, are we committed to ontologically by Taylor's moral phenomenology?

The irony is that Taylor encounters this problem already at the beginning of his academic career. As he says in the early paper on phenomenology: "Merleau-Ponty's descriptions like all descriptions *commit him to a certain ontology*. If so, what status should we give to his ontology?" (1958, 131, italics mine). This fundamental question can also be directed at Taylor's own account: What are we committed to ontologically by his phenomenology of strong evaluation? In this regard, it is especially revealing that Taylor's later ontological view also remains quite exploratory and tentative. The really astonishing thing is that, published forty-five years later, his paper "Ethics and Ontology" is hardly more explicit than the allusions of the early text on Merleau-Ponty. Note the open end that characterizes both texts: the young Taylor dismisses the issue of Merleau-Ponty's ontology as "too complex to be treated here," while the more recent paper breaks off with the comment that "the conceptual means at my disposal are still too crude to explore this in an illuminating fashion" (1958, 132; 2003, 320). In other words, Taylor is reaffirming a crucial uncertainty with which he has been struggling all along. Although his consistency is admirable, it remains doubtful whether Taylor's thinking on the relationship between ethics and ontology has made any real progress down the decades.

2.3.2 Taylor's Rapid Move "Uphill"

Many of Taylor's critics accept his phenomenological account of moral experience, but seem to lose track of what he is trying to do along the ontological axis of his thought.[14] As Bernard Williams brilliantly puts it: "From a strong base in experience, Taylor very rapidly moves uphill, metaphysically speaking" (1990, 48). As has been discussed (in section 1.3.3), Johnston sees more than an argumentative sleight-of-hand in this two-stage approach, arguing that Taylor's conceptualizations "both point towards subjectivism as much as objectivism" in such an ambiguous way that "the nature of his own position becomes fundamentally unclear" (1999, 105). The central worry, it would seem, is not that (part of) Taylor's thought necessarily turns to the subject and its interiority, but that he also makes a move "outwards," raising the issue of the metaphysical underpinnings of morality. Both this outer nonanthropocentric bent and his human-focused analyses are constitutive of Taylor's doctrine of strong evaluation. But it is nowhere clarified—neither by Taylor nor by his interpreters—how these different investigations work together to illuminate the nonanthropocentric features of strong evaluation.

As has been noted (in section 1.1.1), Taylor's doctrine of strong evaluation is primarily a critique of naturalistic approaches to ethics. Rejecting the idea that value simply flows from our natural desires, he opposes any view that sees value as coming from our human responses to a neutral reality. Taylor clusters this type of view under the label "ethical naturalism," and he generally mentions John Mackie and Simon Blackburn as two of its advocates (2003, 306–307). From their perspectives, strong values can only appear as "errors" on our part (Mackie) or as "queer" entities (Blackburn) that we project onto a world that is in itself, properly understood, neutral or meaningless. As Taylor understands them, these naturalists argue that morality must ultimately be compatible with the terms of modern natural science. But this is exactly what Taylor's phenomenology seeks to make clear we cannot do. As he says:

> There is a tension between phenomenology and ontology. The former, properly and honestly carried through, seems to show that values of this higher status [. . .] are ineradicable from our deliberations of how to live. But ontology, defined naturalistically, says that properties of this kind can have no place in an account of things in the world. (2003, 310)

In criticizing ethical naturalism, Taylor thus wants to capture both our moral predicament in phenomenological terms, and to refute a naturalist ontology that cannot accommodate this phenomenology. He then seems to overplay his hand when he seeks to establish the critique of naturalism through transcendental argumentation. In this respect, it is important to note that Taylor characterizes his arguments about strong evaluation not as ontological, but as a combination of phenomenological points and transcendental reasoning. Without getting into the technical details of this view,[15] it is crucial that Taylor himself emphasizes the *limits* of transcendental arguments, arguing that "there remains an ultimate, ontological question they can't foreclose" (1995b, 33). At the same time, however, he defends his transcendental account of strong evaluation as a compelling argument against naturalism as it establishes not only a phenomenological truth, but also an account of "the limits of the conceivable in human life," that is, an account of its "transcendental conditions" (1989, 32).

In his characteristic way, Taylor here explicitly entangles his different approaches, but the nature of their entanglement is far from clear. On the one hand, he argues that ontological questions lie beyond the scope of transcendental arguments because they are grounded in the nature of experience. But on the other hand, Taylor nonetheless insists that *his* distinctive transcendental approach trumps naturalistic ones beyond mere phenomenological necessity, because it defines the conditions of agency. The problem, then, is that Taylor does not present his view as a challenging phenomenological description of human agency in the face of naturalistic explanations—as his method of transcendental argumentation obliges him to do—but rather seeks to *extend* his critique by challenging a naturalist conception of ontology. To use Williams' metaphor, the problem is that Taylor suddenly moves "uphill," *metaphysically speaking*, while acknowledging at the same time that his transcendental method does not allow for such a steep climb up.

As a result, he tries to validate his ontological critique by phenomenological *fiat*, that is, by simply *presupposing* the superiority of his phenomenological approach. This begs the question, because without a compelling argument for the authority of his account, Taylor's opponents can easily pay him back with the same coin by adhering to a naturalist counterdescription. Where does this leave us? If both moral phenomenology and transcendental argumentation cannot reveal ontological facts, then the critique of naturalist ontology is simply not valid. In other words, the problem with Taylor's interwoven phenomenological-transcendental tactic is not that it cannot foreclose ontological questions, but that ontological neutrality is not an option for it, as it seeks to establish "a kind of moral realism" (1991, 242). The later Taylor makes this very clear:

> The question can arise whether the values we espouse can be supported on the basis of the ontology to which we want to subscribe. Maybe [. . .] that would take us beyond the bounds of a naturalist ontology. The battle between phenomenology and ontology would break out again. (2003, 318)

These statements suggest that Taylor somehow seeks to extrapolate claims about *metaphysical* reality (ontology) from facts about *human* reality (phenomenology and anthropology). The question that arises out of all this is whether Taylor's human-focused perspectives do not cut him off from the nonanthropocentric ontological issues that he is trying to delineate at the same time. Is he simply overambitious in his claims? Or is Taylor's predicament rather symptomatic of the problem initially brought forward by his own diagnosis, namely that it is far from clear how to "align our best phenomenology with an adequate ontology" (2007, 609)? Even if we acknowledge that Taylor is trying to unveil the middle ground between "a 'Platonist' mode of moral realism" and "mere subjectivism," he has still to show how we gain access to this area at all (1994, 211).

Although I think Taylor is onto something important, there are several problems here. How to make sense of this rapid move uphill? Since Taylor criticizes naturalist ontology in crucial reference to his phenomenological and transcendental perspectives, we can only conclude that his argument against naturalism is meant to be phenomenological, transcendental, ethical, and ontological all in one. The problem here, I believe, is not that Taylor wants to back up his views on human nature by adding a transcendental tactic. Rather, the error lies in his attempt to establish an *ontological* argument based on his moral phenomenology.

It seems quite clear that neither moral phenomenology nor transcendental argumentation are sufficient ways of dealing with the tension between moral experience and naturalist ontology. Note that this is just one example of conflicting methodologies in Taylor's philosophy. Considering the three levels of the doctrine of strong evaluation, we can ask similar questions of coherence about all of these domains. In other words, what is the relationship between Taylor's philosophical-anthropological, moral-phenomenological, and ontological concerns? Evidently, all these issues are related through "the wider question of what it is to be human" as their common core (Abbey 2000, 57), but how to go from one field to another? It emerges from the above discussion that these connections are far from self-evident. But why, then, does Taylor continue to insist on the connection between ethics and ontology? What is this "intersecting zone" between moral experiences, on the one hand, and ontological commitments, on the other? In this regard, we should take note of the highly tentative manner in which Taylor raises the issue of ontology. As he concludes his paper "Ethics and Ontology":

> The really interesting question that remains is whether the ethic that all of us share, naturalists and anti-naturalists alike, say, the affirmation of universal human rights [. . .] can consort with the evolutionary naturalism that finds such higher goods "queer." [. . .] Here, on the brink of the really interesting question, I have to break off, partly through lack of time; and partly because the conceptual means at my disposal are still too crude to explore this in an illuminating fashion. I hope to return to this at another time. (2003, 320)

When Taylor finally does return to the issue at the end of *Retrieving Realism*, he again arrives at a rather modest conclusion. Despite there being "good reasons, moral and intellectual, to press forward and attempt a unification of perspectives," we cannot but acknowledge that "there remain deep differences of basic ontology" (2015, 167–68).[16]

Against the background of the present discussion one might conclude that, since neither Taylor himself nor his commentators see the need to question his distinctive employment of the concept of ontology, the burden of proof is with those who claim that Taylor's terminology is distorting. This is my claim indeed, for the crucial point is that an overly broad notion of ontology makes invisible the relationships between Taylor's philosophical anthropology and moral phenomenology on the one hand and his nonanthropocentric ontologizing on the other. Resisting the common trend to rate these on a par, I want to push beyond this and defend a more systematic reading of Taylor's doctrine of strong evaluation.

In my view, it is a source of great confusion that Taylor does not clearly separate his anthropological and phenomenological claims from his nonanthropocentric allusions about the metaphysical underpinnings of human nature. Basically, my claim is that you can account for a large part of Taylor's work, both for its philosophical-anthropological and moral-phenomenological levels, without invoking the word "ontology" at all. To conclude this point, what gets lost from view in a relaxed notion of ontology is how Taylor's nonanthropocentric claims are backed up by his arguments, since having recourse to philosophical anthropology, moral phenomenology, and transcendental reasoning does nothing to support them. The really puzzling thing is that Taylor himself insists on this point by arguing that his phenomenological-transcendental method leaves ontological questions unanswered (1995b, 33).

2.3.3 Pursuing the Links Across Taylor's Interwoven Arguments

So far, I have argued that the concept of ontology by itself adds nothing plausible to the project of a philosophical anthropology, nor does it enhance the credibility of a moral phenomenology. However, the fact that the transcendental argument that is supposed to secure Taylor's claims, has, as he says, both a "phenomenological moment" *and* establishes a kind of "realism," suggests at least that there is more at stake than just some conceptual confusion (1994, 209). Yet since Taylor remains open to the charge that transcendental argumentation is simply the wrong method to use in defense of ontological claims, we have still to find out how to explore Taylor's nonanthropocentrism in an illuminating fashion. In this respect, it is worth remembering that having recourse to a more conventional vocabulary does not help to improve understanding, but rather cuts us off from Taylor's interwoven mode of reasoning. This is because canonical methods force us to separate philosophical anthropology, phenomenology, ethics, and ontology rather than to focus on their relationships. White has certainly understood Taylor on this score, clarifying that it was not until he encountered the problem that at this level of interpretation "many familiar analytical categories and operations become blurred or exhibit torsional effects" that he came to realize "the full significance of Charles Taylor's *Sources of the Self*" (2005, 14). As White explains, "the more I pondered the relation between ethics and ontology, the more they seemed mutually constitutive at this level and the less possible it seemed to accord one or the other clear primacy" (2005, 14).

In reply to this uncertainty, I shall be resisting both the temptation of radically separating Taylor's approaches and the temptation of haphazardly lumping his claims together. That is, since Taylor endorses both "weak" anthropological and phenomenological claims and "strong" ontological and realist ones, I believe we can only shed light on the unity of his thinking if we *first* make clear distinctions between his philosophical-anthropological, moral-phenomenological, and ontological views and *then* reconstruct these concerns as different implications of the phenomenon of strong evaluation.

I would like to end by making three supplementary points. First, Taylor's effort of establishing the connections between the different levels of strong evaluation reflects more a "program" than a theory, as he still has to clarify the precise nature of their relationships rather than just to insist on them. As we have seen, the hesitant way in which Taylor begins to explore the connections between his various concerns has not only provoked considerable criticism, but has caused much confusion as well, especially with regard to Taylor's ontology. Second, given the debates about how to understand Taylor's interwoven arguments, one would expect that his nonanthropocentric approaches to ethics and ontology have triggered many commentators. Yet, because the very ways in which his major interpreters have reconstructed Taylor's claims tend to obscure the nonanthropocentric aspect of his positions, most studies do not take his nonanthropocentrism into account. Another reason that might explain why the nonanthropocentric dimension of strong evaluation has remained in the background of Taylor scholarship is that it is only really put to work in his late writings, and, again, in a highly tentative manner in all of these texts.[17] While many discussions have focused on analyzing, clarifying, and criticizing Taylor's views on ontology from a philosophical-anthropological viewpoint, his ontological claims are seldom discussed from a metaphysical perspective, nor is it part of the implicit background of these discussions.

One way of exploring what might be called the "metaphysics of strong evaluation" is via Taylor's latest question of what we are committed to ontologically by our ethical views. Or, coming from the opposite direction, we might ask whether the ontology to which we want to subscribe fits with our deepest moral instincts. Moreover, because the different orders of questions are logically linked via their common core, it would seem that you cannot establish something in relation to one debate without deciding at least some issues about the other. As this suggests, a great advantage of the focus on the links across Taylor's positions is that accepting a certain theory in one domain has strong consequences for the explanatory theories one can consistently adopt in the other, and vice versa. In this way, the connections between the different levels of Taylor's thought might allow access to a whole new area of questions that is opened up by the multilayered nature of strong evaluation, enabling us to see ontological problems in a whole new light. This brings me to the third point, namely that we should start by differentiating Taylor's various concerns in order to fully explore the potential of the doctrine of strong evaluation. That means: to draw the distinctions that Taylor himself fails to provide. The crux of the matter is that the issue of the underlying connections of the levels of strong evaluation can only arise on account of a clear grasp of the *boundaries* that separate them.

2.4 CONCLUSION: HOW TO UNDERSTAND TAYLOR'S INTERWOVEN MODE OF ARGUMENTATION?

This chapter has explored Taylor's distinctive interwoven mode of argumentation in elaborating on his doctrine of strong evaluation. The discussion of how the philosophical-anthropological, moral-phenomenological, and ontological levels of strong evaluation have been discussed in the literature showed that most studies add substantially to our understanding of the first two levels, but generally fail to account for the full scope of Taylor's ontological aspirations. Also, it was made clear that Taylor's nonanthropocentric ontologizing recedes into the background by his own ambiguous use of the concept of ontology, then also more particularly by his habit of equating ontology with philosophical anthropology. As a result, most of Taylor's commentators do not explain how and where his nonanthropocentrism enters in his thought.

In order to get a better understanding of Taylor's ontology, I proposed to replace the connection between philosophical anthropology and ontology with a focus on the relationship between ethics and ontology. Yet, we came up against another problem in doing so, because neither Taylor's phenomenological approach to ethics nor his transcendental argument entitles him to ontological claims. In an attempt to unravel Taylor's doctrine of strong evaluation, we were faced with a crucial problem: If neither philosophical anthropology nor moral phenomenology allows for ontological claims, then how should we understand Taylor's nonanthropocentric defense of moral realism?

If anything, this chapter has demonstrated that far too little attention has been paid to Taylor's attempt to develop interwoven arguments. Although this unusual method might provide access to a dimension in which nonanthropocentric claims are discernible, we should also acknowledge that Taylor's effort of establishing the connections between the different levels of strong evaluation is rather undeveloped, especially with regard to the relationship between ethics and ontology. In this respect, Taylor's suggestion that we might be in need of a stronger ontological foundation for our ethical beliefs than naturalist ontology can provide is a question rather than a statement.

Reflecting on this question, I will deduce three central arguments out of the doctrine of strong evaluation to explore in more detail in the following chapters: a philosophical-anthropological account that resists naturalist explanations of human nature (chapter 3); a moral-phenomenological argument against reductive understandings of morality (chapter 4); and a nonanthropocentric ontological view that challenges naturalist ontology (chapter 5). As this suggests, this means not only separating Taylor's philosophical anthropology from his moral phenomenology and ontology, but also distinguishing his moral philosophy from his ontology. As will emerge, this way of conceptually carving up Taylor's rich philosophical thought not only enables us to get a better grip on the distinct levels of strong evaluation, but also opens up the question of their relationship and the metaphysical status of Taylor's ontological view.

NOTES

1. Taylor used this expression to characterize his arguments about strong evaluation during a seminar at the University of Leuven, Belgium (June 2, 2015).

2. For this point, I am indebted to Fergus Kerr, who already described Taylor's *Sources of the Self* as being "explicitly a 'retrieval' of a non anthropocentric perspective on the good" (2004, 84). Although neglected by many commentators, I show in section 2.1.3 that Taylor has since continued along this path.

3. In this way, we already saw in chapter 1 that the attempts of Flanagan and Johnston to isolate Taylor's different positions crucially distort the meaning of strong evaluation.

4. He makes this point most elaborately in the paper "Overcoming Epistemology," arguing that the epistemological tradition behind modern naturalism is motivated by an implicit "disengaged anthropology," that is, one that centers on "the picture of the subject as ideally disengaged," on "a punctual view of the self," and on "the social consequence of the first two: an atomistic construal of society as constituted by, or ultimately to be explained in terms of, individual purposes." Through these, Taylor continues, modern epistemology connects with the moral ideals of "reflexive, self-given certainty," "self-responsibility," and "freedom as self-autonomy" (1995a, 6–7). See also *Retrieving Realism* for a rearticulation of this analysis (2015, 24–26).

5. The way Taylor introduces the concept of "moral ontology" in the opening pages of *Sources of the Self* gives the impression that it makes a vital point, but he then suddenly drops the term and no longer uses it, not in the rest of this book (with two rather arbitrary exceptions), nor in any of his other works (1989, 8–10, 41, 72).

6. See Saurette (2005, 208), Taylor (1989, 5), Smith (2002, 237), Kerr (2004, 96), and Laitinen (2008, 15).

7. Originally published as Taylor, Charles. 1996, "Iris Murdoch and Moral Philosophy." In *Iris Murdoch and the Search for Human Goodness,* edited by M. Antonaccio and W. Schweiker, 3–28. Chicago: University of Chicago Press; and reprinted in *Dilemmas and Connections* (2011a, 3–23). I refer to the latter version.

8. I am indebted to Jonathan VanAntwerpen for this term, who used it in his talk during the expert seminar "Pluralism and Secularism" at the University of Humanistic Studies in Utrecht on November 7, 2013.

9. See Abbey (2000), White (2000), Smith (2002), Kerr (2004), Saurette (2005), and Laitinen (2008).

10. I discuss White's view in more detail in sections 5.3.2 and 5.3.3.

11. The quotations are from *Sources of the Self* (1989, 523).

12. See Kerr (2004) for a complementary reading. Kerr argues that Taylor's account of morality is a continuation of the work of Elizabeth Anscombe, Philippa Foot, and Iris Murdoch. He notes that Taylor's strategy to "suspend respect for recent philosophical theories" sounds "very much in tune with Anscombe's own famous declaration [. . .] that moral philosophy should be laid aside 'at any rate until we have an adequate philosophy of psychology, in which we are conspicuously lacking'" (Kerr 2004, 91, 85).

13. See, for example, the many references to Heidegger and Merleau-Ponty in the papers "Overcoming Epistemology" and "Retrieving Realism" (1995a; 2013). A slightly revised version of this last text has been republished as the first two chapters of *Retrieving Realism* (2015, 1–54).

14. See, for example, Williams (1990, 48), Kymlicka (1991, 159), Rorty (1994, 199), Weinstock (1994, 174), and Laitinen (2008, 6–7).

15. I discuss Taylor's transcendental argument at length in section 3.3.

16. When asked about the ontological implications of strong evaluation during a seminar at the University of Leuven, Belgium (June 2, 2015), Taylor again demonstrated a strong sense of caution and hesitancy with regard to ontological problems, explaining that "there is a highly debatable meaning of what you have to assume to be able to talk in this domain."

17. See "Ethics and Ontology" (2003), *A Secular Age* (2007, 607–9, 692–93), "Disenchantment-Reenchantment" (2011b), *Retrieving Realism* (2015), and, standing out from the others by its early appearance, "Iris Murdoch and Moral Philosophy" (1996/2011).

REFERENCES

Abbey, Ruth. 2000. *Charles Taylor*. Teddington/Princeton: Acumen Press/Princeton University Press.

Abbey, Ruth, ed. 2004. *Contemporary Philosophy in Focus: Charles Taylor*. Cambridge, MA: Cambridge University Press.

Anderson, Joel. 1996. "The Personal Lives of Strong Evaluators: Identity, Pluralism, and Ontology in Charles Taylor's Value Theory." *Constellations: An International Journal of Critical and Democratic Theory* 3 (1): 17–38.

Flanagan, Owen. 1996. *Self Expressions. Mind, Morals, and the Meaning of Life*. New York/Oxford: Oxford University Press.
Johnston, Paul. 1999. *The Contradictions of Modern Moral Philosophy. Ethics after Wittgenstein*. London/New York: Routledge.
Kerr, Fergus. 2004. "The Self and the Good. Taylor's Moral Ontology." In *Contemporary Philosophy in Focus: Charles Taylor*, edited by Ruth Abbey, 84–104. Cambridge, MA: Cambridge University Press.
Kymlicka, Will. 1991. "The Ethics of Inarticulacy." *Inquiry* 34: 155–82.
Laitinen, Arto. 2008. *Strong Evaluation Without Moral Sources*. Berlin: Walter de Gruyter.
Laitinen, Arto, and Nicholas Smith, eds. 2002. *Perspectives on the Philosophy of Charles Taylor*. Helsinki: Societas Philosophia Fennica.
Olafson, Frederick. 1994. "Comments on *Sources of the Self* by Charles Taylor." *Philosophy and Phenomenological Research* 54 (1): 191–96.
Rorty, Richard. 1994. "Taylor on Self-Celebration and Gratitude: Review of *Sources of the Self*." *Philosophy and Phenomenological Research* 54 (1): 197–201.
Rosa, Hartmut. 1995. "Goods and Life-Forms: Relativism in Charles Taylor's Political Philosophy." *Radical Philosophy* 71 (May/June): 20–26.
Rosa, Hartmut, and Arto Laitinen. 2002. "On Identity, Alienation and the Consequences of September 11th. An Interview with Charles Taylor." In *Acta Philosophica Fennica. Vol. 71. Perspectives on the Philosophy of Charles Taylor*, edited by Arto Laitinen and Nicholas Smith, 165–95. Helsinki: Philosophical Society of Finland.
Saurette, Paul. 2005. *The Kantian Imperative: Humiliation, Common Sense, Politics*. Toronto, OH: University of Toronto Press.
Smith, Nicholas. 2002. *Charles Taylor: Meaning, Morals and Modernity*. Cambridge, MA: Polity.
Taylor, Charles. 1964. *The Explanation of Behaviour*. London: Routledge and Kegan Paul.
Taylor, Charles. 1985. *Human Agency and Language: Philosophical Papers vol. 1*. Cambridge, MA: Cambridge University Press.
Taylor, Charles. 1988. "The Moral Topography of the Self." In *Hermeneutics and Psychological Theory*, edited by Stanly Messer, Louis Sass and Robert Woolfolk, 298–320. New Brunswick, NJ: Rutgers University Press.
Taylor, Charles. 1989. *Sources of the Self. The Making of the Modern Identity*. Cambridge, MA: Cambridge University Press.
Taylor, Charles. 1990. "Rorty in the Epistemological Tradition." In *Reading Rorty. Critical Responses to Philosophy and the Mirror of Nature (and Beyond)*, edited by A.R. Malachowski, 257–75. Cambridge, MA: Blackwell.
Taylor, Charles. 1991. "Comments and Replies." *Inquiry* 34: 237–54.
Taylor, Charles. 1994. "Reply to Commentators." *Philosophy and Phenomenological Research* 54 (1): 203–13.
Taylor, Charles. 1995a. "Overcoming Epistemology." In *Philosophical Arguments*, 1–19. Cambridge, MA/London, England: Harvard University Press.

Taylor, Charles. 1995b. "The Validity of Transcendental Arguments." In *Philosophical Arguments*, 20–33. Cambridge, MA/London: Harvard University Press.

Taylor, Charles. 1996/2011. "Iris Murdoch and Moral Philosophy." In *Dilemmas and Connections*, 3–23. Cambridge, MA/London: Belknap Press of Harvard University Press.

Taylor, Charles. 2003. "Ethics and Ontology." *The Journal of Philosophy* 100 (6): 305–20.

Taylor, Charles. 2005. "The "Weak Ontology" Thesis." *The Hedgehog Review: Critical Reflections on Contemporary Culture* 7 (2): 35–42.

Taylor, Charles. 2007. *A Secular Age*. Cambridge/London: Belknap Press of Harvard University Press.

Taylor, Charles. 2011a. *Dilemmas and Connections*. Cambridge/London: The Belknap Press of Harvard University Press.

Taylor, Charles. 2011b. "Disenchantment-Reenchantment." In *Dilemmas and Connections*, 287–302. Cambridge, MA/London: Belknap Press of Harvard University Press.

Taylor, Charles. 2013. "Retrieving Realism." In *Mind, Reason, and Being-in-the-World. The McDowell-Dreyfus Debate*, edited by Joseph Schear, 61–90. New York, NY: Routledge.

Taylor, Charles (with Ayer, A.J.). 1959. "Phenomenology and Linguistic Analysis." *Proceedings of the Aristotelian Society, supplementary volume* 33: 93–124.

Taylor, Charles (with Dreyfus, Hubert). 2015. *Retrieving Realism*. Cambridge, MA: Harvard University Press.

Taylor, Charles (with Kullman, Michael). 1958. "The Pre-Objective World." *The Review of Metaphysics* 12 (1): 108–132.

Weinstock, Daniel. 1994. "The Political Theory of Strong Evaluation." In *Philosophy in an Age of Pluralism: the Philosophy of Charles Taylor in Question*, edited by James Tully and Daniel Weinstock, 171–93. Cambridge, MA: Cambridge University Press.

White, Stephen. 1997. "Weak Ontology and Liberal Political Reflection." *Political Theory* 25 (4): 502–23.

White, Stephen. 2000. *Sustaining Affirmation: the Strengths of Weak Ontology in Political Theory*. Princeton, NY: Princeton University Press.

White, Stephen. 2005. "Weak Ontology: Genealogy and Critical Issues." *The Hedgehog Review: Critical Reflections on Contemporary Culture* 7 (2): 11–25.

Williams, Bernard. 1990. "Republican and Galilean: Review of *Sources of the Self*." *The New York Review of Books* 37 (November 8): 45–48.

Chapter 3

Philosophical Anthropology of Strong Evaluation

The original context in which Taylor introduces the concept of strong evaluation is philosophical anthropology, that is, "the study of the basic categories in which man and his behavior is to be described and explained" (1964, 4). In fact, as he says in *Philosophical Papers*, philosophical anthropology is the common theme that links his various concerns (1985a, 1). Taylor continues to develop this approach in *Sources of the Self* by highlighting the philosophical-anthropological assumptions that in his view specifically underpin contemporary moral philosophy (1989, 53–62).[1] Labeling this climate as skeptic, relativist, subjectivist, and naturalist, Taylor criticizes a host of ethical theories for failing to make sense of the actual ways in which human beings live their lives. In so doing, he says to be defending an "*ad hominem*" perspective that is not only central to "the whole enterprise of moral clarification" but also illuminates the "transcendental" conditions of human life (1995a, 37; 1989, 32). The cornerstone of Taylor's critique of contemporary moral theory is his belief that selfhood and morality cannot be separated. In line with this, he shows a distinctive *ethical* use of the concept of human being, as he repeatedly discusses questions of agency in connection with moral issues. In this way, Taylor consistently develops his critique by building an argument that steers a course between philosophical anthropology, on the one hand, and ethical theory, on the other.

My purpose in this chapter is to reconstruct Taylor's arguments in between philosophical anthropology and ethics, that is, to clarify how his *ad hominem* and transcendental positions relate to, depend on, and mutually reinforce one another to clarify the connection between human nature and ethics. I first explore the context in which Taylor elaborates his philosophical-anthropological approach by presenting it against the background of his critique of contemporary moral theory (section 3.1). I continue to clarify his view in more detail by drawing a parallel with some early work of Martha Nussbaum, and by putting a spotlight on his distinctive *ad hominem* mode of reasoning in between philosophical anthropology and ethics (section 3.2). I then focus on Taylor's use of transcendental argumentation in support of his *ad hominem* perspective, and finally reflect on the ethical conclusions that can be drawn from these arguments (section 3.3).

3.1 WHAT IS PHILOSOPHICAL ANTHROPOLOGY?

3.1.1 Human Universals

As we saw in chapter 1, the basic assumption of Taylor's doctrine of strong evaluation is that all human beings share an implicit sense of qualitative distinction or higher worth, which allows for a range of incommensurably higher values without which human life would not be possible. On several occasions, Taylor has made it clear that strong evaluation is to be understood as a structural feature of human agency, noting that "the human beings we are and live with are all strong evaluators" and that strong evaluation is "something like a human universal, present in all but what we would clearly judge as very damaged human beings" (1985b, 28; 1994a, 249). Taylor's thesis of strong evaluation is but one example of a larger project to describe those features of human action and experience that in his view are both indubitable and universal. Depicting these central features as "human universals," "human constants," "generic terms," or "category terms," his aim is to capture the permanent structures of human existence in the full knowledge of the diverse particular historical contexts where these structures are current.[2]

As has been discussed at length by Abbey (2000), Smith (2002), and Laitinen (2008), a preoccupation with concepts that are supposed to capture the structural features of human agency is a constant throughout Taylor's oeuvre. He introduces this method in the paper "The Moral Topography of the Self," in which he makes a crucial distinction between "what belongs to human agency as such, in all times and places, and what is shaped differently in different cultures" (1988, 299). On the one hand, Taylor's belief that "what we are as human agents is profoundly interpretation-dependent" allows for a diversity of human self-understandings (1988, 299). On the other hand, he also believes that "a constant is to be found in the shape of the questions that all cultures must address" (1988, 299). He continues this focus in *Sources of the Self* by arguing that the conditions of selfhood (as delineated by Taylor in the second chapter of that book) are to be understood as "inescapable" conditions of human agency (1989, 52).

It is important to note at the very outset that Taylor has been quite clear about the risks of a philosophical-anthropological method, acknowledging that his attempt to distinguish "human universals" from mere "historical constellations" is "always contestable," "forever provisional," and "subject to endless revision and refinement" (Taylor in: De Lara 1998, 111; 1989, 112; 2005, 40). Having made these reservations, though, we must ask what timeless features of human agency Taylor thinks still hold across cultures. Abbey, Smith, and Laitinen have provided helpful analyses here. Abbey notes the following universal features: "the self's moral orientation, the centrality of self-interpretation, the fact that humans are animals with language, the dialogical nature of selfhood, and the significance of embodiment" (2000, 2). Accordingly, Laitinen (who expresses his indebtedness to Smith for his account) adds to the list by reconstructing the following index of human constants:

> Humans are (1) embodied agents and perceivers oriented towards the world, (2) expressive language-using animals, and (3) social animals dependent on each other in various ways. Further, humans are (4) strong evaluators and (5) storytelling animals who grasp the unity of their lives through narratives. Finally, humans are (6) inescapably in contact with moral sources and furthermore they are (7) religious animals who can give meaning to death and suffering. (Laitinen 2008, 75)

With these universals in place, though, Smith warns us that many contemporary philosophers are "suspicious of such talk" and that many theorists see Taylor's invocation of human universals as a warrant for ethnocentrism (2002, 239).[3] Nevertheless, Smith concludes, Taylor's philosophical anthropology sufficiently avoids the pitfall of ethnocentrism through his acknowledgment of "the historical contingency of the limits we do draw rather than abandoning them altogether" (2002, 239).

At first glance, there seem to be at least two basic weaknesses in Taylor's philosophical-anthropological approach. First, his argument seems rather thin as a *philosophical* theory, since most of Taylor's effort goes into explaining and describing what "undamaged" human personhood *is*, rather than actually *justifying* his account (1989, 27). This is a serious concern, because without a convincing argument for the superiority of his account, Taylor's opponents can easily pay him back with the same coin by adhering to their own descriptions. Second and adding to, rather than reducing, the force of the first objection, Taylor's essentialist approach is "untimely" at best, but will seem today (at least to some of us) to be considerably outdated.[4] This means that unless Taylor succeeds in providing a solid and compelling argument for his claims, his philosophical anthropology is very unlikely to yield widespread support. Yet, Taylor is fully aware of the peculiarity of his most pertinent claims in the naturalist climate of thought that he believes is thriving. In the next section, I will therefore concentrate on the particular philosophical discussions in which Taylor situates himself in elaborating his philosophical anthropology.

3.1.2 Against Naturalist Projectivism

In the paper "Explanation and Practical Reason," Taylor starts from the observation that it is commonplace in our culture to adhere to some form of moral subjectivism or skepticism, that is, to adhere to the belief that moral disputes "cannot be arbitrated by reason" and that we all just ultimately have to plump for the values that "feel best to us" (1995a, 34). This climate, he continues, is underpinned by "some rather deep metaphysical assumptions" that can ultimately be traced back to certain relativist and subjectivist ideas about the nature of morality (1995a, 34). "Relativism" here means the belief that all moral goods are of equal value since the only available access to value is simply what we de facto want and care about. "Subjectivism," then, involves the related belief that the superiority of some goods over others can be validated only by subjective desires and choices.

As we have seen in the previous chapters, the doctrine of strong evaluation attacks these views head on. As Abbey points out, Taylor not only "strikes a blow at relativism in moral theory" by insisting that "individuals do not see all their values or desires as being of potentially equal worth," he also "poses a challenge to subjectivism" by arguing that "when individuals experience some goods as inherently more worthy than others, they are responding to their sense that the good is valuable independent of their choice of it" (2000, 25–26). In elaborating on this, Taylor first argues that relativism and subjectivism are rooted in a premise "buried deep in the naturalist way of thinking," namely that values are not *real* as they are in fact a kind of "projection" on our part (1989, 57, 56). This is the central idea, he continues, behind the naturalist temper that is manifest not only in "reductive explanations" but in another way in "classical utilitarianism," then also in the "supposed 'naturalistic fallacy,'" in "various theories of moral judgements as projections," and in "attempts to distinguish 'value' from 'fact'" (1989, 22, 53, 58).

Taylor has been clear from the outset that his main target is the commitment to naturalism that in his view is shared by all reductive theories. He explains his critique by making a distinction between "cruder" reductionist theories and views of a more "sophisticated" naturalism (1989, 67). Taylor defines the crude type of reductionism as the view that understands values as "projections of ours onto a world which in itself was neutral" (1989, 53).[5] For Taylor, John Mackie's "error-theory" is the most important example of this type of position, but he further sees a projectivist view underlying Richard Hare's prescriptivism, which sees the projection of values as being amendable to "voluntary control," and in the work of Simon Blackburn, who tries to reconcile a "non-realist" theory with ordinary moral experience (1989, 6, 53, 60). In Taylor's view, naturalist projectivism paints a distorted picture of moral experience; yet, the inadequacy of this picture tends to be obscured because it is supported by an erroneous model of practical reasoning based on an "illegitimate extrapolation from reasoning in natural science" (1989, 7).

To get clear on this, we must recall Taylor's claim that basic moral reactions have two crucial features. On the one hand, they are so fundamental that they strike us as "rooted in instinct" (1989, 4–5). On the other hand, such reactions involve certain claims about "the nature and status of human beings" (1989, 5). The mistake of naturalist projectivism, then, is that it focuses exclusively on the instinctive aspect; the underlying anthropological claims are altogether neglected. Taylor's point is that projectivist views are nonetheless no exception in that they also rely on certain conceptions of human nature, but shun any articulation of these claims. This is not just incomplete, but also internally inconsistent. A full-blooded naturalism requires the naturalization of our anthropological beliefs, but there are very few philosophers that consistently do so by arguing that beliefs about what a human being "is" have evolved in human evolution simply because of their survival value.[6]

Taylor rejects the assimilation between moral and instinctive reactions because it runs counter to everyday moral practice. Many people believe, for example, that a feeling of revulsion about child pornography is a healthy or fitting reaction, one that we *should* have. But we do not think of ourselves in this way with regard to a dislike of sweets. As Taylor explains, in the moral case the feeling of revulsion strikes us as one *"meriting"* this reaction—a reaction that we would be willing to defend if necessary—whereas in the nonmoral case the feeling of dislike is "just a brute fact" (1989, 6, original emphasis). For Taylor, then, this shows that reductive explanations of moral reactions as simple gut feelings crucially distort our moral experience. Rejecting this approach as a crude type of reductionism, he continues to discuss some more sophisticated projectivist positions.

Among these is what he calls the "involuntary projection view" (which he attributes to Edward Wilson and, again, John Mackie) that understands the projection of values as a deeply involuntary but structural feature of our human experience (1989, 53–54). By this account, grasping the world in value terms is understood as a phenomenon such as color perception, depicting our valuations as a "coloration" that the "neutral universe inescapably had for us" (1989, 54). On either version (crude or sophisticated), Taylor argues, any attempt to offer nonevaluative descriptions of values lacks an essential feature of our value terms, namely that they are not mere descriptions of our perceptions and responses, but also make a *normative* claim. That is, if someone were unaware of the normative point of evaluative terms such as "courage" or "brutality," that person would not be able to understand the sorts of behavior that these terms aim to describe. For Taylor, this shows at once that the whole parallel between values and secondary properties is rather useless, since the "descriptive" meaning of such terms cannot be separated from their "evaluative" point (1989, 54). In line with this, he then makes his well-known claim that we cannot understand the evaluative point of a term such as courage without reference to some language community or society. In other words, what naturalist projectivist approaches fail to recognize is that one needs to take account of the "social interchange" or "common purposes" in the society that uses this particular term (1989, 54).

However, the projectivist might object, even if our strong evaluations make sense only against a larger background of qualitative distinctions developed in a given society, why can one not just continue to insist after all that values are relative and not part of reality? Blackburn's "quasi-realist" view makes a point like this by arguing that we should continue to do "as if" our values are real because of their central place in our lives—despite the awareness that they are in fact subjective projections.[7] Taylor also resists Blackburn's brand of naturalism. In his view, we simply have no better "measure of reality" to explain moral issues than those terms that, after critical reflection, we think make the "best sense" of our lives (1989, 57). He argues, therefore, that the fact that our values are rooted in a given society does nothing to diminish their importance, neither for understanding human agency nor for practical reason. More importantly, Blackburn's quasi-realism runs counter to moral experience. As noted, Taylor argues that we essentially understand moral values as incommensurably higher than our other goals and desires. Because of this, we generally refuse to treat our moral beliefs as subjective projections as it "lies in their nature as strong evaluations to claim truth, reality, and objective rightness" (2011, 298). On Taylor's reading, Blackburn bluntly neglects this reality by making his quasi-realism "*compatible* with moral experience by making this experience somehow *irrelevant* to it" (1989, 60, original emphasis).

On Taylor's reading, what the above discussion does make clear is the basic point that "good and right are not part of the world as studied by natural science" as these are not properties of a neutral world but related to human practices (1989, 56). Yet this result does not seem to him to show anything like what his naturalist opponents say it shows, namely that relativism and subjectivism are the only available options in ethics. In fact, as we will see (in section 3.2), far from leaving moral theory empty-handed, Taylor holds the opposing view that the discontinuity between science and ethics rather gives us an anchor for practical reason.

At this point, it might be helpful to go back to Johnston's critique (as discussed in section 1.3.3) that Taylor blurs the distinction between "having an understanding of the world and having an ethical understanding of the world" (1999, 106). In reply to this criticism, I showed that instead of trying to "assimilate moral judgments and empirical claims" (Johnston 1999, 106), Taylor is in fact driving a wedge between moral and scientific claims. Considering Taylor's wholesale rejection of naturalist projectivism, we can now see that his strategy within this discussion is to shift the level of debate. Instead of simply arguing about whether the distinction between "real" empirical facts and "non-real" phenomenological values is valid or not, he tries to draw attention to the fact that the actual opposition lies between science and ethics.

In other words, Taylor argues that science and ethics must be looked at in their own right as they analyze, clarify, and evaluate human life in their own separate ways. Furthermore, this means that although the distinction between facts and values is crucial to the scientific enterprise, it simply does not hold in the realm of ethics because our moral responses can be understood neither as "crude" gut feelings nor as "sophisticated" colorations of a neutral world, nor as "quasi-real" historically contingent projections. However, as I will show in the following sections, this conclusion has important implications for moral theory. In fact, what emerges from Taylor's rejection of naturalist projectivism and the fact-value dichotomy that underpins this outlook is that we are in need of a wholly different understanding of ethics.

3.2 INTERWEAVING PHILOSOPHICAL ANTHROPOLOGY AND ETHICS

On the whole, Taylor's critique of naturalist projectivism is that it is unsatisfactory in two related ways. It falsely assimilates instinctive and moral reactions and at the same time imposes impossible requirements on moral theory by making scientific modes of validation as criteria for it. The kind of method Taylor thus needs in developing his rival account is one that insists neither on dividing fact from value nor on radically separating descriptive from evaluative meaning, nor is his method one that undermines basic human experiences and responses for explanatory purposes. To meet these criteria, Taylor introduces his philosophical-anthropological approach to ethics.

Against this background, my purpose in this section is to pursue how Taylor uses philosophical-anthropological arguments to substantiate his ethical reasoning. I first draw on some early writings of Martha Nussbaum to explain in more detail the argumentative structure of his argument (section 3.2.1) and continue to show that it is only from what Taylor calls an *ad hominem* viewpoint that his argument yields substantive results (section 3.2.2). It is worth emphasizing here, however, that I am using Nussbaum's work only as a heuristic device, that is, to illuminate Taylor's view on the connection between philosophical anthropology and ethics, instead of employing her as a conversation partner for Taylor.

3.2.1 An Internal-Evaluative Viewpoint

Since mainstream moral philosophy does not seem to leave much room for the alliance between philosophical anthropology and ethics, it should not surprise us that one has to go back a long way in the history of philosophy to find an ethical theory that is able to meet the above criteria. Taylor sees an example in Aristotle, who developed an ethical theory based on "a study of human nature and its fundamental goals" (1964, 4). Although it is clear that Taylor employs his central concept of strong evaluation along similar lines, there has been some discussion about the nature of the argument he has been defending. In this way, Daniel Weinstock emphasizes an ambiguity in Taylor's account of strong evaluation, "having to do with whether that account is to be understood *normatively* or *descriptively*" (1994, 172, original emphasis). He finally concludes that strong evaluation is "best understood as a normative thesis, describing the manner in which human beings deliberate practically *at their best*" (1994, 172, original emphasis). Similarly, Flanagan distinguishes Taylor's "descriptive" claims from a set of "normative" claims (1996, 147). In the light of these distinctions, Abbey concludes that "strong evaluation is both descriptive and normative: Taylor believes that it both describes how people are as well as outlining what is required for full personhood" (2000, 18). Smith adds another interpretation by speaking of the "therapeutic aim" of Taylor's project, that is, "to convince us that there really is such a naturalist mindset at large in modernity" and "to shift the burden of proof in much philosophical debate" by exposing that mindset (2002, 7).

If anything, these characterizations indicate that Taylor's doctrine of strong evaluation cannot be understood as simply descriptive or simply normative. Rather, as I will argue, his argument encompasses both elements in that you cannot consistently withdraw your assent from its *normative* point without withdrawing from the entire *description* of human agency that the doctrine of strong evaluation represents. To clarify this point, I will show in the present section that Taylor has a more contemporary ally in the early work of Martha Nussbaum. Yet this seems to be a connection that Taylor himself has overlooked.[8] I will draw on Nussbaum's view extensively in explaining Taylor's position, because her account of human functioning, her essentialist reply to relativism in political theory, and her insistence on the significance of Aristotle's human nature argument for contemporary debates show many illuminating parallels with Taylor's philosophical-anthropological project. Moreover, Nussbaum repeatedly refers to Taylor as a close relative of her view (1992, 243, 245, notes 12 and 36; 1995, 131, note 65).

In her seminal article "Human Functioning and Social Justice" (1992), Nussbaum sets out to list those capabilities without which human life would not be possible. In so doing, she challenges "contemporary assaults on 'essentialism' and on nonrelative accounts of human functioning" as she aims to delineate "the most important functions of the human being, in terms of which human life is defined" (1992, 203, 214). Nussbaum's argument is related to the thesis of strong evaluation in the following five ways. The first and most striking similarity between Taylor and Nussbaum is that their projects start from the same premise, namely that we all share a basic, intuitive idea of what normal, undamaged human personhood consists in. Whereas Taylor believes that we all have a sense (however dim or inarticulate) of the central place of strong evaluations in our lives, in that we would not recognize as fully human a person that lacked a moral framework altogether (1989, 31), Nussbaum argues that there is a "broadly shared general consensus about the features whose absence means the end of a human form of life" (1992, 215). Second, both authors believe that human life has certain universal features. In the same way Taylor maintains that it is possible to formulate "transhistorical truths on the human subject" (Taylor in: De Lara 1998, 111), Nussbaum asserts that "those who would throw out all appeals to a determinate account of the human being" are "throwing away far too much" (1992, 205). Third, Nussbaum's account of the human being as "one that divides its essential from its accidental properties" (1992, 207) clearly resonates with Taylor's two-dimensional aim of separating the "human universals" from the "historical constellations" (1989, 112). Fourth, both acknowledge the danger of relativist and subjectivist understandings of human action for ethics, and furthermore, they both argue that these views misconstrue moral experience. Similar to Taylor's critique of naturalist projectivism, Nussbaum criticizes what she calls the "assault on ethical evaluation" by contemporary views that "trade tacitly on beliefs and related sentiments that their official view does not allow them" (1992, 211, 239–40).

Fifth and most importantly, in elaborating their distinctive positions, Taylor and Nussbaum both employ a radically different logic from that of their opponents, making their arguments original and challenging, yet in some respects rather difficult to follow. We already encountered this problem when observing that Taylor's doctrine of strong evaluation does not make much sense in terms of a strict separation between descriptive and normative meaning. Nussbaum's account is particularly revealing in this respect, because her terminology perfectly describes Taylor's position in between philosophical anthropology and ethics.

Right at the outset, Nussbaum draws a distinction between what she calls "metaphysical-realist essentialism," which she rejects, and her own "historically grounded empirical essentialism" (1992, 206, 208). She characterizes metaphysical realism as the view that there is "some determinate way that the world is apart from the interpretive workings of the cognitive faculties of living beings," that is, "independently of any experience of human life and human history" (Nussbaum 1992, 206). To rely on metaphysical realism today, Nussbaum continues, would be to pretend that we can be "told from outside" what to be and do, whereas the answers can only come "from ourselves" (1992, 207). Yet in her view the collapse of metaphysical realism does not mean that relativism and subjectivism are the only available options left to us, nor does it necessarily rule out all appeals to an essentialist account of the human being. Taylor makes the same point in his own terms when suggesting that although "Platonism is dead," this does not necessarily mean that we "all have to be projectivists" (1991, 248; 1994b, 210). Following on from this, Nussbaum adds:

> In fact, the collapse into extreme relativism or subjectivism seems to me to betray a deep attachment to metaphysical realism itself. For it is only to one who has pinned everything to that hope that its collapse will seem to entail the collapse of all evaluation—just as it is only to a deeply believing religious person, as Nietzsche saw, that the news of the death of God brings the treat of nihilism. (1992, 213)

Acknowledging the absence of a transcendent basis for judgment should not, then, make us despair or make our strongly evaluative judgments seem any less important—unless, that is, we have not yet overcome metaphysical realism ourselves, clinging to a conception of evaluation that takes only those judgments to be valid which can be justified by a transcendent metaphysical grounding. Although elaborating on it in a slightly different way, Taylor is getting at the same point when he challenges the notion that there is nothing between an "extrahuman ontic foundation for the good," on one hand, and "pure subjectivism," on the other (1989, 342). On the whole, both authors seek to open up the middle ground between Platonic metaphysical realism, on the one hand, and naturalist projectivism, on the other. This means that, rather than accepting the destructive logic that "one is either a Platonic moral realist or a projectivist" (Abbey 2000, 31), Nussbaum and Taylor are reopening the whole question of the relationship between ethics and science, arguing that our predicament still leaves room for ethical evaluation and for essentialism of a certain kind. But what kind of position can make sense of this situation? Put differently, what type of argument allows for essentialist claims and secures our strong evaluations for moral theory while avoiding the extremes of metaphysical realism and naturalist projectivism at the same time?

Nussbaum defines her account as both "internal" and "evaluative" or "normative" (1992, 208, 214). Regarding the *internal* aspect, her essentialism is first and foremost rooted in human experience and has therefore to be contrasted with "external" metaphysical realism in the above sense. As a historically embedded and historically sensitive account, internal essentialism is a way of "looking at ourselves, asking what we really think about ourselves and what holds our history together" (Nussbaum 1992, 208). With regard to the *evaluative* character of her account, Nussbaum explains that separating universal from historical features of human agency necessarily requires an "evaluative" inquiry because "we must ask, which things are so important that we will not count a life as a human life without them?" (1992, 208). Nussbaum justifies this explicit interweaving of descriptive and normative points by arguing that the conception of the human being is *itself* a normative conception, in that it involves "singling out certain functions as more basic than others" (1992, 227).

Nussbaum's explanation of the internal and evaluative character of her account is revealing for the doctrine of strong evaluation in the following four respects. First, concerning the internal aspect, Taylor has been arguing all along that the historical or social embeddedness of our strong evaluations does nothing to undermine their importance. That is, he believes that we can make sense of human agency only "internally," or, using Taylor's term, "*ad hominem*," by having recourse to the actual strong evaluations by which people live their lives. Second, Taylor's critique of naturalist projectivism, his rejection of the fact-value distinction, and his insistence on the difference between science and ethics are clearly in line with Nussbaum's aim to deliberately avoid taking on a neutral stance. Third, Nussbaum's view allows us to acknowledge that Taylor's doctrine of strong evaluation has been a normative investigation from the very outset, as he has been describing human agency by focusing on—and thus evaluating—its most distinctive features. Fourth, these similarities enable us to see that Nussbaum's internal-evaluative viewpoint is precisely the type of approach Taylor thinks we need to come to grips with our moral predicament in between the extremes of Platonic moral realism and naturalist projectivism. This is the context in which Taylor develops his *ad hominem* argument.

3.2.2 Taylor's *Ad Hominem* Strategy

If anything, the comparison with Nussbaum clarifies *why* Taylor's anthropological and ethical views cannot be separated: because he is developing an internal-evaluative argument that centers on the connection between facts of human nature and ethical beliefs. However, we still need to say much more about the distinctive way in which Taylor uses the picture of a strong evaluator to defend normative claims. In this respect, we noted that there is some confusion among Taylor's interpreters about whether strong evaluation is to be understood as a phenomenological description of human agency or as a normative thesis (Weinstock), or as a combination of both (Flanagan and Abbey), or rather as a therapeutic argument that seeks to convince us that human beings need not necessarily be described in naturalist terms, nor that we ought to picture ourselves in this way (Smith). We can now get a clearer view on Taylor's strategy by examining the different steps of his *ad hominem* viewpoint in more detail. Moreover, as we will see (in section 3.3), this analysis sets the stage for Taylor's transcendental justification of strong evaluation.

Taylor's *ad hominem* argument consists of four basic elements. First, it connects human nature to ethical questions. Second, it is both internal and evaluative (in the above sense). Third, it literally appeals "to the person" (*ad hominem*) by invoking issues of personal identity and consistency of beliefs. Fourth, the results of Taylor's argument are established by a kind of "self-validating" procedure. In identifying these elements, I have taken inspiration from Nussbaum's chapter "Aristotle on Human Nature and the Foundation of Ethics" (Nussbaum 1995), in which she distinguishes similar components in Aristotle's views on human nature and ethics. I argue that Taylor's doctrine of strong evaluation, although elaborated in more contemporary terms, encompasses the same basic elements as Aristotle's human nature argument, as Taylor's *ad hominem* strategy implicitly follows an Aristotelian logic.[9]

In the previous sections and chapters, we have already pointed out the first three Aristotelian elements in Taylor's views. The analyses in chapters 1 and 2 clearly illustrate how Taylor discusses human agency in connection with moral issues in developing his picture of human agents as strong evaluators. We further saw (in section 3.1.2) that he contrasts this picture with naturalistic theories that in his view fail to make sense of human and moral agency alike. I then argued (in section 3.2.1) that Taylor's method is best understood in terms of the internal and evaluative dimensions of Nussbaum's capability approach, because he consistently has recourse to ordinary moral beliefs and responses in criticizing his opponents.

Regarding the appeals to personal identity and consistency of beliefs, it became visible (in section 1.2.2) that Taylor's attack on classical utilitarianism consists in exposing and refuting the imagined agent behind utilitarian theory as a paradigmatic weak evaluator. Additionally, he also criticizes utilitarians for being inconsistent by strongly valuing the ideals of rationality and benevolence without being able to incorporate this strong motivation in their moral theory (1989, 31–32). Next, it was shown (in section 1.2.2) how Taylor defends an *ad hominem* mode of practical reasoning in reply to the charge of the naturalistic fallacy by arguing that "*we* would be shown up as insensitive" if we no longer felt the demand of strong values such as respect and benevolence (1995a, 37, original emphasis).

The appeal to a "we" is an appeal to our beliefs about personal identity, further showing how Taylor's argument, like Nussbaum's, is rooted in an internal-evaluative viewpoint that proceeds "*ad hominem*" by having recourse to widely shared preferences and choices, and by working within our own evaluative beliefs about who we are. In the end, Taylor's view is the commonsensical one that we identify ourselves not by our natural desires for food, drink, sex, and sleep, but by the peculiarly human register of evaluations that are constituted by strong value. In this way, he continues to draw attention to beliefs that "we"—including his critics and opponents—deeply hold, simply by being a human respondent. He argues:

> [Strong evaluation] just means that you see your valuing X as something that is itself right or valuable. Ask yourself what it would be like if you lost this preference. In the case that the preference is for ice cream you may not care about losing it, but what if it is for caring about people being tortured? Would you want to degenerate that point? (Taylor in: Rosa and Laitinen 2002, 188)

In other words, if someone really did not see the distinction between respect for human life and a preference for ice cream, and continued to insist that it would not matter to him or her to either stop caring about people being tortured or to lose the preference for ice cream after considering Taylor's *ad hominem* argument, Taylor could reply only that we would not see this as a human possibility, but as pathological. In this way, the appeal to personal identity forces the challengers of the doctrine of strong evaluation to choose between two options: *either* to revise their original view and accept that we recognize some goals as intrinsically more worthy than others independent of our desires *or* to give up the very beliefs by which the opponent defines him or herself.

However, we have also seen (in section 1.3.3) that a critic such as Johnston rejects this approach by criticizing Taylor for neglecting the *logical* possibility of denying moral claims (Johnston 1999, 101). The above discussion should make it clear that to insist on mere logical points as an argument against the doctrine of strong evaluation is to miss Taylor's *ad hominem* strategy entirely. As we have seen in Taylor's critiques of utilitarian and naturalist moral theories, the point is not that these positions are *logically* inconsistent, but that the advocates of these views contradict *existentially* what they proclaim theoretically, insofar as they implicitly endorse evaluative beliefs that their official view does not permit them. The upshot of this argument is that we cannot explain in naturalist terms what the advocates of naturalism themselves are doing as they live their lives.[10] As a result, some moral theories are undermined on account of existential impossibility, as they tacitly trade on a conception of human agency that takes us beyond the bounds of humanness. (In this respect, it is worth remembering that Taylor describes the imagined agent of utilitarian ethics and naturalist theory as respectively an "impossibly" shallow character and as a "monster" (1985b, 26; 1989, 32).) By contrast, on Taylor's *ad hominem* model of practical reasoning, a commonsense claim that it is always wrong to torture children, regardless of the preferences or beliefs that might allow this practice, makes perfect sense: as human beings, we "always already" understand that human life (as we conceive it) rules out certain practices, despite the fact that these are perfectly logically possible.

Ad hominem reasoning is, therefore, far from being fallacious, an important argument when used to explicate unarticulated evaluative beliefs, or when such reasoning relates to the credibility of certain implicit statements about human nature. As Taylor's strategy is implicitly rooted in an Aristotelian view of human nature and ethics, the contrast with modern, scientific modes of rational validation is evident. It should not surprise us, then, that the *ad hominem* appeals to personal identity and consistency of beliefs yields a typical nonmodern result. That is, it establishes, as Nussbaum puts it, not so much a "knock-down proof" but rather "an appeal to the reader to consider whether the opponent's project does not deal in an odd sort of incoherence" (1995, 105).

Having elaborated the third element of Taylor's *ad hominem* strategy, all that remains is to illustrate the fourth and last component: the self-validating procedure of the argument. However, little has been said about this point in the present account of strong evaluation. That is, it still has to be shown that Taylor's argumentation follows a circular line of reasoning that not only avoids the trap of logical fallacy, but also yields substantial normative points. To get clear on this, we must include Taylor's use of transcendental argumentation in support of his *ad hominem* argument, which is the central topic of the next section. If we now return to the questions with which we began, we can see that Taylor's philosophical anthropology incorporates descriptive, normative, and therapeutic points all in one. More specifically, the above analysis explicates that Taylor's *ad hominem* perspective differs from naturalist projectivism in the following three respects.

1. Its criteria are not drawn from the realm of neutral, external facts, since Taylor believes moral reasoning draws on other resources than this. His argument thus takes us beyond conventional methods of rational justification in which empirical observations and logical points are central. But there are still criteria here, for the decisive considerations in Taylor's reasoning are such that they pose a real challenge to his opponents.
2. However, these criteria can be acknowledged only when we see that Taylor makes quite different demands on explanation in moral theory. Rather

than to blur the distinction between gut feelings and moral reactions, the decisive points are principally *ad hominem*, concerning commonsense beliefs that are ethical in a broad sense: beliefs about what is right and wrong, worthwhile and worthless, admirable and contemptible.
3. With these points in place, we also recognize that the success or failure of Taylor's method depends neither upon empirical proof nor upon logical consistency, but upon lucid phenomenological clarification of those values without which human life would not be possible.

3.3 TRANSCENDENTAL JUSTIFICATION

In the present discussion, Taylor's philosophical anthropology has mostly been serving a negative function in that the aim of his *ad hominem* argument is to show the inadequacy of naturalistic approaches to ethics. However, this critique is only the basis of a positive argument that seeks to convince us that strong evaluation is indeed a human universal that is "present in all but what we would clearly judge as very damaged human beings" (1994a, 249). In this respect, Taylor's doctrine of strong evaluation cannot be traced back only to Aristotle but also in an important way to Kant, as he repeatedly has recourse to Kant's transcendental argument form in justifying the doctrine of strong evaluation.

It is important to note at the outset that Taylor's transcendental method follows a different logic from his *ad hominem* argument. However, although my aim has been to differentiate both arguments in order to account for the full breadth of Taylor's strategies, it is clear that these arguments are closely related at the same time. Because of this, their success or failure is, to a certain extent, interdependent. Taylor's *ad hominem* critique of naturalist projectivism can be seen as preparing the ground for his transcendental argument concerning strong evaluation. His next step is to show that the portrait of human beings as strong evaluators poses a "strong challenge to the naturalist picture" as it delineates the "transcendental" conditions of human life (1989, 31–32). However, here we come up against what seems to be a recurrent problem of Taylor's doctrine of strong evaluation: What is the philosophical status of an account that on the one hand starts rather unpretentiously as a *description* of human agency, but on the other hand boldly ensures a more compelling—in this case not normative but transcendental—claim? That is, while we started from the problem that it is not clear whether the doctrine of strong evaluation has to be understood descriptively or normatively, we are now faced with the question of how Taylor's claims about strong evaluation yield certain transcendental conclusions. As we have seen, what is distinctive of the doctrine of strong evaluation is that it links ethics to issues of philosophical anthropology, phenomenology, and ontology. But how does this relate to transcendental argumentation? Does Taylor's characteristic way of interweaving insights from different philosophical domains also involve exploring the implications of his transcendental argument for ethics, philosophical anthropology, phenomenology, and ontology alike? Or is his transcendental method an attempt to connect descriptive and normative claims, on a par with his *ad hominem* argument? Furthermore, granted that Taylor is squarely within the terrain of transcendental argumentation, how should we understand the argument itself? These questions bring us right back to our most central concern: What is the relationship between the several different types of consideration—anthropological, ethical, phenomenological, ontological, descriptive, normative, transcendental—inherent in the doctrine of strong evaluation?

In an attempt to clarify these issues, my aim in this section is to show that Taylor's transcendental argument and his *ad hominem* strategy are mutually reinforcing, and to explain how this multistage tactic serves to strike a double blow at naturalist conceptions of agency and morality. The discussion starts with an illustration of Taylor's understanding of transcendental argumentation, followed by a reconstruction of his tacit use of the transcendental method in support of the doctrine of strong evaluation (section 3.3.1). In view of the many questions that are being raised by this account, I continue to develop a more systematic defense of the transcendental necessity of strong evaluation by drawing heavily on Christian Illies' analysis of the transcendental argument form (section 3.3.2). Finally, I put a spotlight on the ethical significance of Taylor's *ad hominem* and transcendental arguments (section 3.3.3).

3.3.1 Inescapable Evaluations

Taylor's transcendental reasoning is mostly implicit, as he nowhere explicitly announces that he is developing a transcendental argument by insisting that human beings are essentially strong evaluators. Confusingly, he gives a detailed analysis of the overall procedure of transcendental arguments in the paper "The Validity of Transcendental Arguments" (1995c), but nowhere specifies how this account, if at all, relates to his own philosophical claims. In trying to get clarity on this issue, I will start with on overview of the texts in which Taylor explicitly elaborates on transcendental argumentation.

Taylor's first record of transcendental arguments is to be found in the paper "The Opening Arguments of the *Phenomenology*" (1972), in which he discusses the first three chapters of Hegel's *Phenomenology of Spirit* as "an essay in transcendental argument" (1972, 151). This text is helpful for present purposes in that it both gives us a basic idea of how Taylor understands transcendental arguments and describes the tradition in which he situates himself as a transcendental thinker. As he explains: "By 'transcendental arguments' I mean arguments that start from some putatively undeniable facet of our experience in order to conclude that this experience must have certain features or be of a certain type, for otherwise this undeniable facet could not be. Obviously, the best-known examples are to be found in Kant" (1972, 151). Pointing to similar arguments by Strawson, Wittgenstein, and Merleau-Ponty, Taylor notes that this type of reasoning is by no means confined to Kant, but is "very much part of contemporary philosophical debate" (1972, 151–52, 156). He then continues to argue that the transcendental arguments of Kant, Strawson, Wittgenstein, and Merleau-Ponty seem to serve a common purpose, as they are "all directed against one or other aspect of the dualist picture of experience developed and handed down to us by Cartesianism and empiricism" (1972, 156). In other words, transcendental arguments, as Taylor understands them, lend themselves to exploring human experience in the broadest sense, as they were first initiated by Kant as proof of the necessary categories of experience, and have since then been used either to refute established notions of experience or to challenge the picture of human nature that resulted from them. Even though Taylor has still to explain in more detail how these arguments work, he already concedes here that it is "at least tempting to believe that we can delineate facets of experience that are basic and pervasive enough to be undeniable, and these can be the starting points for our arguments" (1972, 156). He continues this discussion in the paper "The Validity of Transcendental Arguments":

> The arguments I want to call "transcendental" start from some feature of our experience which they claim to be indubitable and beyond cavil. They then move to a stronger conclusion, one concerning the nature of the subject or the subject's position in the world. They make this move by a regressive argument, to the effect that the stronger conclusion must be so if the indubitable fact about experience is to be possible (and being so, it must be possible). (1995c, 20)

Against this background, it is rather surprising that this paper takes no account of the concept of strong evaluation, for there is no doubt that Taylor sees strong evaluation as an indubitable feature of human experience when he says that "the capacity for strong evaluation in particular is essential to our notion of the human subject" (1985b, 28). Despite Taylor's not elaborating on the type of argument that would justify his claim, he makes it very clear that a proper understanding of human identity *must* involve "evaluations which are essential because they are the indispensable horizon or foundation out of which we reflect and evaluate as persons" (1985b, 35).

Although there is no explicit reference to transcendental argumentation here, I want to pursue this point about the inescapability of strong evaluation a bit further, because there seems little reason to doubt that this is the pivotal transcendental thesis Taylor has been defending throughout his various writings. Moreover, he continues his tacit transcendental reasoning in *Sources of the Self* by insisting that stepping outside strongly evaluative frameworks would be to step outside our very understanding of "undamaged human personhood" (1989, 27). To strengthen this view, Taylor then invokes the portrait of an agent without any horizon of evaluation to show that this portrait makes a very distorted picture of human agency. He argues that such a person, unable to decide "issues of fundamental importance" and having "no orientation in these issues whatever," would be "in the grip of an appalling identity crisis"; that is, we would see this person as "pathological" (1989, 31).

In order to clarify Taylor's point here, it might be helpful to discuss the critiques of Flanagan and Johnston, who both deny that strong evaluation is inescapable or necessary for human beings. Flanagan makes this point by emphasizing that "evaluation can be nonethical without being counterethical" (1996, 146). As he explains, "a person who lives a life built around love of baseball [. . .] might fully abide what morality, commonsensically construed, demands" without engaging in "strong 'spiritual' evaluation" at all (1996, 146). He backs this point with a second example, arguing that many professional athletes fall prey to identity crises at the end of their playing career, despite our not thinking of such persons as "particularly reflective or as centrally motivated by ethical concerns" (1996, 154). Johnston elaborates a related critique. In his view, anyone who rejects the idea of moral objectivity is in fact avoiding strong evaluation. As he explains, such "anti-moralists" do not necessarily fall victim to identity crises, as Taylor says they would, because "the anti-moralist does know where she stands: she is someone who believes that there are no objective values" (Johnston 1999, 104).

Although these objections are largely based on misrepresentations of what Taylor is trying to say, they are quite helpful because the nature of Taylor's claim emerges far more clearly in considering Flanagan's and Johnston's criticisms. With regard to the baseball enthusiast, Taylor's point is that even shallow or one-dimensional agents may be strong evaluators. In fact, a life that centers on the *love* of baseball is indeed a good example of strong evaluation, as the passion for this sport does provide a standard by which other goals, desires, and choices are judged. In other words, because of the central place of baseball in such a life, baseball is *fulfilling* to this person as it gives them a sense of *dignity* to build their life around it (e.g., by being a baseball player or a coach). This person *respects* people who also engage in it and feels *admiration* for those successful in the world of baseball. The same holds for a life focused on sporting excellence. Really wanting to become a professional athlete is to value this goal in a strong sense, that is, to see it not only as more worthy than other goals, but also as the standpoint from which other, lower goods must be weighed and judged in pursuance of this goal. At the end of their career, the athlete has lost their most important goal in life (being a professional athlete), and, subsequently, the sense of dignity and fulfillment attached to this goal.

However, Johnston's antimoralist counterexample of a strong evaluator seeks to push beyond this by insisting that strong evaluations are nothing but preferences. As Johnston says, even though the antimoralist has certain evaluative beliefs, she "would accept that if she was disposed differently, she would have a different view and that independently of this there is no question of whether the view is correct" (1999, 104). In other words, although the antimoralist does not claim to be evaluation-free, she denies that her framework consists of strong values. In Taylor's view, this type of self-understanding can be sustained only by a certain lack of self-lucidity. Rather than lacking a framework of strong evaluations, Johnston's antimoralist, on the contrary, has a strong commitment to a certain ideal of rationality. However, because she claims a kind of distance from her own value commitments, this horizon cannot be explicated in her own self-understanding as an antimoralist. This allows the underlying motivations to be disregarded altogether, accrediting the picture of a nonevaluative agent. Surprisingly, though, Johnston does not seem worried that this makes a rather distorted picture of a human being. In fact, Johnston's approach is a clear illustration of the projectivism Taylor is fighting against, because it is precisely this type of position that keeps us from connecting with the actual commonsense terms and experiences in which we live our lives. Again, Taylor's point is that the antimoralist falls foul of *existential* possibility, not logical principle. In a word, to be morally orientated is "a condition of being a functioning self, not a metaphysical view we can put on or off" (1989, 99).

Even though the possibility of a nonevaluative human agent seems effectively ruled out by Taylor's logic, it still leaves many questions unanswered. If the generic structure of transcendental arguments is that they proceed from a nonambitious starting point by plausible steps to a stronger conclusion, what exactly is the putatively undeniable fact in Taylor's argument about strong evaluation? Is the thesis of strong evaluation an appeal to an undeniable feature of *moral* experience, exploring the background conditions of morality? Assuming that it is, it is far from evident what this entails, with regard to both the alleged indubitable starting point and the stronger claims that are made on account of it. Does it mean that our actions and choices as strong evaluators presuppose some kind of universal moral consciousness out of which we form explicit judgments? Or, considering Taylor's image of morality as involving higher goods, is it that we simply know from experience that there are goals which are higher than others and therefore demand our respect? Furthermore, even if we would have properly defined Taylor's starting point, what about the more ambitious claims? In other words, what are the enabling conditions and transcendental implications of strong evaluation? In an attempt to answer all of these questions, I propose a more systematic reading of Taylor's claims in the next section.

3.3.2 Transcendental Argumentation

In order to assess the extent to which Taylor's demonstration of the inescapability of strong evaluation satisfies the criteria of a transcendental argument, I will draw not only on Taylor's own criteria as elaborated in "The Validity of Transcendental Arguments" and related comments, but also on a distinction made by Christian Illies, between two broad kinds of transcendental argument. Illies differentiates between what he calls the "explorational" type and the "retorsive" type of transcendental argument (2003, 31–32). Since all of Taylor's definitions of a transcendental argument (1972, 151; 1991, 208–209; 1995c, 20) point toward the explorational type, I shall reconstruct his argument as such. The explorational type of transcendental argument has the same formal structure as *modus ponens*. Illies elaborates:

> q
> q only if p (or: if q then p)
> ∴ p

> In this formal account, "q" is supposed to be a judgment to the extent that some minimal fact exists or some state of affairs occurs. The second premiss, namely, the "transcendental conditional," spells out that p is a necessary condition for q to be the case (whereby "p" is a judgment on some further fact or state of affairs). [. . .] The function of the transcendental conditional is obvious. It is meant to show that someone who accepts q will find himself rationally committed also to accepting p. (2003, 33)

In reply to his commentators, Taylor implicitly concedes the explorational way of moving from premisses to conclusions by speaking of "the initial reality, from which the argument starts, and the inferred reality, which it wants to get to" (1994b, 209). In elaborating on this, Taylor explains that his starting point (q) is the notion of personal identity:

> Now my initial reality is human beings with identities in the Eriksonian sense, that is, a sense of "who they are" which crucially takes the form of some orientation as to where they stand, what is more or less important to them, and so on. [. . .] It is very much a part of my argument that human beings can't be without identities. (1994b, 209)

He then adds a second premise (p) that strong evaluation is a necessary condition of having an identity. As he explains:

> I then want to move to my inferred reality and argue that what can amount for us to an orientation must involve strong evaluation, i.e. the sense that some things are worthy of being chosen or valued or sought or cherished. *Strong evaluation is essential to identity, and identity is essential to being a fully functioning human being.* So we have to have strong evaluation. (1994b, 209, italics mine)

In order to demonstrate the inescapability of strong evaluation, Taylor thus starts from "human beings with identities," because he sees identity as essential to being a fully functioning human being. These explanations can be seen as different formulations of what Taylor sees as an undeniable fact of human nature, namely that "normal" human agents have identities. However, since the force of the argument crucially depends on the strength of the first premise, one can seriously doubt whether this is a safe starting point. After all, as Nussbaum points out, all conceptions of human being are—far from being indubitable and beyond cavil—*normative* conceptions in that it involves "singling out certain functions as more basic than others" (1992, 227). That is, we tend to think differently about this issue because the concept of the human being is neither value-free nor self-evident. Yet we should also take seriously Taylor's objective precisely to *settle* this very issue by invoking our deepest beliefs about what counts as a human life. Seen in this light, his starting point merely reflects his belief that we all share a basic intuition of what "undamaged" human personhood consists in (1989, 27).

However, since objections can be made to the starting points of personal identity and full personhood, we might consider whether the doctrine of strong evaluation provides other possible first premises. We could, for example, draw attention to Taylor's claim that all human beings experience qualitative contrasts, and that although the content of these contrasts differs, people all make (implicit or explicit) distinctions between higher and lower goods. Yet this is no uncontroversial issue either, since it is perfectly possible to endorse a naturalist conception of morality that excludes qualitative contrasts or higher goods by recognizing only desires and preferences. Put simply, this means that, if we want Taylor's argument really to take off, we must start with a premise that is far *simpler* than those mentioned earlier.

Given these points, I think that a slightly different emphasis could strengthen Taylor's position. There is perhaps a less ambiguous (and for transcendental purposes thus stronger) claim in *Philosophical Papers*: that human beings have second-order desires. As has been noted (in section 1.2.1), Taylor paraphrases Frankfurt by arguing that when we reflect on human agency, we come up against "the fact of strong evaluation, the fact that we human subjects are not only subjects of first-order desires, but of second-order desires, desires about desires" (1985c, 220). Yet this claim presupposes another, more basic one, namely that human beings are essentially *agents*. Unlike the more substantial and therefore more questionable notions of personal identity, undamaged human personhood, qualitative contrasts, and higher goods, the limited claim that we are agents may well be taken for granted, since it does not seem to make much sense to deny it. The fact that this statement does not need further argument makes it quite a strong starting point.[11]

With the minimal assumption that we are agents, we have identified the *first* transcendental claim in Taylor's argument (C^1). The next step requires an exploration of this starting point through an analysis of the indispensable conditions for human agency to be possible at all. It is clear that Taylor sees second-order desires as a necessary precondition of distinctively human action. Adding the context of transcendental argumentation now allows us to argue that Taylor's insistence on second-order desires is in fact the formulation of the *second* premise in his transcendental argument (C^2). That is, on Taylor's account, coming to grips with the more rudimentary fact that we are agents *must* include the fact that we care about our desires and deliberate about our actions in a way that other, nonhuman agents do not.

Although the appeal to second-order desires for explanatory purposes is not yet a justification, it would seem that this condition also survives skeptical reflection. For even in face of the most radical naturalist, is it not naïve to maintain that there are no commitments, however tentatively held, beyond our desires for food, drink, sex, and sleep that inform our deliberations and actions? Surely, having second-order desires is not an empirical condition of the way human beings go about in the world. Rather, the transcendental statement that human agency must include second-order desires makes an internal-evaluative claim, invoking commonsense beliefs about who we are and aspire to be. This *ad hominem* reasoning then leads to the *third* and final transcendental claim that human agents are essentially strong evaluators (C^3) and cannot but be so if we want to account for human action in general (C^1) and second-order desires (C^2) in particular.

On the whole, all three claims of Taylor's argument refer to certain commonsensical, self-evident facts of human experience. The first is that we are agents. The second one adds that we cannot make sense of this unless we take into account that we are subjects of second-order desires, demarcating human agents from other kinds of agent. The third claim concludes from this that we must see strong evaluation as inescapable to allow for human agency and second-order desires to be possible. Taylor's argument thus appeals to the reader to consider whether it is consistently possible to acknowledge human agency and to deny second-order desires and strong evaluation simultaneously. That is, only on the basis of what we as human subjects *recognize* as human agency can we assert that strong evaluation is inescapable. This reading of Taylor's transcendental argument clearly reaffirms his central *ad hominem* perspective.

Although the above reconstruction shows that Taylor's reasoning is best understood as an explorational type of transcendental argument, there are also some fundamental "retorsive" antiskeptical considerations that foster the thesis of strong evaluation. The retorsive type of transcendental argument proceeds by "retorting" skeptical objections back against the skeptic himself. It seeks to do so, Illies explains, by showing that skepticism about some claim or judgment leads to an inconsistency or tension between "what is *expressively* stated by the sceptic," on the one hand, and "what is *implicitly* expressed by his act of assertion," on the other (2003, 45, original emphasis). In this way, retorsive transcendental arguments are essentially designed to show that there are claims or judgments that "cannot be rejected rationally" (Illies 2003, 45). To be sure, Taylor does not argue that strong evaluation cannot be rejected on *rational* grounds, but he does make a retorsive move in insisting that it cannot be excluded for *existential* reasons. His claim here is that the particular context that is required by our actions as strong evaluators simultaneously rules out certain ways of life, which shows the impossibility of a consistent skeptical denial of strong evaluation. As we have seen (in section 3.3.1), Taylor's description of a framework-less agent clarifies that an existence without any strong evaluation would be unbearable, and that such an agent would be a "damaged, radically reduced human being, suffering from a pathological disability" (1991, 250–51). In this way, Taylor thus uses skeptical objections to *validate* his claim about the inescapability of strong evaluation, because in his view the incoherent picture of a nonevaluative agent demonstrates precisely that strong evaluation "creeps back in even where it is supposed to have been excluded" (1985b, 33).

3.3.3 The Ethical Significance of the Argument

An important conclusion of Illies's analysis is that transcendental arguments do not seem to be of much use in providing a basis for *normative* claims. The main reason is that a descriptive first premiss cannot possibly lead to a normative conclusion without begging the question. This not only reraises our central question of whether Taylor's thesis of strong evaluation has to be understood descriptively or normatively, but also puts this question in a new context. With regard to the explorational type of transcendental argument, Illies asserts that "in order to avoid the naturalistic fallacy, the starting-point would have to be *normative* if we want to conclude some normative p (like a demand or value)" (2003, 41, original emphasis). Retorsive transcendental arguments, he continues, are equally haunted by the threat of the naturalistic fallacy as the only way to ground normative points via such arguments is to find some self-evident assumption that turns out to be normative rather than neutral (Illies 2003, 63). This means that the only way to salvage explorational and retorsive arguments is to look for a starting point that is both self-evident *and* normative. However, Illies warns us, "we must be aware of the huge burden laid on the starting-point: it must be normative, sufficiently substantial, but also so minimal that it could be seen as self-evident" (2003, 44).

These considerations bring us right back to the heart of Taylor's philosophical anthropology, because his aim is precisely to develop a transcendental argument that is supposed to be descriptive, normative, substantial, and yet self-evident *at the same time*. At this point, it might be helpful to recall the observation that Taylor's *ad hominem* perspective cannot be explained in terms of a strict separation between descriptive and normative meaning. Similarly, we cannot grasp his transcendental argument as either anthropological or ethical, or, using Illies' vocabulary, in terms of either neutral or normative starting points. In this regard, the fact-value dichotomy that implicitly informs Illies' distinction between neutrality and normativity seems to block from view the reality that some descriptions have an implicit *ethical* function in addition to their explanatory purpose. This is where the ethical significance of Taylor's philosophical anthropology starts to emerge.

To recognize this, however, is to move beyond Illies' analysis of the insufficiency of transcendental arguments for practical reason. Integrating the doctrine of strong evaluation into this picture is problematic mainly because Taylor deploys an internal-evaluative logic that resists the distinction between fact and value. As has been noted, the leading notion of Taylor's philosophical anthropology is that our moral beliefs are central to our notion of agency. As a result, his more applied transcendental argument was never intended to be value-free. Instead of exploring neutral facts, its function is to delineate those features of experience that we cannot intelligibly think away without losing the mode of agency we recognize as human. This is a normative function in that it highlights our very *definition* of human life. However, the distinctive ethical significance of Taylor's reasoning can be recognized only by taking account of the *ad hominem* background in which his transcendental argument is rooted. This is where the "self-validating" procedure comes to the forefront of his argument. Let me flesh this out.

As we have seen (in section 1.2.1), Taylor's doctrine of strong evaluation starts from the evaluative question of what demarcates human agents from other kinds of agents. Although this is best understood as a philosophical-anthropological enterprise, it is at the same time an ethical project because any description of human being involves an evaluation of what we believe to be most worthwhile and indispensable in life. Yet since Taylor seeks to answer this question by having recourse to our own beliefs and actions, he is in fact drawing attention to *what we already accept* about our nature as human beings. This is indeed a self-validating or circular mode of justification in that his *ad hominem* and transcendental arguments work only if we have some knowledge of what it implies merely to be a human agent, prior to any deliberate contemplation about it.

Taylor's argumentation is successful precisely because this is not an implausible requirement. That is, we *must* see ourselves as having some minimal understanding of human agency *qua* being human agents, because without this basic awareness we would lose the very possibility of being a prospective purposive agent. This indicates that any attempt to make human agency intelligible presupposes that we know, at least in a minimal sense, what "human" agency consists in. Therefore, we cannot but see the concept of the human being as a starting point that is both self-evident and normative. Taylor's aim, then, is to bring this sense to formulation via transcendental argumentation, that is, to make articulate something we already have an inarticulate sense of: that we are strong evaluators. More importantly—and this is the main thrust of Taylor's self-validating mode of justification—since this issue is not neutral, but evaluative, you cannot consistently reject the normative point of Taylor's philosophical anthropology without withdrawing from the entire transcendental description of human agency that the doctrine of strong evaluation represents.

I already argued that Taylor's *ad hominem* focus underlines the internal character of his normative claims. Now I can add that it is precisely *because* it is internal that his philosophical anthropology can be used to draw ethical conclusions. Again, Nussbaum underlines this point:

> It matters a great deal what we ourselves think about our selfhood and our possibilities; what a being who stands apart from our experiences and ways of life thinks seems to matter little, if at all. Human nature cannot, and need not, be validated from the outside, because human nature just *is* an inside perspective, not a *thing* at all, but rather the most fundamental and broadly shared experiences of human beings living and reasoning together. (1995, 121, original emphasis)

With these points in place, we must ask: What are the ethical results of Taylor's philosophical anthropology? On the whole, the appeal to our nature as strong evaluators feeds into two main normative points. The first is that it serves an ethical function by exposing and discrediting unarticulated evaluative beliefs in naturalist projectivism, about the human being and about the nature of morality. The second point then adds that much contemporary moral philosophy cannot make sense of ordinary human experiences on account of its (implicit or explicit) commitment to ethical naturalism.

Naturalistically oriented philosophers are given a challenge: they must either show that our conceptions of the human being and human agency do not involve strong evaluation or convince us that we need to change our deep beliefs about identity. These challenges are important, because the claim that each of us has, and lives by, a self-understanding according to which we are subjects not only of first-order desires but also of second-order desires, is a claim that a great deal of contemporary (Anglo-American) philosophy has not really taken seriously.

In the end, Taylor seeks to explain how not the best but ordinary human life is lived and what terms are useful in grasping this. His demand is that *any* moral theory must begin with an account of *normal* human personhood, which in his view has to include our sense of higher and lower value. This assumption has either been explained as a problematic slide from fact to value (Johnston 1999, 105–107) or rejected altogether as an "excessively moralistic" claim (Flanagan 1996, 146), but to say that theories about what human beings *ought* to do must remain within the boundaries of an account of what a human being *is*, is not to say anything beyond reasonable limits. This looks like a trivial point, but it emerges from the above discussion that accepting it has important implications for ethics.

3.4 CONCLUSION: PHILOSOPHICAL ANTHROPOLOGY AND ONTOLOGY

This chapter has delineated the philosophical-anthropological implications of the doctrine of strong evaluation. Taylor's conception of strong evaluation as a human universal is rooted in a full-out attack on contemporary moral theory, which he criticizes for being naturalist and projectivist in general and for making the fact-value distinction a criterion of ethics in particular. His counterproposal not only argues that there is a space to stand between the extremes of Platonic moral realism and naturalist projectivism, but also shows how to stand in that space: by adopting an *ad hominem* perspective. Taylor's transcendental mode of reasoning, then, has four basic steps. It starts from the basic premise that we are agents, but then adds that this minimal assumption must necessarily include recognition of the fact that we are subjects of second-order desires to make any sense. This is followed by a third claim, namely, that the perception of strong value is a necessary condition of having second-order desires. A fourth step consists in showing the existential impossibility of a consistent skeptical denial of strong evaluation. This allows the conclusion that we must see ourselves as strong evaluators for human agency and second-order experience to be possible. This conclusion has significant implications for philosophical anthropology and ethical theory alike.

For one thing, it rules out reductive naturalistic explanations of human being and moral agency.

An important limitation of Taylor's *ad hominem* and transcendental arguments is that they cannot foreclose questions beyond human self-understanding and experience. At first glance, Taylor is fully aware of this when he says that "it is clear that there are certain ontological questions which lie beyond the scope of transcendental arguments" (1995c, 26). However, matters become more complex when he argues elsewhere that we have "no good grounds to question the ontology implicit in the terms which allow us our best account of ourselves" and says that his argument for the inescapability of strong evaluation establishes a kind of "realism" (1994b, 208–209). On the one hand, this move should not surprise us since Taylor's doctrine of strong evaluation does not stop at philosophical-anthropological levels. On the other hand, the extension of his philosophical anthropology to decide *ontological* questions is clearly contradictory to the internal-evaluative bent of his *ad hominem* and transcendental methods. That is, if Taylor's philosophical anthropology is first and foremost a thesis about the world as we experience it, then what should be made of the statement that our strong evaluations carry a realist force? In other words, what does it mean, on a *metaphysical* level, that we are inescapably strong evaluators? These issues reraise a central question: What, if any, are the ontological implications of strong evaluation?

If we now turn to the principal issue with which I ended chapter 2—about the links across Taylor's interwoven arguments—we can see that Taylor, despite his *ad hominem* and transcendentally informed philosophical anthropology, does ultimately try to move outside the realm of human experience in order to adopt a realist perspective. Although this just restates the central problem of how to understand the connections between Taylor's philosophical-anthropological, ethical, and ontological claims, we can now say more about these connections by considering the boundaries that result from the present analysis. I have argued in this chapter that Taylor's general strategy is to combine philosophical-anthropological and ethical arguments to claim that an overinvestment in the fact-value distinction has blocked from view the disturbing conceptions of human being and moral agency underlying naturalist projectivism. Although it takes a great effort to show the interdependence of philosophical anthropology and ethics in a climate of thought that tends to separate facts from values, I have been trying to show that this a link that can be rationally justified. However, the connection between Taylor's philosophical-anthropological approach, on the one hand, and his ontological perspective, on the other, is still far from evident.

In fact, there seems to be an unbridgeable methodological gap here. For how can the central methods of Taylor's philosophical anthropology, that is, *ad hominem* reasoning and transcendental justification—both necessarily limited to experience—be used to yield ontological conclusions or to support realist claims? Since it is contradictory to extrapolate extrahuman claims from human experience, it seems safe to conclude that Taylor's philosophical anthropology can *never* serve to justify ontological claims. In what sense, then, could his ethical thought provide a basis for ontological theory? This brings us to the next major issue in pursuance of Taylor's doctrine of strong evaluation: the link between his moral philosophy and his ontological view. In trying to obtain clarity on this connection, I explore the ethical implications of strong evaluation in chapter 4, and its ontological implications in chapter 5.

NOTES

1. Surprisingly though, the very term "philosophical anthropology" has disappeared from Taylor's texts since the publication of *Sources of the Self*.

2. Taylor specifies what is involved in this type of inquiry in Taylor (1988, 299–300; 1989, 11, 112; 1994a, 249; 2005, 40–41), then also in the interview in *Thesis Eleven* (De Lara 1998, 111), and in the afterword of *Varieties of Secularism in a Secular Age* (Warner, VanAntwerpen, and Calhoun 2010, 315–17).

3. Note that Taylor has experienced this type of resistance only recently with regard to his philosophical-anthropological concept of "fullness" (as elaborated on in *A Secular Age*). As he explains: "In talking with people and reading reviews of the book, I've found that I'm often totally misunderstood on this. They thought that fullness could only be applied to explicitly religious positions, *while the whole point was that I was looking for a generic term that applied to all people*, whether religious or non-religious" (Taylor in: Warner, VanAntwerpen, and Calhoun 2010, 12, italics mine).

4. See, for example, the critiques of Olafson (1994, 193) and Flanagan (1996, 154).

5. In a footnote, Taylor explains that the terms "projection" and "projectivism" are used by John Mackie and Simon Blackburn, respectively (1989, 528, note 2).

6. Though the increasing interest in "evolutionary" ethics shows that this is no marginal position either. See, for example, James Scott's *An Introduction to Evolutionary Ethics* (2011).

7. See especially Blackburn (1993).

8. When I speak of the "early" Nussbaum, I am referring to her writings on human capabilities, the quality of life, and Aristotle in the 1990s, more particularly to the paper "Human Functioning and Social Justice. In Defense of Aristotelian Essentialism" (Nussbaum 1992) and her chapter "Aristotle on Human Nature and the Foundation of Ethics" (Nussbaum 1995). Although this last text appears in a collection of papers in which Taylor makes an appearance as well, he scarcely refers to Nussbaum's work when elaborating on his views. When he does mention her (for the most part in *A Secular Age*), almost all references are to Nussbaum's late writings.

9. In this respect, Laitinen's characterization of Taylor's account of strong evaluation as a type of "modernized and individualized Aristotelianism" (2008, 33) is spot

on. Given the great similarity between both approaches, it is quite puzzling why Taylor scarcely mentions Aristotle in his writings.

10. Taylor makes this point most elaborately in the paper "Overcoming Epistemology," as he seeks to show that the epistemological tradition in which naturalism is rooted tacitly trades on "some of the most important moral and spiritual ideas of our civilization" (1995b, 8). Here we see Taylor extending his *ad hominem* strategy, arguing that overcoming epistemology involves coming to grips with epistemology's underlying moral ideals of "reflexive, self-given certainty," "self-responsibility," and "freedom as self-autonomy" (1995b, 6–7).

11. See, for example, the arguments of Alan Gewirth (1982) and Deryck Beyleveld (1991), who also depart from the notion of agency to elaborate on a transcendental claim.

REFERENCES

Abbey, Ruth. 2000. *Charles Taylor*. Teddington/Princeton: Acumen Press/Princeton University Press.

Beyleveld, Deryck. 1991. *The Dialectical Necessity of Morality: An Analysis and Defense of Alan Gewirth's Argument to the Principle of Generic Consistency*. Chicago: University of Chicago Press.

Blackburn, Simon. 1993. *Essays in Quasi-Realism*. Oxford: Oxford University Press.

De Lara, Phillipe 1998. "From Philosophical Anthropology to the Politics of Recognition: an Interview with Charles Taylor." *Thesis Eleven* 52: 103–12.

Flanagan, Owen. 1996. *Self Expressions. Mind, Morals, and the Meaning of Life*. New York/Oxford: Oxford University Press.

Gewirth, Alan. 1982. *Human Rights: Essays on Justification and Applications*. Chicago, IL: University of Chicago Press

Illies, Christian. 2003. *The Grounds of Ethical Judgement. New Transcendental Arguments in Moral Philosophy*. Oxford/New York: Oxford University Press.

Johnston, Paul. 1999. *The Contradictions of Modern Moral Philosophy. Ethics after Wittgenstein*. London/New York: Routledge.

Laitinen, Arto. 2008. *Strong Evaluation Without Moral Sources*. Berlin: Walter de Gruyter.

Nussbaum, Martha. 1992. "Human Functioning and Social Justice. In Defense of Aristotelian Essentialism." *Political Theory* 20 (2): 202–46.

Nussbaum, Martha. 1995. "Aristotle on Human Nature and the Foundation of Ethics." In *World, Mind, and Ethics. Essays on the Ethical Philosophy of Bernard Williams*, edited by J. Altham and R. Harrison, 86–131. Cambridge, MA: Cambridge University Press.

Olafson, Frederick. 1994. "Comments on *Sources of the Self* by Charles Taylor." *Philosophy and Phenomenological Research* 54 (1): 191–96.

Rosa, Hartmut, and Arto Laitinen. 2002. "On Identity, Alienation and the Consequences of September 11th. An Interview with Charles Taylor." In *Acta Philosophica Fennica. Vol. 71. Perspectives on the Philosophy of Charles Taylor*, edited

by Arto Laitinen and Nicholas Smith, 165–195. Helsinki: Philosophical Society of Finland.
Scott, James. 2011. *An Introduction to Evolutionary Ethics*. West Sussex: Wiley-Blackwell.
Smith, Nicholas. 2002. *Charles Taylor: Meaning, Morals and Modernity*. Cambridge, MA: Polity.
Taylor, Charles. 1964. *The Explanation of Behaviour*. London: Routledge and Kegan Paul.
Taylor, Charles. 1972. "The Opening Arguments of the *Phenomenology*." In *Hegel: A Collection of Critical Essays*, edited by Alasdair MacIntyre. Garden City, New York, NY: Doubleday
Taylor, Charles. 1985a. *Human Agency and Language: Philosophical Papers vol. 1*. Cambridge, MA: Cambridge University Press.
Taylor, Charles. 1985b. "What is Human Agency?" In *Human Agency and Language: Philosophical Papers vol. 1*, 15–44. Cambridge, MA: Cambridge University Press.
Taylor, Charles. 1985c. "What's Wrong With Negative Liberty." In *Philosophy and the Human Sciences: Philosophical Papers vol. 2*, 211–29. Cambridge, MA: Cambridge University Press.
Taylor, Charles. 1988. "The Moral Topography of the Self." In *Hermeneutics and Psychological Theory*, edited by Stanly Messer, Louis Sass and Robert Woolfolk, 298–320. New Brunswick, NJ: Rutgers University Press.
Taylor, Charles. 1989. *Sources of the Self. The Making of the Modern Identity*. Cambridge, MA: Cambridge University Press.
Taylor, Charles. 1991. "Comments and Replies." *Inquiry* 34: 237–54.
Taylor, Charles. 1994a. "Reply and re-articulation." In *Philosophy in an Age of Pluralism: The Philosophy of Charles Taylor in Question*, edited by James Tully and Daniel Weinstock, 213–57. Cambridge, MA: Cambridge University Press.
Taylor, Charles. 1994b. "Reply to Commentators." *Philosophy and Phenomenological Research* 54 (1): 203–13.
Taylor, Charles. 1995a. "Explanation and Practical Reason." In *Philosophical Arguments*, 34–60. Cambridge, MA/London: Harvard University Press.
Taylor, Charles. 1995b. "Overcoming Epistemology." In *Philosophical Arguments*, 1–19. Cambridge, MA/London: Harvard University Press.
Taylor, Charles. 1995c. "The Validity of Transcendental Arguments." In *Philosophical Arguments*, 20–33. Cambridge, MA/London: Harvard University Press.
Taylor, Charles. 2005. "The "Weak Ontology" Thesis." *The Hedgehog Review: Critical Reflections on Contemporary Culture* 7 (2): 35–42.
Taylor, Charles. 2011. "Disenchantment-Reenchantment." In *Dilemmas and Connections*, 287–302. Cambridge, MA/London: Belknap Press of Harvard University Press.
Warner, Michael, Jonathan VanAntwerpen, and Craig Calhoun, eds. 2010. *Varieties of Secularism in a Secular Age*. Cambridge/London: Harvard University Press.
Weinstock, Daniel. 1994. "The Political Theory of Strong Evaluation." In *Philosophy in an Age of Pluralism: the Philosophy of Charles Taylor in Question*, edited by James Tully and Daniel Weinstock, 171–93. Cambridge, MA: Cambridge University Press.

Chapter 4

Ethics of Strong Evaluation

This chapter investigates the ethical dimension of the doctrine of strong evaluation. How does Taylor understand morality and ethics? How does he characterize moral experience? And how do these views relate to his claims about ontology? We have seen that the starting point of Taylor's moral philosophy is phenomenology, as he presents his view as an exercise in "moral phenomenology" (1989, 68, 74, 81). Unfortunately, unlike his various comments on the *ad hominem* and transcendental methods that authorize his philosophical anthropology, he does not provide a clear explanation of the aims, procedures, and results of moral phenomenology. On the one hand, it is clear that Taylor's moral philosophy steers a course between ethical, phenomenological, and ontological inquiries. On the other hand, it is not so clear what can actually be achieved, *ontologically*, by a phenomenological approach to ethics. In line with his interwoven mode of argumentation, Taylor explicitly seeks to draw ontological conclusions from his moral phenomenology, both in criticizing naturalistic approaches to ethics and in adopting a nonanthropocentric perspective on the good. Yet it remains to be argued out whether Taylor can justify this "move uphill," that is the move from phenomenology to ontology. His conspicuous silence about this tactic seems not only due to Taylor's own uncertainties about moral phenomenology but also generally there has been little discussion about this particular method of ethical inquiry in mainstream philosophical debates.[1] In the face of this confusion, the aim of this chapter is to answer one central question: Is Taylor's interweaving of ethical, phenomenological, and ontological claims justified?

In preparation for this question, I will not only shine a spotlight on Taylor's distinctive brand of morality, but also have recourse to Maurice Mandelbaum's (too-little-known) book, *The Phenomenology of Moral Experience* (1955), which, to my knowledge, is the first and only attempt to develop a systematic and complete moral phenomenology.[2] I first discuss Taylor's broad definition of morality and his explanation of the deeper "moral sources" and "constitutive goods" in the background of moral life, while also highlighting his ambiguous use of phenomenological and ontological terms in clarifying these conceptions (section 4.1). I continue to discuss Taylor's views in more detail by comparing it with Mandelbaum's understanding of moral phenomenology (section 4.2). Finally, I argue that Taylor's strategy of interweaving moral-phenomenological and ontological claims can be understood only by including his nonanthropocentric perspective on the good (section 4.3).

4.1 THE BROAD AND DEEP CHARACTER OF MORALITY

4.1.1 Morality, Broadly Conceived

As noted (in section 1.2.2), Taylor defines morality in a broad sense to highlight the diversity of strong evaluations that define our identities. In his view, morality not just consists in the conventional notion of how people should treat one another, but also covers questions of dignity and what is a good or worthwhile life (1989, 53). Taylor's broad definition goes hand in hand with a critique of (what he sees as) the narrow focus to morality given by philosophers such as Richard Hare, John Rawls, and Jürgen Habermas (1989, 3). In brief, his critique is that these authors are all too narrowly concerned with "what we ought to *do*," and not with "what is valuable in itself, or what we should admire or love," thereby leaving room neither for "our different visions of the qualitative higher" nor for "strong goods" (Taylor 1995c, 145–46, original emphasis). In reply to these theories, Taylor strategically defines morality in terms of strong evaluation to cover both moral issues in the narrow sense (respect and obligation) and broader ethical questions about fulfillment and dignity. In this way, he employs a broad conception of morality precisely to highlight that there are issues of strong evaluation beyond the moral that are of central concern to us, that is, issues of what constitutes a rich, worthy, or meaningful human life (1989, 14).

On the whole, Taylor argues that human beings share a framework consisting of at least three moral concerns that we recognize as the "axes" of our moral life (1989, 14). The first is the sense that human beings command universal respect (1989, 11). The second axis concerns our understanding of what makes a full, worthy human life (1989, 14). The third axis revolves around personal dignity (1989, 15).[3] Even though Taylor claims that every culture recognizes these three axes, his account still lives up to moral diversity as there are "great differences" in how these axes are explained and experienced (1989, 16). The sense of respect for others, for instance, applies to all human beings in some societies but only to one's kin in others. Another example is that secular societies tend to place greater emphasis on the first axis by insisting on the importance of universal respect and autonomy, whereas in religious cultures the issue of human fulfillment on the second axis might be more central (e.g., in feeling called to God or the divine as made clear in revelation). Strong evaluation in a warrior culture (to take yet another historical example) is more likely to arise along the third axis, in terms of dignity, self-esteem, and admiration. However, Taylor argues, despite these differences, it is precisely because we all recognize these three central axes that cross-cultural debates become possible. As he says: "Both Nazi and myself accept some version of the principle 'thou shalt not kill,' together with a different set of exclusions" (1995a, 53).

The novelty of Taylor's broad definition of the moral lies primarily in including questions of fulfillment and dignity. Evidently, we do recognize the notions of a good and worthwhile life, fullness, and dignity, but these are usually not seen by us as *moral* concerns since most theories define morality strictly along the first axis, that is, in terms of respect and obligation. Taylor thus adds the second and third axes in order to put the notions of fullness and dignity in a more *ethical* context.[4]

Ultimately, this means that Taylor's moral phenomenology does not aim at providing a system or procedure that can help us to define our obligations toward others. Nor is his phenomenological approach an attempt to provide us with a complete alternative moral framework. This is because the more established moral goods of, say, utilitarian and Kantian theory (producing the best consequences, universalizability, and obligation) do not stand in opposition to the doctrine of strong evaluation. Rather, since strong evaluations are central also in a simplified domain of benefit maximization or obligation, these theories in fact presuppose strong evaluation. Taylor's aim to extend our notion of what is relevant to morality will therefore not lead us to reject solving moral issues in terms of benefit maximization or the universal applicability of maxims of action. But it may make us reconsider their role in moral life, and the way we weigh these kinds of moral deliberation against other strong concerns.

At this point, it may be helpful to separate the basic universal *structure* of moral experience from the specific *content* of particular moralities in history, that is, to differentiate between the background that we draw on when we try to explain our moral responses, on the one hand, and the commonly accepted moral rules, ideals, and virtues of a given society, on the other.[5] In Taylor's case, this means recognizing the distinction between the three universal axes of morality—respect, fulfillment, and dignity—and "our" late modern moral outlook. With regard to the three axes, Taylor first argues that we are all "universalists" about respect for human life; second, that the aspiration to fulfillment is not an "optional" matter for us and that, therefore, questions along the second axis can arise in "any" culture; and third, that the issue of personal dignity is "no more avoidable" than respect for human life and the aspiration to fulfillment (1989, 6, 11, 15, 16, 42). Considered against these three axes, Taylor continues to argue that the most characteristic demands of *our* historically developed moral common sense are "universal justice," "beneficence," "equality," "freedom," and "self-rule" (1989, 495). With these points in place, we are now in a good position to investigate Taylor's moral phenomenology a bit further. Although its broad scope is indeed an essential feature of his understanding of ethics, we would be telling only half the story if we overlooked the other cornerstone of Taylor's moral phenomenology: its depth.

4.1.2 Life Goods, Constitutive Goods, and Moral Sources

Given Taylor's broad view on morality, one might object that his doctrine of strong evaluation is simply too broad as a theory of *ethics*. In this respect, he has been criticized for failing to provide a standard or criterion to separate the categorical from the merely optional.[6] How, so the objection goes, can the concept of strong evaluation capture the moral, if this notion simply covers the *whole* range of qualitative distinctions that we make? On such a broad spectrum, what place is there left for practical reason and moral argument? Taylor holds two positions here. On the one hand, he clearly rejects the insulation of moral goods from other, so-called "nonmoral" considerations. On the other hand, he does allow for the categorical character of morality by making a qualitative distinction *within* the realm of strong evaluations, that is, to separate first-order "life" goods from second-order "constitutive" goods that function as deeper "moral sources." Let me flesh this out.

The main reason Taylor's moral phenomenology does not stop at the notions of strong evaluation, respect, fulfillment, and dignity is his view that the crucial moral debate turns on our understanding of the "motivations" that define the good life for us. Taylor describes these underlying motivations both as moral sources and as constitutive goods, and stresses that they are not exclusively handed down by tradition but can also be "rooted in moral phenomenology, i.e. our experience of our moral predicament" (1988, 302). He employs the concepts of moral sources and constitutive goods mainly to describe the distinctive way in which human beings stand in contact with the good, namely by recognizing higher-order values. That is, "our sense of what we ought to do or be is shaped by the (strongly valued) goods we acknowledge" (1995c, 134).

The image of strong goods as moral sources brings us to Taylor's distinction between two types of goods. He uses the term "life goods" to articulate "what actions, modes of being, virtues really define a good life for us" and employs the notions of "constitutive goods" and "moral sources" to depict the "higher-order" goods that inspire life goods (1989, 92–93; 1997, 173).[7] Although Taylor admits that the relationship between life goods and constitutive goods is "rather hard to state" (1989, 308), his classification of goods still makes sense if we grant that individuals *have* to rank competing goods if they want to make a nonarbitrary choice in the face of the different goods they espouse. Seen in this light, the category of higher-order constitutive goods merely reaffirms Taylor's view that higher goods are central to the moral life as most people not only recognize multiple goods but feel that they have to rank them. That is, we acknowledge "second-order qualitative distinctions which define higher goods, on the basis of which we discriminate among other goods" (1989, 63).

Taylor's central claim about higher-order motivation is that we take some goods as primary because we see them as higher than others in the sense of more worthy, while deciding about others only from these overriding commitments. Regardless of the actual goods one espouses, the sense is that (lower-order) life goods need crucial reference to (higher-order) constitutive goods by virtue of which these life goods are recognized as "good." That is, if I see devotion to God as a crucial part of the good life, I am articulating a life good. But, Taylor argues, this makes sense only in the (constitutive) context of seeing ourselves as creatures of a loving God. Similarly, universal human rights cannot be separated from a worldview in which human beings are of equal worth. For the same reason, it would not be intelligible to espouse life goods such as a good marriage and a successful career without some underlying recognition of mutual love and personal development as the main sources of a full human life. These examples indicate that life goods define *what* we find of moral importance, whereas constitutive goods explain *why* we believe this to be so. Constitutive goods must therefore be seen not just as crucial motivations to act in some ways rather than others, but also as deeper articulations of the life goods one espouses. This does not mean, however, that constitutive goods are primary in the sense that they always have priority in practical reasoning. Rather, they are the notions that we start from, providing the standpoint from which other goods must be judged.

On the whole, the central objective of Taylor's moral phenomenology is to capture both the broad and the deep character of our strong evaluations. Rather than separating one conception of the moral (respect for others) from other strong concerns (fulfillment and dignity), he seeks to widen and deepen the moral domain by arguing, first, that human beings share a broader framework than what we normally think of as moral, and, second, that we can make sense of this only by including our recognition of constitutive higher goods as moral sources. However, despite the emphasis on the substantial overlap in our strong evaluations, Taylor does not gloss over the fact that moral outlooks can be quite diverse, granting that our experience along the three central axes varies from person to person and from culture to culture.

4.1.3 Constitutive Goods: Phenomenological or Ontological?

With these points in place, Taylor's moral phenomenology is best understood as a descriptive project, as its main goal is to articulate the universal moral background we all draw on for our particular actions and beliefs. Consequently, Taylor's primary task as a moral phenomenologist is to *clarify*. Seen in this light, it would seem that his moral phenomenology lays a much weaker claim than his philosophical anthropology. Whereas Taylor backs the latter with *ad hominem* and transcendental arguments (as explained in the previous chapter), the former is essentially descriptive. Having said that, though, the real problem is that Taylor—neither as a philosophical anthropologist nor as a moral phenomenologist—does not confine himself to a search for mere clarity. We recall his nonanthropocentric view (as introduced in section 1.2.3 and discussed in more detail in section 2.1.3) that strong evaluations track a reality beyond human life. We also saw (in section 2.3.2) how Taylor strategically moves "uphill" in developing this view, that is, to move from phenomenological descriptions to ontological claims in order to refute naturalistic approaches to ethics and ontology. Unlike the humbler project of phenomenological description, this is a claim about understanding our world *correctly*, and this not just on philosophical-anthropological and moral-phenomenological levels but also on an ontological one.

In trying to grasp Taylor's strategy now from the perspective of his moral phenomenology, it might be helpful to examine his conception of constitutive goods more closely. As it turns out, Taylor uses this concept not only to elaborate on his moral phenomenology, but also to open up an ontological perspective. This tactic is most explicit in his paper "Leading a Life" (1997). In line with the above analysis, this text again stresses the need to add the deeper dimension of constitutive goods for gaining a fuller understanding of the life goods one espouses. As Taylor argues, the basic level of life goods connects to a "second" level where we "try to clarify what it is about human beings, or their place in the universe, or our relation to God, or whatever else, that makes it the case that such and such are the highest life goods" (1997, 173). He then explains the need for this second level by asserting that a life good, properly understood, requires "a certain kind of picture of the universe, our capacities, and the possible stances toward this universe they make possible for us" (1997, 173).

On the one hand, it is clear that this is the context in which we have to situate Taylor's central criticism of the overall "suppression of moral ontology" by his opponents (1989, 10). On the other hand, we should also note that this criticism is no longer confined to moral phenomenology, as it principally enters the terrain of ontology. This means that Taylor criticizes contemporary moral philosophy not just for eschewing the articulation of its own goods, but also for suppressing its "picture of the universe" (1997, 173), that is, the implicit *ontology* behind its ethical views. This is particularly explicit in Taylor's dismissal of Rawls' theory of justice on account of its aim to "re-edit something of the Kantian theory, *without the 'metaphysics'*" (1997, 174, italics mine). In this regard, it is telling that Taylor loses no time in launching a direct attack on the "naturalist attempt to deny ontology altogether" in the opening pages of *Sources of the Self* (1989, 10).

This is where Taylor's nonanthropocentrism comes to the forefront of his thought. As we have seen at length in the previous chapters, he not only criticizes the suppression of ontological issues but also endorses the much stronger criticism that a naturalist ontology must be *rejected* if we are to hold on to our moral experience. As Taylor says, "there remains the tension between the phenomenology of the incommensurably higher and a naturalist ontology which has difficulty finding a place for this" (2003, 316). From here it is only a small step to his more explicit rejection of "the ontology we allow ourselves as post-Galilean naturalists," and the question of "whether the values we espouse can be supported on the basis of the ontology to which we want to subscribe" (2003, 318, 319). Here we come up against the recurrent problem in Taylor's doctrine of strong evaluation that we encountered twice in the previous chapter: What is the philosophical status of an account that, on the one hand, starts rather unpretentiously as a phenomenological description of moral experience, but, on the other hand, boldly ensures a more compelling—in this case not normative nor transcendental but ontological—claim?

Taylor's interweaving of phenomenological and ontological reasoning in developing his account of constitutive goods has evoked a variety of interpretations. Abbey, for example, concedes that familiar analytical categories do not capture Taylor's conception of constitutive goods as "the usually discrete categories of knowledge, action, and emotion must be fused when it comes to appreciating the role and power of constitutive goods" (2000, 47). Regrettably, though, despite Abbey's acknowledgment of both the "phenomenological features" of Taylor's moral theory and her discussion at length of the "ontological dimensions" of his thought (2000, 27, 58–72), she nowhere discusses the tension between these different modes of reasoning. Smith, however, notes that even if it were true that all human beings express "some desire to be in 'contact' with moral sources," this "would not of course prove that there is anything in *reality* corresponding to the desire" (2002, 115–16, original emphasis). Quite to the contrary, Smith continues, it may well be that "the desire exists solely at the phenomenological level, that is, as a truth of human subjectivity without foundation in non-human reality" (2002, 116). Unfortunately, Smith does not elaborate on this last point, because it emerges from the above discussion that this is precisely the kind of view Taylor calls into question by rejecting a naturalist ontology and by adopting a nonanthropocentric perspective on the good. Again, instead of driving a wedge between truths and desires (or facts and values), he argues—*pace* Smith—that our strong evaluations "track some reality" and can be *criticized* for "misapprehension" of it (2011, 297). Given this view, it seems safe to conclude that Taylor understands constitutive goods not as merely subjective but as connecting with an extrahuman reality in the background of our life goods.

Others have proposed more radical solutions. Joel Anderson, for example, chooses to speak simply of "goods" in discussing Taylor's views, since "there is no standpoint from which to say that a particular good is a constitutive good rather than a life good that only appears to be beyond further backing" (1996, 37, note 24). At first glance, Taylor seems to agree with this point when he says that the relationship between life goods and constitutive goods is hard to explain (1989, 308). But despite this uncertainty, he also asserts that it is exactly by *distinguishing* life goods from constitutive goods that we "could hope to come clearer about how we recognize a diversity of goods and how we try to make a unity of our lives in the face of them" (1997, 175). From this perspective, Anderson's strategy of deliberately ignoring the distinction between life goods and constitutive goods is to deny the problem rather than to solve it. Taylor, on the other hand, employs this distinction precisely to account for the sense that we make nonarbitrary choices when faced with different goods.

Perhaps the boldest response to Taylor's dual phenomenological-ontological explanation of constitutive goods is Laitinen's rejection of the entire concept. Laitinen separates constitutive goods from what he calls "ontological background pictures" to make the case that once this distinction is made, "no second-level constitutive goods or moral sources are needed" (2008, 8, 265). However, Laitinen emphasizes, "this is not to claim that ontological issues are irrelevant. The central claim is to distinguish the so-called ontological background pictures from the ontologized sources of value" (2008, 8).

Two points can be made here. First, the expressions "ontological sources" or "ontologized sources of value" are nowhere to be found in Taylor's writings. Rather, he speaks of the "ontological accounts" that try to articulate the claims implicit in our moral reactions and of the explanatory "ontology" that explains these reactions (1989, 5). This might seem only a minor difference, but it does undermine Laitinen's interpretation to the extent that saying that these ontological explanations articulates what Taylor calls "constitutive goods" is quite different from saying that these goods *themselves* are "ontological," as Laitinen argues.

Second, Laitinen's aim of upholding the "layer of strong evaluations" while dropping the notion of constitutive goods flies in the face of Taylor's point that espousing a life good without reference to constitutive goods would be dealing with a "compulsion," not a moral obligation (1996/2011, 9). To make this point, Taylor draws a parallel with the neurotic necessity to "wash one's hands" or to "remove stones from the road" (1996/2011, 9). That is, just as the acts of washing one's hands and removing stones from the road become unintelligible when separated from an underlying motivation that includes their point (e.g., to have clean hands and to keep the road passable), so too does a life good require an explanation of why one should live up to the norms that it brings about. This further clarification, then, articulates what Taylor calls both "constitutive goods" and "ontological accounts." As he argues, "a moral obligation comes across as moral *because it is part of a broader sense* which includes the goodness, perhaps the nobility or admirability, of being someone who lives up to it" (1996/2011, 9, italics mine).

This is why Taylor differentiates between Kant's own theoretical framework and the neo-Kantian philosophy of Rawls, arguing that "Kant himself did not similarly restrict the scope of his theorizing" (1997, 174). As noted above, Taylor rejects Rawls' view precisely because it seeks to revise the original Kantian theory by eliminating the "metaphysics" (1997, 174). In criticizing this move, Taylor's point is that just saying *that* autonomy (or benevolence, or universal rights, or whatever) is really important by itself does nothing to explain *why* we ought to respect others. This is why, as Taylor puts it, "you need to be operating on *both* levels"—that is, both life and constitutive—to make full sense of your conception of the good life (1997, 173, italics mine). Because of this, "reflection at either of these levels is hard to carry on without touching on the other" (1997, 173). For these reasons, it seems unlikely, *pace* Laitinen, that we can make sense of Taylor's doctrine of strong evaluation without the dimension of constitutive goods.

Laitinen also criticizes Taylor for suggesting that "the source of the meaning of life in general can be captured in one single ontological account of 'constitutive reality,'" whereas "one can think, *pace* Taylor, that the content to life comes from a plurality of sources" (Laitinen 2008, 268). I find this interpretation of Taylor's account of constitutive goods very confusing. In contrast (as explained in section 4.1.1), I understand Taylor's moral phenomenology as deeply pluralist because it allows for the diversity of goods people espouse (both life and constitutive), while also leaving room for multiple ontological accounts that define these goods. However, these points still do not explain Taylor's view that constitutive goods both make reference to our metaphysical predicament and connect with an extrahuman reality (1989, 307; 2011, 297). This view definitely needs further clarification. Moreover, if, as Taylor insists, we should treat our moral experience as giving us "access to the world in which ontological claims are discernible" (1989, 8), then how should we understand the relationship between moral phenomenology and ontology? This is the topic of the next section.

4.2 METHODS FROM MANDELBAUM

The former section clearly illustrates Taylor's characteristic interwoven line of thought. His leading question is: If moral phenomenology demonstrates (1) that constitutive goods exist and (2) that their experienced source does not come from human experience alone, then "where" do our strong values come from? This question, as Taylor understands it, can be answered adequately only by taking into account the *ontological* conditions that allow for the experience of strong value. However, in the following sections, I show that he is walking into very uncertain territory by drawing ontological claims from his phenomenological approach to ethics. Put simply, having recourse to moral phenomenology by itself does nothing to validate ontological claims. I elaborate on this, first, by highlighting the striking resemblance between Taylor's and Mandelbaum's moral phenomenology (section 4.2.1), and, second, by taking due account of the subtle difference between them regarding the source of moral experience (section 4.2.2).[8]

4.2.1 The Scope of Moral Phenomenology

The American philosopher Maurice Mandelbaum (1908–1987), mentored and influenced by Wolfgang Köhler (one of the founders of "gestalt psychology"), is generally situated in the tradition of "American critical realism," which goes back to the 1920s. However, this seems somewhat of an uneasy fit because it overlooks Mandelbaum's achievements outside his central historical interest, especially in phenomenology. Even though Mandelbaum's phenomenological project shows a striking overlap with Taylor's approach to ethics, Taylor does not mention Mandelbaum in any of his writings, and also generally, there seems to have been some neglect of Mandelbaum's theories.[9] Mandelbaum's *The Phenomenology of Moral Experience* consists of three main tasks. The first is "to show the necessity for grounding any ethical theory upon a phenomenological analysis of moral experience" (1955, 7). The second is "to analyze the nature of that experience and of the moral controversies to which it gives rise" (1955, 7). The third and final aim is to argue that "one can discriminate between those moral judgments which are valid and those which are not" (1955, 43).

In the following sections, I shall concentrate on only two aspects of Mandelbaum's view to evaluate Taylor's move from phenomenology to ontology, namely his explanation of the *scope* of moral phenomenology and his clarification of the *source* of moral experience. As will emerge, moral phenomenology, as Mandelbaum envisages it, is simply the wrong method to use to defend ontological claims. Yet at the same time, he agrees with Taylor that moral demands are not explicable simply in terms of human responses, as they emanate from sources beyond our desires and inclinations. I will argue later on (in section 4.2.2) that this observation has important implications for Taylor's critique of naturalist ontology. At this stage, however, I will first compare Taylor and Mandelbaum in general terms.

There is no doubt that Mandelbaum's focus on the nature of moral experience (rather than the vocabulary used in describing that experience), his explicit rejection of the fact-value distinction, and his view that the results of ethical inquiry must be consonant with other, nonethical theses show many illuminating parallels with Taylor's doctrine of strong evaluation. More particularly, Mandelbaum's phenomenology is related to Taylor's view in the following five ways. The first similarity between Mandelbaum and Taylor is a methodological one. They both argue that ethics should not be concerned with finding a universally valid standard for conduct, but with the explanation of concrete moral experiences. Mandelbaum defines the general task of ethics as "the attempt to gain a systematic and complete understanding of moral experience," a task that can be fulfilled only by "a careful and direct examination of individual moral judgments" (1955, 41, 31). Similarly, Taylor has recourse to "our experience of our moral predicament," which he also describes as an analysis of the "inescapable" features of moral language (1988, 302; 1989, 68). Second, they both believe that moral experience has certain universal features. In the same way Taylor characterizes strong evaluation as a generic feature of human agency, Mandelbaum describes his method as "a 'generic' approach to the nature of moral judgments," that is, to "abstract from these judgments the specific content of their affirmations [. . .] to discover the generic characteristics of all moral experience" (1955, 35–36).

The third similarity is that both authors are dissatisfied with the major moral theories of their time. In the first chapter of his book, Mandelbaum criticizes metaphysical, psychological, and sociological approaches to ethics, while Taylor takes issue with naturalist-inspired moral theories. In so doing, they both take a critical distance from rigid analytic or linguistic approaches that, rather than analyze moral experiences, focus exclusively on the clarification of normative statements. Fourth, both Mandelbaum and Taylor reject the fact-value distinction in endorsing their phenomenological approaches to ethics. As we have seen (in section 3.1.2), Taylor argues that the attempt to split fact and value creates a distorted picture of the way human beings experience moral goods. In his view, thinking within the framework of the fact-value dichotomy to explain moral issues is to get off on the wrong foot, because moral reasoning simply cannot be understood in terms of such a "radical" distinction (1989, 58). Mandelbaum makes the same point when he says that it is a crucial mistake to believe that the task of ethics, being a normative discipline, is "to deal not with 'what is' but with 'what ought to be'" (1955, 13), that is, with normative statements as *opposed* to descriptive ones. In Mandelbaum's view, there are two main problems with dichotomizing normative and descriptive statements and disciplines. First, such a distinction glosses over the reality that "the facts with which ethics deals are (to put it paradoxically) normative facts" (1955, 41). Second, it makes all attempts to connect the results of ethical inquiry with other fields look highly suspicious, for such attempts "would of course break down the distinction between normative and descriptive disciplines" (1955, 15).

Mandelbaum's rejection of the distinction between normative and descriptive disciplines is closely related to the fifth and last parallel between both authors. Mandelbaum continues to emphasize the relevance of moral phenomenology for other disciplines, arguing that his endorsement of a phenomenological approach to ethics is "not to deny that the results of an ethical inquiry must also be consonant with metaphysical, psychological, and sociological theses" (1955, 31). By refusing to isolate moral phenomenology from other fields of inquiry, he implicitly mirrors Taylor's interwoven line of argumentation. In elaborating on this, he makes a connection between what he calls the "metaphysical" approach to ethics and his own phenomenological approach. As it turns out, Mandelbaum's explanation of this connection is highly instructive for coming to grips with Taylor's move from phenomenology to ontology.

The metaphysical approach to ethics, as Mandelbaum defines it, is characterized by what can be called a "top-down" structure, as it seeks to "discover the nature of a *summon bonum* or of a standard for moral obligation through recourse to a consideration of the ultimate nature of reality" (1955, 16). At first, Mandelbaum defends the metaphysician's attempt to connect reality and value against the charge of the naturalistic fallacy—to confuse "what is" with "what ought to be"—because, as he says, "no matter where we start, we must in the end reconcile our conceptions of value and of obligation with what we conceive to be true of the world" (1955, 17). That this is so, Mandelbaum explains, that the goods we value must ultimately be aligned with our conception of reality, emerges from "the fact that we prize that which strikes us as being real—not sham, illusion, mere artifice, or appearance—*because* it is real" (1955, 17, original emphasis). As we have seen, Taylor makes a similar move by arguing that "our best phenomenology" must in the end be aligned with an "adequate ontology" (2007, 609). However, in Mandelbaum's view, one major weakness of the metaphysical approach is that reference to the nature of ultimate reality by itself does nothing to validate a system of ethics.

To make this point, he explains that the metaphysical approach to ethics is "not self-sufficient" as its validity must be "tested" through an appeal to moral common sense, in this way arguing that *any* metaphysical ethics must in the end be aligned with the phenomenological approach to ethics (1955, 17–18).

In other words, to be convincing, a *metaphysical* ethics needs to be supported by *moral-phenomenological* evidence. In fact, Mandelbaum continues, moral phenomenology deserves to take priority over the metaphysical approach in that it "starts from a point which all paths must eventually cross: a direct examination of the data of men's moral consciousness" (1955, 30). Methodologically speaking, this means that the procedure of moral phenomenology is best understood as "bottom-up," as opposed to the top-down structure of metaphysical approaches to ethics, as the phenomenological method states that "a solution to any of the problems of ethics must be educed from, and verified by, a careful and direct examination of individual moral judgments" (1955, 31). On the whole, Mandelbaum concludes, although the phenomenological approach dictates that the proper basis for any normative claim is to be found in moral experience, this does not mean that moral-phenomenological results have no implications for other fields of inquiry: "All that the phenomenological approach demands is that the solution to the problems of ethics must not be dictated by a prior acceptance of hypotheses drawn from the other fields" (1955, 31). Therefore, he adds, there is "no ultimate opposition between a phenomenological approach to ethics and a willingness to connect the results of ethical inquiry with non-ethical hypotheses" (1955, 32).

Mandelbaum's reasoning here almost perfectly articulates the concern for the connections between philosophical areas that is central to Taylor's interwoven line of thought. Moreover, Taylor implicitly follows Mandelbaum by arguing—against naturalism—that we should not let our language be dictated by the commands of science in making the "best sense" of our lives (1989, 57). However, Mandelbaum and Taylor are of different minds on the question of *how* moral phenomenology connects with other fields. As we have seen (in section 2.3.2), Taylor's distinctive move "uphill" clearly states that (bottom-up) phenomenological approaches *must* eventually cross (top-down) metaphysical ones when considering the drawbacks of naturalist ontology for explaining morality. Yet for Mandelbaum, this move reaches beyond the scope of moral phenomenology. Reflecting on this issue, I will show in the next section how Taylor and Mandelbaum ultimately draw different conclusions from their (very similar) moral phenomenologies.

4.2.2 The Source of Moral Experience

A central element of Taylor's and Mandelbaum's views is that they emphasize the special nature of moral goals in comparison with other goals.

Given Taylor's understanding of ethics as involving incommensurably higher values, the merit of Mandelbaum's account is that it illuminates *why* moral goods are experienced as being higher than simple preferences. As Mandelbaum explains, "in some choices we feel that one of the alternatives places a *demand* upon us, that we are obliged, or bound, to act for it," that is, in a way that strikes us "not as a preference but as an 'objective' demand" (1955, 50, original emphasis). In Mandelbaum's view, the element of demand is something many moral philosophers take for granted. As he argues, "most deontological theories have taken the element of a direct moral demand as being a phenomenon which is not capable of further analysis" (1955, 51). However, one of the greatest achievements of both Mandelbaum and Taylor is that they provide a phenomenological analysis precisely of this central element in our moral experience. Echoing Kant, both authors are clear about the desire-independent nature or "objective feel" of moral goods. Mandelbaum defines moral demands as essentially "objective" and "independent of preference, inclination or desire," while Taylor adds they therefore "represent standards by which these desires and choices are judged" (Mandelbaum 1955, 57; Taylor 1989, 20). Mandelbaum then goes one step further when he asserts that "it is impossible adequately to describe this feeling without taking into account what appears to us to be its *source*" (1955, 55, italics mine). In this respect, he notes that

> the demands which we experience when we make a direct moral judgment are always experienced as *emanating from "outside" us*, and as being directed against us. They are demands which seem to be *independent of us* and to which we feel that we ought to respond. (1955, 54, italics mine)

Mandelbaum holds two positions here. First, objective demands are real, not a façade. As he says, "we prize that which strikes us as being real [. . .] *because it is real*" (1955, 17, original emphasis). Second, these demands are a class in itself, not some human projection onto the world, as the felt demand in moral situations is such that "it appears to place a demand upon us because of *its* nature, not because of ours" (1955, 60, original emphasis). Taylor, in turn, makes similar remarks about strong evaluation when he says that "there is something objectively right about this response" because "this response genuinely motivates us, it is not simply a cover, or a rationalization, or a screen for some other drive" (2011, 300). Taylor's and Mandelbaum's clarifications of the human-independent source of moral experience fly in the face of the naturalistic view that value comes into the world with us, as a function of how we as human agents operate. For Taylor, then, this moral phenomenology only sets the stage for his more controversial idea that, although moral demands make sense only in *relation* to us, this does not mean that they are necessarily *dependent* on us, ontologically speaking. This feeds into the twofold explanation that moral demands appear only within human experience, but that we come up against a human-transcendent reality within this experience. Here Taylor's interwoven line of thinking emerges in full force, as this explanation starts from *phenomenology* and ends in *metaphysics*.

At first glance, this is where the assumed philosophical affinity between Mandelbaum and Taylor starts to unravel. From Mandelbaum's perspective, Taylor is making a crucial methodological mistake by connecting phenomenological and ontological questions in elaborating on the source of moral experience, because this move contradicts the very purpose of the moral-phenomenological method, namely to investigate "the data of men's moral consciousness"—and these data alone (Mandelbaum 1955, 30). Because of this starting point, moral phenomenology (as Mandelbaum defines it) is necessarily limited to "the phenomenal world," that is, that which is "directly experienced by me or by others" (1955, 313, note 18). This means, as he clarifies, that both the "origin of an experience or object" and a discussion of "its ontological status" are principally "excluded from phenomenology" (1955, 313, note 18).

However, when elaborating on the source of objective moral demands, Mandelbaum is in no doubt that such demands are, as he puts it, "emanating from 'outside' us," as they are experienced as being "independent of preference, inclination, or desire" (1955, 54, 57). In my view, this observation is not only spot on, but also makes a cogent and convincing case for Taylor's contention that these demands take us beyond ourselves. This raises a further question: If for Taylor and Mandelbaum the main point is that we need to take due account of the human-independent nature of moral demands if we are to hold on to our moral experience, then what are the implications of this phenomenology for the *metaphysical* order in which we are set? Yet for Mandelbaum, merely to raise this very question is to take a wrong turn. As he says, "the fact that the demands of duty are experienced as issuing from outside us does not [. . .] permit one to infer that what we experience as our duty has any ontological status independently of our experience of it" (1955, 58). To clarify this view, Mandelbaum draws a parallel with our perception of color to argue that, although the color red is apprehended as being "objective," it is clear that "a color-blind person does not experience red, and that red has no ontological status—does not exist—outside of the realm of the experience of certain groups of percipients" (1955, 58).

This is where the alliance between Mandelbaum and Taylor breaks down. As noted in discussing Taylor's attack on naturalist projectivism (in section 3.1.2), assimilating moral qualities to empirical properties is precisely what moral phenomenology shows we cannot do. Surely, for Taylor a color-blind person who lacks the experience of "redness" is perfectly possible. But, so his argument goes, this is totally different from—and incompatible with—the moral case. To give a phenomenological explanation of where the comparison between sensory and moral perception breaks down is not difficult. It is grounded in the fact that our perception of nonnormative data (like color) simply does not work as an image for moral experience. If we imagine a person insensitive not to the difference between colors, but, say, to the experienced difference between feeling hungry and feeling the need to save a child from drowning, it is unlikely that anyone could convince us that we are imagining a *moral* agent. Put simply, this means that we are "changing the subject" by conducting this type of thought experiment: once we have abstracted from the inherent normative nature of moral experience by giving a nonnormative example, we have lost our initial topic, that is, to understand moral experience. In other words, if moral experiences must be clearly distinguished from other, nonmoral types of experience because the former cannot be reduced to the latter, then, by logical principle, it simply does not follow that moral demands have the same ontological status as nonnormative properties.

If this be true, it follows that the boundary between moral phenomenology and ontology is an open question. This is of theoretical importance, since many contemporary ethical theories seek to account for morality without having recourse to ontological issues at all.[10] Taking this argument to its final conclusion, this means that a more promising type of moral phenomenology would indeed involve an inquiry into the ontological conditions under which moral judgments are made. Surprisingly perhaps, these implications *support* rather than weaken Taylor's move from phenomenology to ontology. This brings us right back to the topic that launched the doctrine of strong evaluation: Taylor's attack on naturalism. In the end, he takes up a nonanthropocentric perspective on the good precisely because reductive explanations of value as our "error," "projection," or "coloration" of a neutral world do not seem fit in the light of our experience of objective moral demands. But how should we understand the nonanthropocentric outlook that in Taylor's view makes better sense of this experience? Put differently, how can we explain the ontological conditions of morality without reducing strong evaluations to mere preferences and without postulating supernatural entities?

4.3 ETHICS BEYOND THE SELF

As noted (in the Introduction), Taylor defines his nonanthropocentric view as steering a middle course between "a 'Platonist' mode of moral realism" and "mere subjectivism" (1994, 211). Reflecting on this unusual position in the following sections, I argue that Taylor's view is best understood as a phenomenological attempt to connect Murdochean ethics and Heideggerian ontology.[11] In so doing, I show that Taylor's nonanthropocentrism starts from a Murdochean view on ethics (section 4.3.1) only to make room for his more Heideggerian concern for the ontological background conditions within which moral agency takes place (section 4.3.2).

4.3.1 A Murdochean Viewpoint

As noted (in section 2.1.3), Fergus Kerr rightly argues that Taylor's appeal to a nonanthropocentric perspective is not coincidental but indicates the central role of the sovereignty of good in his thinking as a whole. Put simply, Taylor starts from an analysis of human *subjectivity* only to open up a *nonsubjectivist* perspective on the good. The clearest example of this strategy is his assertion that the claims of the "nonhuman" cannot be heard in the "human-centered" frameworks of contemporary moral theorizing (1989, 103). Next to his familiar point that many moral theories occlude the goods they are inspired by, Taylor further claims that especially the neo-Nietzschean outlooks appeal to subjectivism in ethics (1989, 103). Notably, Taylor explicitly mentions Iris Murdoch in criticizing these views: "Does the 'self-forgetful pleasure' that we can take 'in the sheer alien pointless independent existence of animals, birds, stones, and trees' bring us closer to the moral good, as Iris Murdoch claims" (1989, 102)? Besides Kerr, several other commentators acknowledge Taylor's Murdochean viewpoint. Abbey, for example, mentions "Taylor's method of defending a nonsubjectivist account of morality" and stresses his attempt to "transcend subjectivism or anthropocentrism in ethical thinking by adumbrating a moral ontology that makes room for sources of moral motivation and allegiance that are non- or extrahuman" (2004, 9–10). Michael Rosen, on the other hand, sees Taylor's view more as an antisubjectivist and antirealist maneuver than as an ontological thesis about the objective order of reality, as he sees Taylor mainly adopting a nonanthropocentric view to argue against nonrealism and subjectivism in ethics (Rosen 1991, 184–85). Richard Rorty's interpretation seems to be somewhere in between the interpretations of Abbey and Rosen, conceding to Taylor the belief that "we cannot give up on the urge which led to moral realism" despite that "we can no longer be simple realists in our metaphysics or our theology" either (Rorty 1994, 199). Ultimately, as Rorty understands him, Taylor is rejecting all possible kinds of nonrealism because such views are "just not enough to satisfy our *moral realist* urges" (1994, 200, original emphasis).

In his reply to Rorty, Taylor makes two central points. The first is that, rather than being acknowledged only by moral realists and theists, constitutive goods are also recognized by "contemporary unbelieving and 'postmetaphysical' naturalists" (1994, 212). For them, however, these strong goods do not involve God (or some other supernatural entity) but "features of the human predicament and human potentialities" (1994, 212). For Taylor, this testifies to the fact that we simply cannot help "bringing before ourselves pictures of the human predicament which show the goodness and rightness of the things we feel bound to seek" (1994, 212).

Again, Taylor here argues—nonanthropocentrically—that our experience of being moved by certain goods (either religious or nonreligious) makes sense only because it is part of a broader ontological picture that explains the worth and validity of these goods. His second reply to Rorty, then, is that especially this last point—that there *is* a metaphysical picture in play here whether we recognize this or not—has been "unacknowledged by contemporary forms of naturalism" that want to "slither away from the recognition of constitutive goods" (1994, 213). In Taylor's view, the problem here is not just the "continuing self-delusion" of these naturalistic views, but, more importantly, that "every anthropocentrism pays a terrible price in this regard" (1994, 213). He then continues to explain that his own nonanthropocentric view is inspired not only by "deep ecologists" and "theists" (1994, 213), but also by a poet such as Rilke, who suggests that the world is not simply an "ensemble of objects for our use, but makes a further claim on us" (1989, 513).

Taylor also insists, somewhat dramatically perhaps, that to reject this Rilkean kind of thinking *tout court* is to incur a "huge self-inflicted wound" because it articulates something "extremely important" (1989, 513). Perhaps a more down-to-earth explanation of Taylor's Romanticist position is that he sees human life not as freely invented but as embedded in something that both constrains and orients it. As he explains elsewhere: "Your feeling a certain way can never be sufficient grounds for respecting your position, because your feeling can't *determine* what is significant" (1992, 37, original emphasis). That is, it is only by finding ourselves "always already" within some larger framework that we can define what is important to us and what is not. Seen in this light, the shape of Taylor's nonanthropocentrism is that it makes no sense to deny the existence of the limitations that, in his view, inescapably preexist for us. If we now return to the issues with which we began, we can see that Taylor's nonanthropocentrism is not only indebted to Murdoch and cultivated alongside the formulation of a moral phenomenology, but also seeks to incorporate a Romanticist perspective. As we will see, this is where Heidegger enters the scene.

4.3.2 The Importance of Heidegger

Granting Taylor's Rilkean point above about the way the world makes demands on *us*, how should we understand the commitment to *these*—extrahuman—goods? That is, how can we be connected to a reality that on account of its constitutive nature exists *independently* of our intuitions? Put differently, what does it mean to articulate goods that stand independent of human experience, for they principally offer *standards* by which our desires and feelings can be judged? (1989, 4) Even if we take note of Taylor's principal aim to interweave moral-phenomenological points and nonanthropocentric claims, we must still conclude that his moral phenomenology by itself leaves it unclear how and where phenomenological truths feed into ontological ones.

Given these observations, Carlos Thiebaut provides two ways of making sense of Taylor's view. The first is to describe it as a mere negative position that rejects "the most obvious forms of subjectivism and relativism" in defense of the claim that "it is not certain that values are merely contingently subjective" (Thiebaut 1993, 133–34). However, Taylor's point that our own feelings can never be the basis of the reality of constitutive goods cannot be upheld without buying into a nonanthropocentric viewpoint. This is why Thiebaut offers an "appellative" characterization of Taylor's ontology that aims to "eliminate its ontological sting," as it sees Taylor simply insisting on the "unquestionable existence of a variety of goods to which we *appeal* in order to judge, valorize, and live" (1993, 133–34, original emphasis). For Thiebaut, this type of moral realism involves a return to the *subject* more than anything else since he argues that "this inward movement is crucial, for it defines and constitutes the whole history of our historical constitution as moral subjects" (1993, 134–35). Given his recognition of Taylor's "nonsubjective calling to the good," however, Thiebaut ultimately explains Taylor's ontology as being characterized not by a simple return to the subject but rather by a *double* "simultaneous movement":

> In the first place, this realism appears to imbue the world with morality and to constitute, *outwardly*, the good as a component of the real; but, secondly, this appellation appears to provoke also an *inward* movement, towards the subject, before which alone this reality has any sense. (1993, 134, italics mine)

This explanation is spot on as it accounts for both Taylor's phenomenological starting point and the metaphysical thrust of his views. Moreover, Thiebaut underlines the deeply interwoven character of Taylor's "inward-outward" focus by adding that "the process that affirms ethical realism is the same process that affirms the nature of the moral subject" (1993, 135). It therefore says a lot about the depth of Thiebaut's analysis that his discussion of *Sources of the Self* already anticipates the context out of which Taylor's later concern for the tension between moral phenomenology and naturalist ontology will emerge.

At the same time, however, Thiebaut could not yet foresee the breadth of Taylor's nonanthropocentrism. Whereas Thiebaut's analysis mainly draws attention to Taylor's conception of the human subject, the present discussion has shown that this is not his only concern, as Taylor also seeks to explore the metaphysical underpinnings of morality. In this respect, it would seem that Thiebaut's image of Taylor's ontology as "more an anti-subjectivism and anti-naturalism than a metaphysical thesis about the reality in itself of the good" (1993, 135) has been surpassed by Taylor's nonanthropocentric moves. As his attack on naturalist ontology makes plain, his "double, simultaneous movement" ultimately consists in the *phenomenological* retrieval of moral experience for the *ontological* purpose of examining the nonanthropocentric origin of value.

We can come closer to understanding this complex tactic by including Kerr's insightful reading of Taylor since his main concern is precisely to provide an overview of Taylor's nonanthropocentric approach to ethics. Kerr's analysis is revealing in at least three respects. First, whereas most commentators only briefly take notice of Taylor's tendency toward nonanthropocentrism in ethics and ontology, Kerr provides a detailed analysis precisely of this important yet relatively unexplored aspect of Taylor's thought. Second, Kerr rightly draws attention to the fact that Taylor is highly indebted to Heidegger in elaborating his nonanthropocentric moral phenomenology. Third, he raises the vital question of how Taylor's nonanthropocentric ethics relates to his ontological beliefs.

In line with the present analysis, Kerr first emphasizes the close relationship between Taylor and Murdoch by noting that Taylor follows Murdoch in refuting "emotivism, prescriptivism, projectivism, and other forms of nonrealism" (2004, 90). In fact, Kerr continues, the issue that really concerns Taylor is the reality that "we remain stubbornly attached to unreconstructed moral realism" in our everyday practice, for our everyday moral intuitions "operate perfectly naturally and uncontentiously with assumptions about our nature and predicament that are more than anthropocentric" (2004, 92). Kerr then makes an interesting connection between Taylor's position and "Heidegger's philosophy of ecology," arguing that both Taylor and Heidegger seek to challenge the "anthropocentric humanism" that "culminates in Nietzschean claims to the effect that reality is simply what we human beings make of, or project onto it" (2004, 99). In this way, Kerr explains, Taylor takes up this Heideggerian theme to cast light on the way strong goods lay claims on us, arguing that "a proper understanding of our ways of dealing with the natural world has to take us 'beyond ourselves'" (2004, 100).[12]

Unfortunately for the purpose of understanding Taylor's nonanthropocentrism, though, both Kerr's analysis and Taylor's paper "Heidegger, Language, and Ecology" (to which Kerr repeatedly refers) are more about ecology than ethics. That is, they both conclude by saying that Heidegger's thoughts can be the basis of an "ecological politics" rather than elaborating on the implications of Heidegger's antisubjectivist position for ethics (Kerr 2004, 100; Taylor 1995b, 125). In this respect, Kerr also notes that "plainly Taylor's thinking here is quite exploratory and tentative" (2004, 101). At the same time, though, Taylor is very clear (in the introduction to *Philosophical Arguments*) about being "very much a proponent of the 'Romantic' view," but he has also admitted that his position in "Heidegger, Language, and Ecology" is still somewhat premature (1995d, x). As he says, although his paper about Heidegger "evokes" nonanthropocentric themes, they are "not extensively explored anywhere" (1995d, x). The introduction to *Philosophical Arguments* is quite informative with regard to this uncertainty. In this text, Taylor explains his position by contrasting Locke's "instrumental" view of language with the Romanticist "expressivist" understanding of language (1995d, ix). In criticizing the instrumentality of the Lockean conception, Taylor continues, it is crucial to the Romantic view that it stresses the "constitutive" nature of language (1995d, ix). In so doing, Romanticists see language not primarily as an instrument but rather as "what allows us to have the world that we have" or as something that "makes possible the disclosure of the human world" (1995d, ix). On the one hand, it seems clear that this is the context in which Taylor's nonanthropocentrism starts to make sense. On the other hand, when he says that "there is a combination here of creation and discovery *which is not easy to define*," we also recognize the roots of his later uncertainties about the ontological commitments behind our ethical views (1995d, ix–x, italics mine).

That is, if our moral language must be seen as "creative" rather than "instrumental" in that it "makes possible the disclosure of [. . .] this human world of thick and strong evaluations" (1995d, ix; 2003, 312), and if "discovering here depends on, is interwoven with, inventing" (1989, 18), then how to relate the elements of creation and invention to those of disclosure and discovery? In other words, if the disclosure of the demands the world makes *on* us depends on *our* powers of expression, then how to mark the distinction between this extrahuman reality and our human experience and articulation of it?

Indeed, we might want to hear much more about the ontological implications of this nonanthropocentric ethics when Taylor says that "the purposes in question are not simply human" and that "our goals here are fixed by something we should properly see ourselves as *serving*" (1995b, 126, italics mine). This raises a further question: If for Taylor the main point is that we need to be in contact with the extrahuman dimension of our world so as to hold on to our identities as strong evaluators, then what are the implications of his view for the metaphysical order in which we are set? In this respect, Kerr ultimately criticizes Taylor for leaving it "unsettlingly unclear how independent his moral philosophy ultimately is of Christian religion" (2004, 84). Yet he nevertheless concludes that Taylor's paper on Heidegger also indicates an account of "something external to human beings" that might "shape and sustain" a way of being in the world beyond "all anthropocentric subjectivism yet without buying into the supernaturalism of biblical religion" (2004, 84, 102).

4.4 CONCLUSION: MORAL PHENOMENOLOGY AND ONTOLOGY

Where does this leave us? Taking the above analyses together, the present discussion has highlighted the following central points:

1. Taylor's moral phenomenology starts from a broad definition of morality that includes our sense of respect and obligation as well as issues of fullness and dignity.
2. It articulates structural features of morality across ages and cultures: strong evaluation, the three-axised structure of moral life, and the distinction between life goods and constitutive goods.
3. It seeks to account for value pluralism by leaving room for the diversity of goods people espouse and the particular cultural contexts in which they seek moral orientation.
4. It draws attention to the depth of moral experience, first, by highlighting the crucial role of constitutive goods as moral sources in the background of our moral beliefs, and, second, by arguing (in the wake of Mandelbaum) that we can make full sense of these strong motivations only by acknowledging that their source does not come from us alone.
5. In so doing, Taylor gradually moves beyond moral phenomenology by laying out a nonanthropocentric perspective that is simultaneously rooted in a Murdochean understanding of ethics and a Heideggerian conception of ontology, albeit elaborated in a highly exploratory and tentative fashion.

If we now turn to the vital issue with which chapters 2 and 3 ended—about the links across Taylor's interwoven arguments—we now see him adopting an ontological perspective for a second time; in this case, not by taking in realist claims in developing his philosophical anthropology, but by using his moral phenomenology to raise ontological questions. This means that, although Taylor's human-focused perspectives in philosophical anthropology and moral phenomenology lucidly demonstrate that you can account for a large part of the doctrine of strong evaluation without invoking the word "ontology" at all, the discussion has now reached a point where ontological reflection can no longer be avoided.

One of the results of the former two chapters is that they show in great detail that Taylor's philosophical anthropology and ethics are deeply interwoven and interdependent, as they have several explanatory and argumentative implications for one another. That is, accepting Taylor's moral phenomenology has strong consequences for the philosophical-anthropological views one can consistently adopt in the light of this phenomenology. In the same way, his thesis of the transcendental necessity of strong evaluation cannot be upheld without also having an impact on one's conception of morality. As a result, Taylor's philosophical-anthropological and ethical arguments effectively work together to strike a double blow at reductionist understandings of human agency and morality. However, it also emerges from the above discussions that these arguments only implicitly inform Taylor's nonanthropocentric viewpoint. Although his thinking in this domain is highly tentative, the pursuit of Taylor's interwoven line of thought in comparison with Mandelbaum nonetheless makes it clear that the ontological implications of morality remain an open question when reflecting on the source of moral experience. I conclude from this that, since the distinction between phenomenology and ontology will be hard to draw in any unequivocal terms, Taylor's uphill move from phenomenology to ontology is ultimately justified. For one thing, this means that he is right to criticize naturalistic ontological commitments by having recourse to moral phenomenology.

As we have seen, Taylor criticizes naturalistic explanations of value precisely because they neglect the experience that moral demands take us beyond ourselves. However, even if he is quite right to argue that the naturalist suppression of ontological reflection has fostered a "kind of eclipse of ontological thinking" in moral theory (1995d, 39), then what could it mean to undo this suppression? Or, to put it in Mandelbaum's terms, where does a bottom-up phenomenological approach to ethics eventually cross a top-down metaphysical one in reflecting on the source of moral experience? This is where Taylor's central question of how to align our best phenomenology with an *adequate* ontology emerges in full force. Although this is a valid question, the present analysis demonstrates that far too little attention has been paid to Taylor's ontological perspective to answer it properly. Entering into the final stage of the attempt to shed light on Taylor's interwoven arguments, we now need to take the analysis only one step further—that is, to focus exclusively on the ontological implications of the doctrine of strong evaluation. This is the topic of chapter 5.

NOTES

1. By this I do not mean, of course, that the works of major phenomenological thinkers are not of moral significance, but that inquiry into concrete moral experiences as a specific *method* of philosophical investigation has not generally been part of

moral philosophy as practiced in the continental and analytic traditions. However, for a useful discussion of the contributions to ethical thought by the phenomenological tradition, see Drummond and Embree (2002).

2. I thank Mark Timmons for bringing this book to my attention.

3. Löw-Beer provides a helpful summary of the three axes, explaining that the strong evaluations that give answers to the following range of questions define the scope of morality for Taylor: "(1) Meaning of life: What is the meaning of life, what is it to lead a fulfilled life? (2) Ideals: What should I strive for? What kind of person would I like to be? (3) Rights: What makes others worthy of respect? What are our obligations to others?" (1991, 225). In the introduction of *A Secular Age,* however, Taylor argues that the issue of the "meaning of life" is not an essential but a typically *modern* phenomenon, to be distinguished from the universal experience of "fullness" (thanks to Guy Vanheeswijck for this point).

4. In this regard, Taylor's approach can also be seen as a retrieval of an *ancient* understanding of ethics, resisting the modern reduction of what morality is as a dimension of human life. As Julia Annas notes in her book on ancient ethical theory: "In our society we have to turn to popular self-help manuals to find extensive discussion of questions of the best life, self-fulfillment, the proper role of the emotions, personal friendships and commitments, topics which in the ancient world were always treated in a more intellectual way as part of ethics" (1993, 10).

5. This distinction largely corresponds to Bernard Gert's distinction between "morality" and a "moral theory": "It is important right at the beginning to distinguish between morality and a moral theory that makes explicit, explains, and, if possible, justifies morality. I use the phrase 'moral system' to mean the same as 'morality' and regard morality or the moral system as the system people use, often unconsciously, when they are trying to make a morally acceptable choice among several alternative actions or when they make moral judgments about their own actions or those of others" (Gert 1998, 3).

6. According to several critics, strong evaluation is too broad a concept to capture the moral. Laitinen discusses some of these critiques (2008, 33–43).

7. Taylor initially writes about "hypergoods" as much as "constitutive goods" and "moral sources," but while upholding the notions of constitutive goods and moral sources, he scarcely refers to hypergoods after *Sources of the Self.* I will therefore use the expression "constitutive goods" or simply "higher goods," rather than hypergoods, in presenting Taylor's moral phenomenology.

8. Parts of the discussion in section 4.2 first appeared in Meijer (2017a).

9. Some exceptions are Christopher Lloyd (1989), Ian Verstegen (2000; 2010), the latter a collection of essays about Mandelbaum's work, and Mark Timmons and Terry Horgan (2005), who develop their "cognitivist expressivism" in crucial reference to Mandelbaum's moral phenomenology.

10. See, for example, the illuminating title of Hilary Putnam's *Ethics Without Ontology* (2004).

11. This argument first appeared in Meijer (2017b).

12. The quotation is from Taylor's paper "Heidegger, Language, and Ecology" (1995b, 126).

REFERENCES

Abbey, Ruth. 2000. *Charles Taylor*. Teddington/Princeton: Acumen Press/Princeton University Press.
Abbey, Ruth, ed. 2004. *Contemporary Philosophy in Focus: Charles Taylor*. Cambridge, MA: Cambridge University Press.
Anderson, Joel. 1996. "The Personal Lives of Strong Evaluators: Identity, Pluralism, and Ontology in Charles Taylor's Value Theory." *Constellations: An International Journal of Critical and Democratic Theory* 3 (1): 17–38.
Annas, Julia. 1993. *The Morality of Happiness*. Oxford: Oxford University Press.
Drummond, John, and Lester Embree, eds. 2002. *Phenomenological Approaches to Moral Philosophy. A Handbook*. Dordrecht, SC: Kluwer Academic Publishers.
Gert, Bernard. 1998. *Morality: It's Nature and Justification*. New York/Oxford: Oxford University Press.
Kerr, Fergus. 2004. "The Self and the Good. Taylor's Moral Ontology." In *Contemporary Philosophy in Focus: Charles Taylor*, edited by Ruth Abbey, 84–104. Cambridge, MA: Cambridge University Press.
Laitinen, Arto. 2008. *Strong Evaluation Without Moral Sources*. Berlin: Walter de Gruyter.
Lloyd, Christopher. 1989. "Realism and Structurism in Historical Theory: A Discussion of the Thought of Maurice Mandelbaum." *History and Theory* 28: 296–325.
Löw-Beer, Martin. 1991. "Living a Life and the Problem of Existential Impossibility." *Inquiry* 34: 217–36.
Mandelbaum, Maurice. 1955. *The Phenomenology of Moral Experience*. Paperback 1969 ed. Baltimore/London: The John Hopkins Press.
Meijer, Michiel. 2017a. "A Phenomenological Approach With Ontological Implications? Charles Taylor and Maurice Mandelbaum on Explanation in Ethics," *Ethical Theory and Moral Practice* (online first article, DOI: 10.1007/s10677-017-9837-7).
Meijer, Michiel. 2017b. "Human-Related, not Human-Controlled: Charles Taylor on Ethics and Ontology." *International Philosophical Quarterly* 57 (3): 267–85.
Putnam, Hilary. 2004. *Ethics Without Ontology*. Cambridge, MA: Harvard University Press.
Rorty, Richard. 1994. "Taylor on Self-Celebration and Gratitude: Review of *Sources of the Self*." *Philosophy and Phenomenological Research* 54 (1): 197–201.
Rosen, Michael. 1991. "Must We Return to Moral Realism?" *Inquiry* 34: 183–94.
Smith, Nicholas. 2002. *Charles Taylor: Meaning, Morals and Modernity*. Cambridge, MA: Polity.
Taylor, Charles. 1988. "The Moral Topography of the Self." In *Hermeneutics and Psychological Theory*, edited by Stanly Messer, Louis Sass, and Robert Woolfolk, 298–320. New Brunswick, NJ: Rutgers University Press.
Taylor, Charles. 1989. *Sources of the Self. The Making of the Modern Identity*. Cambridge, MA: Cambridge University Press.
Taylor, Charles. 1992. *The Ethics of Authenticity*. Cambridge, MA: Harvard University Press.
Taylor, Charles. 1994. "Reply to Commentators." *Philosophy and Phenomenological Research* 54 (1): 203–13.

Taylor, Charles. 1995a. "Explanation and Practical Reason." In *Philosophical Arguments*, 34–60. Cambridge, MA/London: Harvard University Press.

Taylor, Charles. 1995b. "Heidegger, Language, and Ecology." In *Philosophical Arguments*, 100–26. Cambridge, MA/London: Harvard University Press.

Taylor, Charles. 1995c. "A Most Peculiar Institution." In *World, Mind, and Ethics. Essays on the Ethical Philosophy of Bernard Williams*, edited by J. Altham and R. Harrison, 132–55. Cambridge, MA: Cambridge University Press.

Taylor, Charles. 1995d. *Philosophical Arguments*. Cambridge/London: Harvard University Press.

Taylor, Charles. 1996/2011. "Iris Murdoch and Moral Philosophy." In *Dilemmas and Connections*, 3–23. Cambridge, MA/London: Belknap Press of Harvard University Press.

Taylor, Charles. 1997. "Leading a Life." In *Incommensurability, Incomparability and Practical Reason*, edited by Ruth Chang, 170–83. Cambridge, MA: Harvard University Press.

Taylor, Charles. 2003. "Ethics and Ontology." *The Journal of Philosophy* 100 (6): 305–20.

Taylor, Charles. 2007. *A Secular Age*. Cambridge/London: Belknap Press of Harvard University Press.

Taylor, Charles. 2011. "Disenchantment-Reenchantment." In *Dilemmas and Connections*, 287–302. Cambridge, MA/London: Belknap Press of Harvard University Press.

Thiebaut, Carlos. 1993. "Charles Taylor: On the Improvement of Our Moral Portrait: Moral Realism, History of Subjectivity and Expressivist Language." *Praxis International* 13: 126–53.

Timmons, Mark, and Terry Horgan. 2005. "Moral Phenomenology and Moral Theory." *Philosophical Issues* 15: 56–77.

Verstegen, Ian. 2000. "Maurice Mandelbaum As a Gestalt Philosopher." *Gestalt Theory* 22 (2): 85–96.

Verstegen, Ian, ed. 2010. *Maurice Mandelbaum and American Critical Realism*. London/New York: Routledge.

Chapter 5

Ontology of Strong Evaluation

Taylor's nonanthropocentrism has evoked a variety of interpretations and misunderstandings. One of the most persistent errors is perhaps the attempt to "read off" Taylor's claims some kind of ontological *theory*. Such attempts are doomed to fail because he simply does not have one—at least not in the sense of a systematic and complete set of ideas that is intended to explain certain truths about the world. It should therefore be noted from the outset that Taylor's thoughts on ontology are far less refined than his positions in philosophical anthropology and ethics (as set out in the foregoing chapters). A large part of the problem could well be that his first engagement with ontology ends in a state of aporia, where Taylor finds himself forced to conclude that ontological questions are both "unavoidable" and "unanswerable" (1959, 128, 139). However, there is no doubt that the nonanthropocentric thrust of strong evaluation needs and demands bold, persistent ontological experimentation at the same time.

Abbey seems to anticipate Taylor's nonanthropocentric moves on the last page of her study. After a discussion of Taylor's (at that time early) investigations of secularity in the Gifford lectures and in "A Catholic Modernity?" (Taylor 1999/2011),[1] she suggests that a new universal feature of selfhood might be inferred from these studies, namely "that humans aspire to some form of transcendence" (2000, 212). As Abbey concludes, "it seems to me that what is only intimated in his previous writings acquires a firmer role in his analysis of secularity," namely, "a view of human nature as including a fixed need for contact with the transcendent as harboring a permanent desire to go beyond the all-too-human" (2000, 212). Commentators who insist on the foundational role of theism in Taylor's ethical writings might say that this represents nothing new in his thought. For example, in "The Concept of a Person," Taylor already expresses his belief that "the aspiration to spiritual freedom, to something more than the merely human, is much too fundamental a part of human life ever to be simply set aside" (1985a, 113). Elsewhere, he argue that "human beings have an ineradicable bent to respond to something beyond life" and, moreover, that "denying this stifles" (1996/2011, 20). To this day, however, many commentators are puzzled about the ontological implications of Taylor's theistic anthropology, as it remains unclear what metaethical position he means to defend in support of his theistic viewpoint. As Abbey explains Taylor's renewed philosophical predicament:

> in previous writings his claim has been that humans feel their strongly valued goods to be grounded in something more than individual choice. But this is presented as part of his "best account" of moral experience, and as something that could be disproved. The suggestion that humans need to surpass anthropocentrism does not enjoy the ontological status it seems to acquire in these later works. (2000, 212)

In the face of this crucial observation—that the later Taylor seems to modify his view beyond moral phenomenology—I believe it is far too easy simply to equate Taylor's ontology with his theistic affirmations as a practicing Roman Catholic. However, this seems to be a fairly widespread interpretation, often formulated as an accusation that Taylor either wants to return to a Platonic type of moral realism or tries to sneak the Christian God in within his ontology.[2] Although Taylor's Catholicism troubles some critics far more than others, it is clear that there is no consensus on the shape of his theism, varying as the opinions do from the observation that Taylor is "wonderfully unpreachy" and "very unpretentious" (Williams 1990, 45) to caustic talk of "his reason for urging the Judaeo-Christian religion upon us" (Skinner 1991, 149). Unfortunately, by focusing exclusively on Taylor's Catholicism and mistakenly charging him with moralism, many critics miss the subtlety of his moral realism and the very caution with which he develops his ontological view. Starting from the crudest misconceptions, I first consider what I believe Taylor's ontology is *not* (section 5.1).[3] Next, I give an overview of his ontological claims throughout his diverse writings, starting from his very first essay on ontology and his major writings up to his more recent publications (section 5.2).[4] I then continue to discuss some interpretations and critiques of Taylor's ontology (section 5.3). In the final section, I examine Taylor's latest views in *Retrieving Realism* (2015) and *The Language Animal* (2016) against the background of his thinking as a whole (section 5.4).[5]

5.1 MISUNDERSTANDINGS OF TAYLOR'S ONTOLOGY

5.1.1 Taylor the Platonist

One approach to Taylor's ontology is to see it as being "guided more by his Platonic model than by anything else" (Olafson 1994, 193–95). However, Taylor's response to the charge of Platonism is clear. Already in *Sources of the Self* he is in no doubt that no one today can accept Plato's metaphysics of Ideas since the Platonic fusion of scientific explanation and ethical insight lies "irrecoverably shattered" by the rise of natural science (1989, 73, 96). He repeats this point in reply to his commentators by arguing that Platonism "*in this sense*" is "dead"—that is, in the sense that the inquiry into the universe and the inquiry into the good have been forced apart since the seventeenth century (1991, 248, original emphasis). Although Taylor's language is deliberately precautious, the last sentence—note the italicized clause "*in this sense*"—suggests at least that there is *another* sense in which Platonism is still very much alive. This is indeed Taylor's view. But because his delicate approach of Platonism—opposing it in one sense, endorsing it in another—has caused a great deal of confusion among his commentators, we must ask: In what sense does Taylor believe that Platonism still has a viable role to play in moral philosophy?

In brief, his claim is that the demise of Plato's ontology of Ideas does not simultaneously rule out the Platonic notion of a moral good as the object of empowering love. Taylor elaborates on this most directly in *Sources of the Self*. In a discussion of the continuing manifestation of strong evaluation throughout history, he argues that the evident collapse of Platonism as an ontological model does not diminish its major historic impact, and this happens for two reasons. First, Plato's doctrine of the Good represents one of the first articulations of strong evaluation. Second, it provides one of the most intelligible ones. As Taylor envisages it, Plato's conception of the Good exemplifies the very definition of a moral source as the "ultimate" source of strong evaluation because it is intrinsically "worthy of being desired" and provides the "standard" of the desirable beyond our de facto desires (1989, 122).

Taylor's more controversial claim, then, is that such sources of strong evaluation have an analogous place in the ethical life of our modern contemporaries to that of the Idea of the Good among Platonists. As he says, it is not just that Christian and Jewish theism conceive a constitutive good as a moral source in this Platonic way, but also "modern humanist" views that strongly value a form of human life which is built around facing a "disenchanted" universe (1989, 93–94). Taylor's point here is that also an entirely immanent view of the good is compatible with a Platonic conception of ethics as involving objects that merit our respect and call for a commitment beyond mere desirability. In the case of modern humanism, the moral source (or constitutive good) is human beings capable of courageous disengagement, and it is the respect and admiration for this capacity that empowers us to live up to it. Whatever fills this role is playing the part of a moral source in Taylor's sense, allowing him to argue that the move to an immanent ethic does not mean that this role stops being played.

To be sure, this view draws a great deal from Plato. However, what needs to be added is that Taylor is indebted not just to Plato's understanding of moral motivation, but also to Murdoch's conception of the sovereignty of good over the moral agent and to Kant's notion of *Achtung* that we experience before the moral law. As shown in the previous chapters, the ethics of strong evaluation draws heavily on both authors. Taylor first expresses his commitment to Murdoch in *Sources of the Self* (1989, 534, note 4) and declares later on that he sees her as one of his teachers in the paper "Iris Murdoch and Moral Philosophy" (1996/2011, 23). Taylor's debt to Kant is more difficult to pinpoint, as he mentions him with both criticism and approval. At any rate, the indebtedness to Murdoch and Kant shows at least that the doctrine of strong evaluation draws on more resources than just Plato. In other words, Olafson is only partly right when he concludes that Taylor conceives moral sources in a "markedly Platonic way" because "the vital fact about them is that their goodness owes nothing to our espousal of them" (1994, 193).

But if Taylor's nonanthropocentrism does not commit him to full-blown Platonism, and if we should overstate neither Murdoch's nor Kant's influence on Taylor either, the question we need to ask is: What type of position is left? Given Taylor's wholesale rejection of antirealism in ethics, he must embrace moral realism, and if he rejects Platonism, he must embrace some non-Platonic type of moral realism. In other words, since Taylor rejects both Platonism and all reductionist types of moral theory (relativist, subjectivist, utilitarian, procedural, naturalist, projectivist), he is committed to thinking that there is room for a non-Platonic and nonreductive form of moral realism. After all, as has been mentioned (in section 2.3.1), although Taylor is somewhat reluctant to label himself a moral realist, he ultimately claims to defend a "kind of moral realism" and to think of himself as a "moral realist" (1991, 242, 246).

Against this background, he seeks to make room for his ontology by describing it as a "third alternative between Platonism and projectivism" (1994b, 210). At this point, it may be helpful to note that some critics reject altogether the intermediate space in which Taylor defines his position. Taylor himself makes this point, for example, in a reply to Stephen Clark: "Clark seems to hold that what I identify as the middle ground between Platonism and naturalist projectivism does not exist. [. . .] How do you convince someone that we do not all have to be projectivists if Platonism is ruled out" (1991,

247–48)? Adding to this challenge, Taylor picks up a similar sense of resistance in Olafson's reading of his position. As Taylor explains, Olafson has "trouble placing my position" because he "seems to allow only two positions: a kind of Plato-type realism, on one hand, or some version of nonrealism on the other" (1994b, 209–10). Johnston is perhaps a third example of such "either-or" readings, as he believes that Taylor's conceptualizations "both point towards subjectivism as much as objectivism" in such an ambiguous way that "the nature of his own position becomes fundamentally unclear" (1999, 105). In any case, the fact that some theorists tend to simply *equate* Platonism and moral realism without any further ado, without any search for other kinds of realism and without asking what more moderate cognitive and ontological demands *can* be met, puts Taylor in a rather difficult argumentative position—though this at least partly explains his reservations about styling himself as a moral realist.

5.1.2 Taylor the Theist

Whereas some commentators see Taylor as a Platonist, others dismiss the charge of Platonism as flawed. However, a large number of them do so only to make the claim that Taylor is best understood as an advocate of theism. Numerous reviews of *Sources of the Self* raise the worry that Taylor is, if not a Platonic metaphysician in disguise, more like a hidden Christian theologian. In this spirit, Quentin Skinner notes that "Taylor's final message, like that of the Churches, is that we cannot hope to realize our fullest human potentialities in the absence of God" (1991, 133). Melissa Lane concurs when she says, first, that Taylor advances "a normative argument that only theism is an adequate moral source" and, second, that he "fashions a theory requiring God, or something very like God, to be complete" (1992, 46, 48). Accordingly, Bernard Williams characterizes *Sources of the Self* as a "Catholic tale" (1990, 45). Others simply insist that we should be wary of "the theism that lurks ever more prominently" in Taylor's writing (Flanagan 1996, 154). For yet others, the real problem is that "Taylor's argument about the indispensability of theism" boldly states that "atheist moral sources are inadequate" (Skinner 1991, 149; Johnston 1999, 111). Paul Johnston seems to express the most radical interpretation, for his reading goes so far as to conclude that Taylor's attempt is "to show that everyone should believe in God" (1999, 112).

One of the phrases that have triggered such frantic responses is Taylor's expression of the "incomparably higher." In Skinner's reading, Taylor strategically employs this term to render incontestable his theism. He argues that if, as Taylor insists, we really stand in need of "something awe-inspiring and completely incomparable in order to give meaning to our lives, then it is certainly hard to see how we can hope to attain that meaning in the absence of God. For who else is completely incomparable?" (Skinner 1991, 147). For Williams, however, the problem lies not so much in Taylor's account of the incomparably higher,[6] but more in his "uphill" move from phenomenology to ontology (1990, 48).

At least three problems emerge from the above readings. First, what does Taylor's conception of the "incomparably higher" mean to express? Second, how does he evaluate the difference between theistic and nontheistic moral sources? Third, how should we understand Taylor's move "uphill," that is, the move from moral phenomenology to moral ontology? The first issue, the status of the incomparably higher, is perhaps the easiest one to respond to. As has been shown at length in the previous chapters (most notably sections 1.2.2 and 4.1.2), Taylor uses this phrase in a generic sense, not to set out a substantive moral vision. It simply means that we need some sense of qualitative discrimination to live a normal human life. The fact that this meaning is spelled out in detail at the beginning of *Sources of the Self* (1989, 19–20) makes it rather difficult to accept some of the above interpretations. Unfortunately, Taylor notes in retrospect, although the expression "incomparably higher" was meant to describe a common feature of all moral views, namely "the incommensurability between what is strongly and what is merely weakly valued," several critics have missed this meaning (1991, 241).

With this issue out of the way, we come to the objections that pose a more serious challenge to Taylor's ontology. We can illustrate the second problem by looking at Lane's observation that Taylor, "while he considers the Romantic self and modern art as other possible sources," nonetheless assures us that "only the believers in God can be sure that their moral source, if existent, is adequate" (1992, 48). Lane's remark draws attention to a section in *Sources of the Self* that has caused quite a stir among commentators. Toward the end of the book, Taylor distributes the moral sources of his historical analysis into three large domains: one theistic, a second one that centers on a "naturalism of disengaged reason," and a third area that finds its sources in "Romantic expressivism" (1989, 495). These three general types of moral source set the stage for his highly controversial claim that the sources of disengaged reason and expressivism are in a quite different situation from theistic ones. As Taylor says, "no one doubts that those who embrace [theism] will find a fully adequate moral source in it," whereas it remains doubtful whether the same is true of nontheistic sources, that is, whether the adherence to such sources is in fact "enough to justify the importance we put on it" (1989, 317).

For Skinner, this claim is simply shocking as "many of 'us'" have come to recognize that our craving for meaning "will somehow *have* to be satisfied by whatever meanings we can find in everyday life"; in fact, "there are no other meanings to be had" (1991, 149, original emphasis).[7] Johnston goes one step further, dismissing Taylor's theistic views as a kind of joke to which we should not attach too much importance: "Here, Taylor's challenge to modern philosophy reaches heroic proportions, for belief in God, which is generally dismissed as obsolete, turns out to be the only view open to contemporary individuals" (1999, 111). These responses are not merely biased. They also treat the claim that nontheistic meanings are the only ones left for us (Skinner) because belief in God is obsolete (Johnston) as if it were the consequence of a philosophical argument that shows any theistic outlook to be just absurd; but these "criticisms" ultimately consist in denying the hazy commitments that many contemporary individuals rely on. Of course, the fragility of our valuations affects believers and nonbelievers alike. As a theist, Taylor has no problem in acknowledging this reality. In this regard, he is acutely aware that critical questions could be directed at theistic views as well—notwithstanding his "hunch" that the potential of theism is "incomparably greater" (1989, 518).

But we can still ask: What does it mean to say that *only* theism provides a fully adequate moral source for those embracing it, and that it appears doubtful whether the same is true of, say, secular humanist sources? Ultimately, Taylor's position is that "high standards need strong sources" (1989, 516). While he raises this major issue very—perhaps too—quickly in the last chapter of *Sources of the Self*, it is elaborated upon more clearly in the follow-up lecture "A Catholic Modernity?" (1999/2011). In this lecture, Taylor argues that we are living in an "extraordinary" moral culture, historically speaking, in which "suffering and death, through famine, flood, earthquake, pestilence, or war, can awaken worldwide movements of sympathy and practical solidarity" (1999/2011, 177). Reflecting on the history of this culture, he first asserts that "the Christian roots of all this run deep," referring to the missionary efforts of the Counter-Reformation and Protestant churches (1999/2011, 178). However, Taylor continues, at some point, philanthropic actions cease to be simply Christian inspired. That is, the practice of giving aid to those in need gradually becomes part of a much larger movement, where it comes to be inspired not merely by Christianity, but by a great variety of moral outlooks. At a certain point, Taylor explains, this habit of mobilizing for the relief of suffering worldwide becomes part of our very "political culture," causing a massive increase in our philanthropy (1999/2011, 178). Given this history, he concludes, "our age makes higher demands for solidarity and benevolence on people today than ever before" (1999/2011, 182).

In the light of all this, Taylor's daring hypothesis is that our increasingly secularizing culture might be aiming higher than its moral sources can sustain. To be sure, we live up to the standards of benevolence and justice to the extent that we do because they have become part of what we understand as a "normal" civilized human life. However, Taylor reminds us, this makes a rather fragile motivation: "A solidarity ultimately driven by the giver's own sense of moral superiority is a whimsical and fickle thing. We are far, in fact, from the universality and unconditionality which our moral outlook prescribes" (1999/2011, 182). In other words, if merely having "appropriate" beliefs is no guarantee for sustaining affirmation of the high demands of benevolence and justice, how, then, Taylor asks, will we face the moral challenges of our age? In making this point, he does not spare himself, as a theist, a certain amount of self-criticism:

> Just having appropriate beliefs is no solution to these dilemmas, and the transformation of high ideals into brutal practice was demonstrated lavishly in Christendom, well before modern humanism came on the scene. [. . .] It is perhaps not an accident that the history of the twentieth century can be read either in a perspective of progress or in one of mounting horror. Perhaps it is not contingent that it is the century both of Auschwitz and Hiroshima and of Amnesty International and Médicins sans Frontières. (1999/2011, 185, 187)

Although there is room to disagree about the ways in which Taylor ties these issues together, we need only to think of the various unwelcoming responses to refugees in "liberal" and "enlightened" Europe to see that he is touching on something very real and important.

Taylor's theism has also been criticized in another way. According to some critics, his theistic understanding of human nature—which states that human beings have an "ineradicable bent to respond to something beyond life" (1996/2011, 20)—is not simply a distortion, but simply wrong. The charge is generally formulated as a concern that Taylor is blind to the lives of many contemporary individuals. This objection is expressed in various ways. One is that "many people in antiquity, many people now, no doubt a few in the times in between, have lived with a sense that nothing they know of is incomparably higher than other things or infinitely valuable" (Williams 1990, 48). Another formulation is that "many people have come to grips with the contingency of their selves, with their fallibility, and with their naturalness" (Flanagan 1996, 160). A third expression states that "many of us have come to realize that, since there is no God, we shall somehow have to manage on our own" (Skinner 1991, 149).

For Williams, then, "to move as determinedly as Taylor does to the transcendental level is to freight the moral consciousness with demands that it not only can live without, but has lived without quite successfully" (1990, 48). For Flanagan, "there is no incoherence in the idea of persons [. . .] operating effectively and happily within frameworks that they simply do not see or experience as final or foundational" (1996, 160). And for Skinner, it is not only evident that the feeling of having to manage "on our own" has become "widely and deeply embedded in our culture"; it is also evident that its prevalence "casts considerable doubt on Taylor's argument about the indispensability of theism" (1991, 149). Taylor's replies to Skinner speak to all of these criticisms. His overall response remains that many critics misinterpret his central line that people with theistic beliefs find a fully adequate moral source in their theisms. As Taylor puts it, "what I was rather saying was that it was clear that those who accept theism don't see themselves as needing further moral sources, whereas it is a property of other world-views that they may see human beings as still lacking such sources" (1991, 241). In another reply to Skinner, Taylor explains further how this point connects with his "hunch" that theistic sources might be more adequate than nontheistic ones for the affirmation of human beings as worthy of respect, benevolence, and justice. He argues: "In my view, this is the question: How much *can* you affirm? Just talking of 'opportunity' or 'duty' is beside the point. As though you could just turn it on" (1994a, 255–56, original emphasis).

However far removed this tentative question may be from "a normative argument that only theism is an adequate moral source" (Lane 1992, 46), the objection can nevertheless be made that Taylor is walking into very uncertain territory here, as he tries to make a statement about how different people experience different moral sources. Again, the concluding chapter of *Sources of the Self* only very briefly touches on these major themes. Yet Taylor has explained his view elsewhere in more detail. In an interview (De Lara 1998, 112), he says that our civilization is in need of a certain theistic perspective ("strong sources") precisely because it demands so much philanthropy from us ("high standards"). Given these points, it comes as no surprise that Taylor's hunches toward theism depend largely on a hopeful view on human nature. Yet what happens to our self-understanding once we no longer share Taylor's hope? Williams makes this point when he says that Taylor seems not to have taken seriously enough "Nietzsche's thought that if there is, not only no God, but no metaphysical order of any kind, then this imposes quite new demands on our self-understanding" (1990, 48). Anticipating this type of concern, Taylor ensures us on the very last pages of *Sources of the Self* that human history might also be read in a much darker way, invoking the notion that the great spiritual traditions have also been the causes of "untold misery and even savagery" (1989, 519). Although this comment comes a little late, it still is helpful as it shows that Taylor is not blind to darker visions, but simply disagrees with them.

However, Williams' point about Taylor's omission of Nietzsche is well taken when we consider the highly ambiguous views on Nietzsche in Taylor's writings as a whole. Granted that Nietzsche is without doubt Taylor's most important interlocutor on the issue of adequate sources, the apologizing final footnote of *Sources of the Self* is most revealing of this uncertainty. After his brief discussion of the "challenge" posed by Nietzsche in the concluding chapter, Taylor notes that Nietzsche's thought is "as always, more many-sided and complex than this" (1989, 593, note 32). Setting aside the many invigorating questions that emerge from this topic,[8] and returning to the principal issue from which the discussion started—the issue of adequate sources—we can now (hopefully) understand better not only the spirit in which Taylor expresses his doubts regarding secular sources, but also why he continues to insist that high standards need strong sources. That is, he raises the issue of adequacy not to decide who is ultimately "right" (humanists, anti-humanists, believers in transcendence, etc.), but to draw attention to a range of ethical-political dilemmas pressing on Western culture as a whole.

5.2 TAYLOR THE ONTOLOGIST

In the hope of having redeemed Taylor from being both an outmoded Platonist and a deluding priest, I would now like to focus on what I see as the "hard problem" of his ontology.[9] The difficulty with overstating Taylor's theistic views is not only that this often makes a caricature of his moral thought; it has the further disadvantage of obscuring his dominant line that we cannot make full sense of our moral predicament without also deciding certain ontological issues. Although this topic was briefly raised by invoking Williams' apt phrase that "Taylor very rapidly moves uphill, metaphysically speaking" (1990, 48), the present analysis has still not made much progress in this area. For Williams, to extrapolate ontological claims from facts about human experience is to "freight the moral consciousness with demands that it can not only live without, but has lived without quite successfully" (1990, 48). That is, Taylor's ontological urge goes "a long way beyond what, in its first steps, it rightly said was necessary to any moral consciousness at all" (1990, 48).

Even after taking into account the analyses of strong evaluation in the previous chapters, Williams' point still stands. How do we make sense of the ontological pretensions allegedly possessed by Taylor's moral phenomenology? What are we committed to ontologically by the doctrine of strong evaluation? What ontology can underpin the phenomenology of higher goods? Should we ultimately conclude with Williams that those who use phenomenological reflections to defend ontological views are moving all too rapidly from those particular reflections to claims about how to understand the world? Or are there crucial aspects of Taylor's ontology that his critics have missed, aspects that could serve to justify his nonanthropocentric perspective? This will be the topic of the following sections: What does Taylor actually say about ontology (section 5.2) and how have his commentators discussed his ontological views (section 5.3)?

5.2.1 The First Attempt

Taylor's first publication on ontology is a little-known paper he wrote at the age of twenty-eight, simply entitled "Ontology" (1959). Showing admirable consistency, this paper already prepares the way for Taylor's "pluralistic robust realism" in *Retrieving Realism* and his latest defense of "Ethics in the broad sense" in *The Language Animal* (2015, 154; 2016, 212). The young Taylor argues that the search for one single determinate language in which to talk about man and world has been confusing rather than clarifying ontological problems, anticipating his latest ideas that "there could well be *many* languages each correctly describing a different aspect of reality" by invoking different "kinds" of independent reality (2015, 153–54, original emphasis; 2016, 262). Moreover, Taylor's first thoughts on ontology shed considerable light on the question as to why this topic has been such a hazardous issue in his writings as a whole.

His paper sets off with the statement that there is no unique and determinate meaning of concepts such as "being," "is," or "exist." That is, when we make statements like "time exists" or "redness exists," we rarely know what we are actually saying or what "exist" is meant to express (1959, 125). Taylor then separates what he calls the "pseudo-problem of ontology" from the "real" problem (1959, 125–26). One way of dealing with the question of what "time" and "redness" mean in statements of the above kind is to reject this question as a pseudo-problem, posed for us by language. As long as we try to treat time and redness as entities inhabiting the world along with empirical entities such as tables, chairs, and stones, we will remain forever perplexed by their ontological status. Yet this problem simply disappears, Taylor notes, "once we overcome the belief that all substantives stand for some kind of particulars," which has the further advantage that "we no longer have to invent 'third realms' or 'objectives' or remake language over in the image of a calculus" (1959, 125). This is an acceptable approach to ontology for many philosophers. Hilary Putnam, for example, defends a "pragmatic realism" that takes this argument to its final conclusion. Since it is neither necessary nor sufficient to posit "mysterious entities which somehow guarantee or stand behind correct judgments," we should rather reject the idea of ontology altogether as obsolete "Platonizing" (Putnam 2004, 70).

However, for the young Taylor this is not real the issue because ontological questions "also arise in connection with concepts in their use as predicates, and not simply in connection with substantive expressions" (1959, 128). He elaborates on this by discussing statements such as "the children are sleeping" and "the children are insolent" (1959, 126–28). In explaining *this* type of ontological claim, it will just not do to refer to substantives such as the children's closing their eyes (sleeping) or sticking out their tongues (insolent). Without knowing what they *mean*, these facts cannot explain all that much.

Neither will it help to invoke such features as being awake, disobedient, or rude. This would only move the issue from one place to another, from the issue of explaining the meanings of "asleep" and "insolent" to the issue of explaining what it means to be "awake," "disobedient," or "rude." Therefore, Taylor continues, if we had to reply to someone who does not understand these concepts, it is clear that we would have to move to a "different level of argument" to explain them (1959, 126).

This means, in other words, that ordinary language is intelligible only to those who are involved in it, allowing our interlocutors to recognize certain acts as "sleeping" or "insolent" from within their practice-internal perspectives. Yet, in Taylor's view, there still remains an uncertainty here when we reflect on the ontological implications of our ordinary language. Difficulties start to emerge, he explains, when considering that everyday language involves "behavior by sentient beings," which, in being endowed with meaning, differs from movements of material objects or natural processes (1959, 128–129). This means that a *different* ontological problem arises when we reflect on the presuppositions behind our language—that is, when we reflect on the ontological background in which our terms make sense. This is the issue that really concerns Taylor: for behavior to be meaningfully recognized as "insolent," we must be presupposing a background that is somehow different from an ontology that recognizes only "natural" processes devoid of such meanings. Children can be insolent, molecules cannot.

On the one hand, these deliberations can be seen as a preparation for Taylor's general argument against psychological behaviorism in *The Explanation of Behaviour* (1964) and his philosophical-anthropological agenda in *Philosophical Papers* (1985c): since human beings are living, responsive beings, perceptive of certain meanings, their behavior is fundamentally different from the operations of machines and natural processes. Yet, on the other hand, Taylor also seeks to include ontological questions of a nonanthropocentric kind by invoking "the status of so-called 'metaphysical' statements about ontology" (1959, 139). With these observations, we come to what Taylor identifies as the "real" ontological problem: How does the ontology of human behavior, expressed in ordinary language, relate to the ontology of natural processes and material objects, expressed in terms of science? As he himself puts it:

> Ontological questions are not, however, always the result of whimsical objections to ordinary concepts. [. . .] Some are in a sense *unavoidable*, i.e. they are posed for us by certain dilemmas which arise out of the use of our language; when, e.g. two different kinds of particular, one incompatible with the other, seem to have equal right to occupy the same logical space, or when we seem to be able to say two or more incompatible things about a given particular. (1959, 128, emphasis added)

Reflecting on this issue, Taylor notes that the problems are posed by the scientific conception of the world that increasingly dominates our views and explanations. He therefore makes a distinction between "M-language," that is, the terms we use to describe "material objects, including of course human beings in so far as we speak of them as material objects," and "P-language," that is, the terms by which we describe "persons (and some animals) and their behavior" (1959, 129). From *this* ontological perspective, it is a crucial mistake to ask which language is the *real* one (ordinary or scientific) or whether "time," "redness," and "insolence" *really exist,* because such questioning fails to recognize the wide variety of uses of "there is" and "there exists." The issue is therefore not whether we can talk meaningfully about human behavior in ordinary language, but, given our faith in science and scientific terminology, how ordinary language differs from, and is related to, events and processes in nature. In Taylor's view, this problem is "unavoidable" in the sense that human beings can be *adequately* described by *multiple* explanations, which, in this case, is by both ordinary, commonsense terms ("insolent," "obedient," "hostile," "friendly") and scientific, objectifying languages (biological, physiological, psychological, psychiatrical). As he says, "the children are, after all, also material objects, and their sticking out the tongues, and chanting of rude melodies are also events in the world just as a stone's rolling, or a leaf's falling, are" (1959, 129).

This means that even after considering the multiple uses of the term "exist" and differentiating between different truth claims within different languages, the issue of their *relationship* remains. Unlike the pseudo-problem dealt with earlier, Taylor insists, this problem does not simply disappear by a clarification of the logic of our language, because, as he puts it, "our ontological commitments *clash*" (1959, 136, emphasis added). This problem—that some ontological commitments are in conflict with others—is, I believe, at the root of Taylor's interwoven mode of thought as it is both deeply metaphysical and phenomenological. In fact, as we will see later on, this is the crucial theme he *continues* to debate as "our ontological problem" also in later works (1959, 130). In this way, the young Taylor's approach to ontology also sheds new light on his overall insistence on the links across different disciplines: How do different truths and languages relate to one another? That is, how can we ever understand the various insights of the human sciences and philosophy if we do not understand their relationships to ordinary language and to one another? And, granted that we do not want to stick with just one of these viewpoints, how should we respond to the metaphysical problem that the ontological commitments of these different languages *exclude* one another at times?

As we have seen at length in the previous chapters, Taylor gradually develops this interwoven mode of reasoning into an argument that the phenomenology of moral experience is not intelligible from a scientific-naturalist ontological viewpoint.[10] Similarly, if we take our stand in moral phenomenology, the language of the human sciences cannot be given an interpretation, and nor can, say, the statements of Nietzsche and Foucault. Ultimately, Taylor's belief is that "there is no justification for this civil war. For we can and do learn to use all these languages" (1959, 136).

But we can still ask: How do we even manage to do this? Perhaps we do not manage all that well, and the important question might be: How *should* we use these different languages? To answer this question, though, we need first to understand the role of these "ontological civil wars" in everyday life. In this respect, Taylor already noted that the meaning of "insolent" can be explained only to someone who understands the human behaviors in which this term makes sense, just as explanations in terms of "neurosis," "psychosis," "depression," and "hysteria" could only be given to someone who already has some understanding of this terminology, that is, has an understanding of "the ontology of the language stratum in which these terms figure" (1959, 136). But if such explanations are intelligible only *within* a given language, that is, in terms that share the same ontological presuppositions, then how do we pick up a *new* language? Taylor gives two explanations. First, we learn new languages by making "non-logical leaps" (1959, 137). Second, we all sometimes live "unreflectively" by temporarily retreating from the more sophisticated level at which different languages clash (1959, 138). With regard to the first point, he makes clear that

> we do manage somehow to get inside. We do so by the same kind of non-logical leap by which we first entered the universe of speech of our parents. The child just "catches on" to a new aptitude or the point of a joke. The discontinuities in our language occasioned by the ontological gaps require that we make "leaps" of this kind later in life, as well, but in the latter cases as in the first, we leave no logical footprints by which we can trace our progress in a series of logical relations. (1959, 137)

Taylor clearly states how *not* to deal with such ontological "gaps": by trying to assimilate everyday explanation to scientific statements and concepts. The gap that lies between ordinary language statements and claims of science can be illustrated by looking at a phrase such as "My unforgiving attitude was the cause of his death, which made her very unhappy" (1959, 133). Believing that this statement can be explained in objectifying terms is failing to recognize the difference in ontology. A similar mistake is made when I point to the table and say "molecules," and my two-year-old brother takes this to mean what I mean by "table," because "molecules are not just parts of the table which we refer to in everyday speech" (1959, 137). In this way, Taylor continues, "some of the problems of the philosophy of science, as well as some of those of the philosophy of mind arise from a failure to recognize ontological 'gaps'" (1959, 135). These points bring us right back to the initial problem that we cannot explain the explanatory language *in itself*, except in terms of its individual concepts. For the young Taylor, this confusion is just part of the human predicament as the world of physics and the world of everyday will not converge into "single images," leaving us with an "askew" logical focus (1959, 137). Here we come up against Taylor's second answer to the question as to how we manage to cope with conflicting descriptions of our world, namely by having recourse to what he calls "primitive language," that is, "language before the introduction of the most rudimentary science" (1959, 137). However, when he adds that we "cannot help but pose ourselves ontological problems when we reflect on our language" (1959, 138), it would seem that the only way to escape ontological gaps and clashes is to just stop *articulating* them, that is, by refusing to say anything more sophisticated than what can be said in primitive ordinary language.

The problem is that this puts us in a very peculiar ontological position. Either we pick up new languages by logically untraceable "leaps" (as a child picks up language for the first time) or we stay locked in an imaginative pre-reflective state prior to all description. If this is really our predicament, the question that arises is whether there is any role left to play for ontological inquiry. Both of Taylor's explanations suggest that the answer to this question is a simple "no." His notion of nonlogical leaps seems to annihilate the very idea of ontological reflection: if we cannot help but "jump" from one ontology to another without leaving "logical footprints by which we can trace our progress" (1959, 137), there is no more point debating ontological claims. The second option, then—to remain within the confines of primitive ordinary language—closes off the entire area within which ontological claims are discernible. As Taylor makes himself plain in opposing Merleau-Ponty, the very attempt to enhance our primitive ontology seems to destroy it (1958, 113).

Is this the last word? If so, it would seem that ontological theory has simply outlived its usefulness. Surprisingly perhaps, for the young Taylor it does not follow from this discussion that ontological questions are empty *tout court*. As he says, "when we turn to reflect on the progress we have made, we sometimes have an experience somewhat similar to double vision," that is, "we might say that we learn to see the world in a new light, to look at it from a new point of view" (1959, 137). On the one hand, this view clearly demonstrates Taylor's notorious optimism. On the other hand, it is a constructive reminder that a critical look does not mean that we should prejudice matters either by jumping all too rapidly to the conclusion that ontological questions are pseudo-problems. Perhaps the bottom line is, therefore, that we simply have to accept that this is as far as progress in ontological inquiry can take us: a new point of view.

Yet Taylor's paper has a somewhat different ending. The last part goes back to its central problem of how to understand the relationship between the ordinary language of persons ("P-language") and the materialist languages of science ("M-language"). Taylor concludes his discussion by briefly comparing—and, finally, rejecting—two rivaling approaches of this problem: Ryle's philosophy of language and Merleau-Ponty's phenomenology (1959, 139–41). For present purposes, what is most striking is the strong criticism of Merleau-Ponty. As Taylor reads him, "Merleau-Ponty is trying to find a new scientific language which will embody the ordinary language ontology of persons," ultimately resulting in "a mixture of scientific terminology and P-language used in a poetic way" (1959, 139–40). Taylor's critique is that this method confuses rather than clarifies, because Merleau-Ponty's invention of a new, phenomenological language stratum, while illuminating, cannot possibly "replace" the languages of psychology and physiology (1959, 140). In retrospect, this criticism comes somewhat unexpected because Taylor will develop his *own* phenomenology later in his career, equally adding to the confusion by inventing new concepts such as "strong evaluation," "constitutive goods," and "moral sources." Even more puzzling is that Taylor here attacks the very argument that he will later defend, namely that the reductive explanatory languages of the human sciences have no place for human meanings. In this respect, he criticizes Merleau-Ponty for neglecting that the languages of physiology and psychology have achieved their success precisely by *excluding* P-language, and, moreover, that they must continue to do so if they are to remain usable at all for the scientific inquiries in which they occur (1959, 140). However troubling these points may be for placing Taylor's later critique of the human sciences (in *The Explanation of Behaviour* and *Philosophical Papers*) and his moral-phenomenological approach (in *Sources of the Self*), there is at least one belief that seems to have stood the test of time. As it turns out, the young Taylor criticizes not just phenomenology but the attempt itself to find some general language that will supersede all others. As he concludes:

> We have ceased to say that some particular language is the "real" way to talk about things. But we have not really answered the question raised by the introduction of new language strata in doing so. We are still perplexed when we try to understand the relations between what we talk about in one stratum and what we talk about in others. In a sense, the questions we ask in this domain are unanswerable. But they are not, for all that, imaginary questions. (1959, 139)

As mentioned at the beginning of this section, Taylor's exploratory paper "Ontology" embarks on issues that are elaborated on in more detail in *Retrieving Realism* and *The Language Animal*.[11] Even though we have only just begun to explore Taylor's ontological thought, it says a lot about its consistency that these later works build further on elements from this very paper. They do so not only by urging us to consider that "there are several ways of describing nature all of which may be true," but also by allowing different semantic logics that describe "different kinds of reality" (2015, 153, 160; 2016, 262).

Considering the aporetic result of Taylor's first paper on ontology—that we are just "perplexed" when we try to align our languages of self-understanding—it is intriguing that he is still absorbed in this very problem at the end of his career. The issue is: What are we committed to by the fact that we speak the languages that we do? What are we forced to recognize the existence of by the way we live our lives and deal with the things and people around us and ourselves? Apparently, the mere lack of satisfactory answers does not stop Taylor from continuing to ask these questions. Why? Perhaps because he believes that for all the diversity of our languages they form a family nonetheless. What they have in common is that they focus our awareness of our world, grasping the reality in which we are set. On Taylor's model, ontology is much more an effort to bring this sense to formulation than a matter of finding knockdown proofs. His paper "Ontology" leaves the possibility open that there is a way to learn beyond "non-logical leaps" and "askew" ontological images. It should not surprise us, then, that the young Taylor concludes with the hope that new languages "enable us to see and understand things about human beings that we wouldn't otherwise" (1959, 141).

At this early stage of the analysis, it remains to be seen whether Taylor's ontology can be spelled out in sufficient detail in order to be evaluated. A possible future concern is that his latest notion of *plural* revealing perspectives on the world only *intensifies* the problem of their relationship and does nothing to solve ontological conflicts. For now, I will set aside this concern and pursue Taylor's ontological thinking in more recent writings. Before doing so, however, it is important to realize that his debut in ontology—an attempt to show that ontological questions are both "unavoidable" and "unanswerable"—sets a rather tricky stage for the further development of his thought. On the one hand, his belief that we are in an epistemic situation that unavoidably burdens us with ontological questions spells out his continuous concern with ontology. On the other hand, since he also maintains that these problems are perplexingly impossible to answer, it will be very difficult, if not altogether hopeless, to decide whether Taylor's ontological view has made any progress. Ironically, this is precisely the predicament he describes as "our ontological problem" (1959, 130), namely that it is notoriously unclear when we have reached a gain in insight and when we have just bumped into new ontological question marks.

How does one explore questions that one does not know how to answer or debate? This is now the peculiar task Taylor has set for himself as an ontologist. We might say, therefore, that Taylor's ontology is more a "program" than a theory, as he has still to show that this project can be carried out at all. Moreover, as will emerge, Taylor gradually revises his ontological view in the course of his writing. Whereas the younger Taylor argues that there simply is "no justification" for resolving ontological gaps and clashes (1959, 136), the later Taylor sets out to *arbitrate* rivaling languages and ontologies. He does so, first, by arguing that "interpretive plausibility is the ultimate criterion for any hermeneutic explanation" (1985c, 7), and, second, by defending his view that the "Best Account" of human action is trumps (1989, 58). However, the initial pluralist sense is never far away. As the young Taylor concludes, "there may be other [languages] which will teach us more. Our metaphysical craving for *the real* language remains unsatiated" (1959, 141, original emphasis). This means, in other words, that Taylor's hard-won ontology is not all that different from his theistic hunches after all: it is a *question* rather than a statement.

5.2.2 Haphazard Ontologizing in Taylor's Major Writings

As we have just seen, the thrust of Taylor's first essay in ontology is to point out that taking a stand in a single language blocks out the ontologies of others. After this initial "linguistic" approach to ontology, it is not until *Philosophical Papers* that Taylor again takes up ontological discussions.[12] As we will see, he employs the concept of ontology to discuss a wide variety of issues. In an attempt to explicate these issues, I focus in the present section on the different contexts in which Taylor expands his approach after the paper "Ontology." As will emerge, he uses the concept of ontology to raise linguistic questions as well as issues of philosophical anthropology, ethics, epistemology, political theory, ecology, phenomenology, and, in the background of all of these, metaphysics.

In *Philosophical Papers* (1985c), Taylor generally employs the concept of ontology in what I called earlier an "anthropological" sense, that is, he uses it to discuss certain (implicit) beliefs about what a human being is and what human agency consists in. This can be illustrated by briefly looking at the papers "How is Mechanism Conceivable?" (1985b) and "Interpretation and the Sciences of Man" (1985d). The former criticizes the "ontological" argument of mechanism. That is, it criticizes the thesis that human behavior must be ultimately explicable in terms of body chemistry and neurophysiology because "human beings are after all physical objects" (1985b, 181). Similarly, the latter makes the case that we cannot come to understand important dimensions of human life within the bounds set by the "ontological" belief that "reality must be susceptible to understanding and explanation by science so understood" (1985d, 21).

At first glance, Taylor seems to continue this anthropological conception of ontology in *Sources of the Self* when elaborating his notions of "ontology of the human" and "moral ontology" in the opening pages of the book (1989, 5–10). At the same time, however, he steadily widens the meaning of ontology by also including other topics in the employment of this term. As he explains his objectives out of the introductory notions of "ontology of the human" and "moral ontology" (which he uses only until the third chapter), Taylor's aim becomes redefined first as exploring the background picture of our "spiritual nature and predicament," then as exploring the background picture lying behind our "moral and spiritual intuitions," and then, some pages later, as both exploring the background assumptions to our "moral reactions and judgements" and the "contexts which give these reactions their sense" (1989, 3, 8, 41). In my view, it is a mistake to rate this second, broader range of definitions on a par with the first. This is because an overinvestment in "ontology of the human" and "moral ontology" loses from view that Taylor's ontologizing explicitly crosses the boundary between the human and the nonhuman at other points in *Sources of the Self*.[13]

The most explicit example of this wider focus has already been mentioned in the analysis of Taylor's debt to Murdoch for his nonanthropocentric understanding of ethics (section 4.3.1). As noted, he criticizes contemporary moral theory for neglecting the claims of the "nonhuman" by recognizing only "human-centered" goods such as freedom, benevolence, and universal rights (1989, 102–103). It is here, or so I argue, that the ontological discussion in *Sources of the Self*—addressed to all those who are influenced by a "naturalist-inspired *metaphysical* picture" (1989, 59, italics mine)—tentatively picks up where it left off in the early paper "Ontology," in that Taylor seeks to restore his initial focus on "the status of so-called 'metaphysical' statements about ontology" (1959, 139). This is no small feat. Unlike the limited philosophical-anthropological use of the concept of ontology in *Philosophical Papers* in explaining human behavior, Taylor now starts to press ontological questions in a way that bursts the boundaries of any one established academic discipline, as it cuts right across the distinction between the human and the nonhuman.

Philosophically speaking, Taylor's questioning straddles philosophical anthropology and metaphysics; and where the sciences are concerned, he freely crosses the boundaries between the natural and the human sciences.[14] A possible way of stating this expansion is to distinguish between Taylor's "ontology of the human" (or philosophical anthropology) and what we might call his "ontology of the non-human" (or metaphysics), where the former is used for the narrower domain concerned with our self-understanding and behavior and the latter for the wider domain where anthropological, phenomenological, ethical, and ontological issues coincide—including the principal question of how we should understand the reality beyond the human world. But perhaps the question as to whether such a distinction allows for the full range of Taylor's ontological thought should not be hurried at this stage. In reply to his commentators in this period, Taylor admits that *Sources of the Self* sketches not even the beginnings of an argument on these matters, explaining that this book, "particularly towards the end, contains affirmations or hints of affirmations which go beyond what I made any systematic attempt to argue for" (1994b, 203).

Adding to the confusion, Taylor introduces *new* meanings of ontology in *Philosophical Arguments* (1995f). We can illustrate these meanings by differentiating between "epistemological," "political," and "Heideggerian" uses of the concept. The first usage is part of Taylor's critique of modern epistemology, that is, the view that we can first "come to grips with the problem of knowledge," and then "later proceed to determine what we can legitimately say about other things" (1995f, vii). Although he sees Descartes and Locke as the founding fathers, Taylor argues that this image still holds us captive today as many contemporary authors (he mentions Quine and Derrida) who think they have overcome Descartes' dualism are still giving priority to epistemology by "defining their ontology, their view of what is, on the basis of a prior doctrine of what we can know" (1995f, viii).[15]

Taylor elaborates on this in "Overcoming Epistemology" (1995e) and in "Lichtung or Lebensform: Parallels between Heidegger and Wittgenstein" (1995d). In brief, his point is that classical epistemology is not simply a vehicle for producing valid and reliable beliefs in practicing philosophy and science, but part of a broader view which determines a way of being in the world, that is, which forces upon us a certain ontological stance. This is what Taylor calls the "ontologizing" move of epistemology, visible in Locke, that is, "the reading of the ideal method into the very constitution of the mind" (1995d, 64). In other words, with Locke the stance of disengagement loses its initial methodological function, as it is understood as the *actual* way the mind operates in perceiving the world. Passing over the many complex details of this debate, it suffices to note here that Taylor's tireless effort to show that epistemology in this way "dictates" ontology refers back to his central interwoven mode of argumentation, which insists that our accepted ontology programs our thinking on various other issues. As he explains this point decades later, this is "far from being a bloodless debate over scientific method. It is deeply involved in the contrary ethical and metaphysical passions of the modern age" (2015, 26).

One of these "ethical and metaphysical passions" is invoked in the paper "Cross-Purposes: The Liberal-Communitarian Debate," opening up another, in this case "political," type of ontological discussion. This text explores the difference between "ontological issues" and "advocacy issues" in social theory (1995a, 181). Advocacy issues concern "the moral stand or policy one adopts," whereas ontological issues concern "what you recognize as the factors you will invoke to account for social life," that is, "they concern the terms you accept as ultimate in the order of explanation" (1995a, 181–82). From this starting point, though, Taylor largely continues his anthropological use of the concept of ontology by invoking issues of self-understanding. In this way, he characterizes Michael Sandel's *Liberalism and the Limits of Justice* as an "ontological" book in that it tries to show how different political proposals are "linked with different understandings of self and identity" (1995a, 182). The first point echoes Taylor's basic claim that underlying ontologies stipulate our thoughts on other issues (in this case, political ones); the second parallels and continues his anthropological use of the concept of ontology by invoking issues of self-understanding.

Taylor also develops a familiar type of ontological critique in elaborating on the liberal-communitarian debate, namely that there is a great deal of motivated suppression of social ontology among liberalists. To make this point, he argues that the issues of advocacy and ontology have been inadequately appreciated. In Taylor's view, it is not just that the distinction between ontological and advocacy questions remains largely unarticulated, but also that many commentators misperceive the impact of the ontological by neglecting the reality that taking an ontological position helps to "define the options it is meaningful to support by advocacy" (1995a, 183). Following a line of thinking drawn largely from *Sources of the Self*, Taylor ultimately argues that the confusion of advocacy and ontological issues has contributed to an "eclipse of ontological thinking in social theory," convincing his readers that the debate between liberals and communitarians can only be opened if the ontological issues are clarified (1995a, 185, 203).

Another employment of ontology can be found in the paper that we briefly considered in the discussion of Kerr's reading of Taylor (in section 4.3.2), "Heidegger, Language, and Ecology" (1995c), which I will therefore simply call Taylor's "Heideggerian" use of the concept of ontology. In this text, Taylor intends to forsake language theory for ontological inquiry by exploring Heidegger's philosophy of language in the following way. He first locates Heidegger's thought in the "expressive-constitutive" language theory of Herder and then transposes language theory into *ontological* reasoning by asking "what" is being manifested in our strong evaluations (1995c, 101). Against this background, Taylor ultimately defends Heidegger's conception of "*language speaking* rather than human beings speaking" as a "vitally important" new line of thinking about our relation to the cosmos (1995c, 101, 126, original emphasis).

Taylor's paper begins by emphasizing Heidegger's importance for the ecological protest against technological society. That is, Heidegger's "antisubjectivist" philosophy of language can be made relevant for ecological debates in that it argues, first, that "something beyond the human makes demands on us" and, second, that "this source cannot be identified with nature or with the universe" (1995c, 100–101). To clarify this view, Taylor first sets Heidegger against the background of the constitutive theory of language, which sees language as "making possible new purposes, new levels of behavior, new meanings" (1995c, 101). Taylor explains this tradition in crucial reference to Herder, who argues that language enables its users to move beyond a mere "response" to some object to the attribution of certain "properties" to it, thereby not just describing but *constituting* new meanings (1995c, 103). This Herderian constitutive view of language as making possible new meanings adds up to Taylor's leading idea that human agency can be understood only from within the dimension of a "deep" type of reflection and articulation, concerning issues of worth rather than mere desirability. As he argues a few pages further on, "only language beings can identify things as *worthy* of desire or aversion" (1995c, 106, original emphasis).

Taylor then introduces Heidegger as an heir to the Herder tradition who both continues and *reverses* the constitutive conception of language by no longer speaking in terms of reflection or consciousness (Herder) but to see language as "opening access" to meanings (Heidegger), that is, to see language as "the condition of the human world being disclosed" (1995c, 111–12). Standing back from this Herder-Heidegger comparison, Taylor seems to be concerned about the question he reads between the lines: If one of the fundamental functions of language is that it "constitutes" our world by introducing new meanings and by making possible strong value, how should we understand the *ontological* status of these meanings? As he says, Heidegger is not talking about "the cosmos out there," that is, the world of natural science which is indifferent to us, but about "the world of our involvements, including all the things they incorporate in their meaning for us" (1995c, 107).

In the remainder of the paper, Taylor tentatively explores this question by discussing Heidegger's "manifestationist reading" of the space of expression, a reading that at the same time rejects all "ontic underpinnings" of this space (1995c, 120). Although presenting him as an "uncompromising realist" (1995c, 120), Taylor's Heidegger mainly endorses a negative argument, namely that strong value flows neither from an enchanted universe nor from human subjects alone, in this way steering a course between Platonism, on the one hand, and subjectivism, on the other. Put simply, in Taylor's view, Heidegger criticizes Platonism for neglecting the "human" aspect of being—our being-in-the-world or *Dasein*—while also criticizing subjectivism for *overstating* the human aspect by ignoring that being is "not simply our doing," as any of our doing "supposes as already there the disclosure of things in language" (1995c, 115). In a word, both Platonism and subjectivism fail to recognize the true nature of being as "*Dasein*-related, yet not *Dasein*-controlled" (1995c, 115).

However instructive these points may be for Taylor's reading of Heidegger, it is somewhat of an anticlimax that they nowhere refer to the doctrine of strong evaluation. For there is no doubt that Taylor *himself* embraces the constitutive view in developing his nonanthropocentric perspective on the good, while also holding a middle position between "a 'Platonist' mode of moral realism" on the one hand, and "mere subjectivism," on the other (1994b, 211). Moreover, as we have seen in the previous chapter (section 4.3.1), Taylor makes it clear that he is following the example of deep ecologists, theists, and a poet such as Rilke in adopting the view that the world does not simply exist for human purposes, but makes a "further claim" on us (1994b, 213; 1989, 513). In fact, Taylor admits to believing that "every anthropocentrism pays a terrible price in impoverishment in this regard" (1994b, 213). Unfortunately, though, he does not clarify how his nonanthropocentric understanding of strong evaluation relates to his endorsement of Heidegger's takes on language and ontology.

As a result, the present analysis of Taylor's ontology still cannot explain the problem with which the previous chapter ended, namely how Taylor applies Heideggerian ontological reflections in developing his Murdochean nonanthropocentric view on ethics, as it remains unclear how Taylor's claims about constitutive language help to substantiate his ontological view. That is, if a world of qualitative contrasts is disclosed through languages of worth, which is also a locus of constitutive goods, how should we understand the nature of these goods, ontologically speaking? Put differently, what is the metaphysical status of values that are human *related* insofar as we feel their appeal, but not human *controlled* as they principally offer standards of conduct? At this point of the discussion, it no longer suffices simply to refer to the interwoven character of Taylor's arguments. Intriguingly, Taylor already knows that he has this problem in *Philosophical Papers*. In fact—unlike his conspicuous silence in "Heidegger, Language, and Ecology"—he makes it clear that his thought at that time is still too premature to grasp the relationship between morality, language, and ontology in full:

> I do not know how clear I can be about this at the present stage, but perhaps I can gesture towards the question in this way: if one of the fundamental uses of language is to articulate or make manifest the background of distinctions of worth we define ourselves by, how should we understand *what* is being manifested here? Is what we are articulating ultimately to be understood as our human response to our condition? Or is our articulation striving rather to be faithful to

something beyond us, not explicable simply in terms of human response? [. . .]
I would dearly like to be able to cut through the clutter and confusion that we all
labour under so as to be able to explore this question, but I have to admit that I
am far away from this at present. I need, among other things, to be much clearer
about language and meaning. (1985c, 11–12, original emphasis)

Yet since Taylor continues to face the same problem ten years later in *Philosophical Arguments*, and given that his alternative philosophical-anthropological, ethical, epistemological, and political approaches to ontology do not solve this issue either, it would seem that his strategy so far is to leave his nonanthropocentric perspective unexplained, and therefore to admit to an explanatory gap within his doctrine of strong evaluation.[16]

However, we find another hint about Taylor's nonanthropocentrism in the paper "Iris Murdoch and Moral Philosophy" (1996/2011). In this text, he first praises Murdoch for criticizing the "narrowness" of theories of obligatory action and for taking us "beyond morality to issues about the good life" (1996/2011, 4). But he also invokes another aspect of Murdoch's work—albeit in a far more tentative and exploratory fashion—when he says that she takes us even beyond the question of the good life to the consideration of a good which would be "beyond life" in her investigations of the "almost untracked forests of the unconditional" (1996/2011, 4–5). I will focus here only on the latter issue, that is, Taylor's exploration of what he calls the "forest" beyond the "field" of ethics which Murdoch has opened up for us (1996/2011, 5, 15). Not all that different from that in his paper about Heidegger, Taylor's language here is more poetic than philosophical. In this respect, it is telling that his discussion begins with the apologetic note that it is hard even to *talk* about this subject, "above all, hard to talk about it clearly and in a recognized common language" as the forest of ethics is "virtually untracked" (1996/2011, 15). However, Taylor continues, we need "new trails" for at least two reasons. First, because we have grown into a "different civilization from our medieval and even early modern forebears" and, second, because human beings are constantly "blazing new trails" as we find "very different ways to God, or the Good, or Nirvana, ways that seem to involve incompatible assumptions" (1996/2011, 15–16).

For Taylor, then, "entering the forest" is acknowledging that life is "not the whole story," that is, to acknowledge that "the point of things is not exhausted by life, the fullness of life, even the goodness of life" (1996/2011, 16). He then continues to explain how this nonanthropocentric mode of thinking goes against dominant conceptions of human flourishing by invoking the conflict between "modern culture and forest-dwelling" (1996/2011, 18). In this regard, Taylor criticizes modern moral culture for overemphasizing the "primacy of life" in its supreme concern with our "humanitarian, 'civilized' world," in which life and happiness must be recovered at all costs, against the threats of death and suffering (1996/2011, 19). But what could it mean, then, to *challenge* the primacy of life? In elaborating on this, Taylor makes a distinction between challenging the "practical" primacy of life and challenging the "metaphysical" primacy of life. The practical type of challenge means to "displace the saving of life and the avoidance of suffering from their rank as central concerns of policy" (1996/2011, 19). This is not Taylor's concern. Rather, he challenges the primacy of life in the *metaphysical* sense of "opening the way for the insight that more than life matters" (1996/2011, 20). These points, then, prepare the ground for Taylor's main thesis that "human beings have an ineradicable bent to respond to something beyond life," and, moreover, that this thesis is "radically at odds with that of secular humanism" (1996/2011, 20).

Considering his later picture of a three-cornered battle between secular humanists, "anti-humanist" neo-Nietzscheans, and believers in transcendence in "A Catholic Modernity?" (1999/2011), it should not surprise us that Taylor here already specifically presents Nietzsche as the most influential challenger of the primacy of life. After all, Taylor argues, like no other Nietzsche opposed the metaphysical primacy of life against secular humanism (even though he goes one step further by also rejecting it in the practical sense), rebelling "against the idea that our highest goal is to preserve and increase life, to prevent suffering" (1996/2011, 21). Once again, Taylor sees himself as defending an intermediate position, in this case not between Platonism and subjectivism but between secular humanism and anti-humanism. He ultimately criticizes both these views for failing to recognize that, although the practical primacy of life has been a great gain for humankind, the metaphysical primacy of life is still "wrong and stifling" in that it "puts in danger the practical primacy" (1996/2011, 22).

What is most striking in these last paragraphs is the peculiar reference to Nietzsche. As Taylor develops his nonanthropocentric perspective out of this notion of a forest, Nietzsche principally enters the stage as his central supporter against the metaphysical primacy of life (1996/2011, 20). Yet, two pages later, Taylor compares and contrasts his view not with Nietzsche but with "the anti-humanism of Nietzsche's heirs" and with secular humanists who "together condemn religion and reject any good beyond life" (1996/2011, 22). Unfortunately, Taylor's probing paper about Murdoch explains neither the complex role of Nietzsche in this debate nor the need for exploring the "forest of ethics" in much detail. It would seem, therefore, that his tribute to Murdoch parallels his account of Heidegger in that Taylor's mixed use of ontological and poetic language ("forest-dwelling," "the clearing") avoids rather than authorizes a clear statement about his *own* ontological position.

What emerges from this outline so far is that (1) Taylor's ontological inquiries involve linguistic, anthropological, ethical, metaphysical, epistemological, political, ecological, nonanthropocentric, Heideggerian, and Murdochian considerations all in one; (2) Taylor's argumentation grows rather thin precisely when it comes to explaining his own ontological beliefs; and (3) he acknowledges this by explicitly apologizing at times for being incomplete. Although these points bring together several elements of Taylor's tentative ontology, they still do not exhaust his thoughts on this subject. As we will see in the next section, he has one more ontological trump card to play.

5.2.3 More Recent Writings

After his first essay on ontology in 1959 and the above-mentioned exploratory writings (1985–1996), it takes Taylor a good long time to broach the subject of ontology again. However, his more recent writings are well worth waiting for since they open up an additional strategy: a *phenomenological* approach to ontological problems. This tactic begins in "Ethics and Ontology" (2003), without doubt Taylor's most forthright text about ontology. For one thing, he stops using the confusing, haphazard ontological rhetoric of earlier writings. Furthermore, he is more open about his central disagreement with naturalism, arguing that the difficulty consists in a *metaphysical* dispute more than anything else. It is therefore somewhat disappointing that there has been so little discussion about "Ethics and Ontology."[17] Taylor's renewed focus emerges early on from the refreshingly clear opening of the paper: "What are we committed to ontologically by our ethical views and commitments? One common temptation of modern philosophy has been to answer: nothing; moral commitments and factual beliefs are in different spheres" (2003, 305).

He then notes that the many attempts to split fact and value have generally been motivated by one central concern, namely to do justice to what Taylor calls our "post-Galilean" worldview, which stipulates that "value comes into the world with us, the human agents who evaluate" since the universe itself has been seen as "devoid of meaning and value" (2003, 306). Against this background, Taylor's paper picks up his old theme of naturalism by arguing that our moral culture sets us the following challenge: either we correct our naturalist ontology or we must revise the most salient features of our moral experience. To clarify this tension, he stresses that the attribution of value is fundamentally different from attributing other qualities, such as color, in that "questions of *merit* now arise" (2003, 308, original emphasis). That is, we can be asked to demonstrate the "rational grounds" of a normative statement such as "you are dishonest" in a way that we would never be asked to show that the table is really red (2003, 308). The problem for ethical naturalism, then, is precisely to account for this "qualitative status of the ethical" that defines our sense of morality, that is, the sense that moral values are "in some way special, higher, or incommensurable with our other goals and desires" (2003, 308, 309). His criticism is, in other words, that post-Galilean naturalists such as Mackie and Blackburn annihilate our sense of value by depicting it as "error" or "projection," in that way denying the incommensurably higher altogether (2003, 309). Taylor then presents his moral phenomenology as a *problem* for naturalist ontology:

> There is a tension between phenomenology and ontology. The former, properly and honestly carried through, seems to show that values of this higher status [. . .] are ineradicable from our deliberations of how to live. But ontology, defined naturalistically, says that properties of this kind can have no place in an account of things in the world. (2003, 310)

Here we find Taylor embarking on a new, more determined mode of "ontological reasoning." That is, instead of his previous exploratory uses of the term, he now employs the concept of ontology as a full-out attack on naturalist-inspired metaphysics. In fact, Taylor heightens the tension by insisting that we must suffer one of two things: the pain of "resisting the phenomenology" or the pain of "challenging the ontology" (2003, 310, 312). Given his continuous effort to show how strong evaluation is inescapable for human beings, Taylor quickly rejects the first option. As he says, "even the most stripped-down utilitarian holds a value like 'rationality' as a virtue in the ethical sense; that is, she sees this quality in people not just as useful, not just as desirable, but also as *admirable*" (2003, 310, original emphasis). He also rejects Mackie's and Blackburn's half-hearted acceptance of moral phenomenology, that is, to accept that "this is how it looks" but to insist at the same time that "it is not really like this in the objective world" (2003, 311). For Taylor, the difficulty with this strategy is that it boldly decides beforehand that everything in nature is to be explained in terms of post-Galilean science, without even formulating it as a basic assumption—let alone arguing for it—and only *then* concludes that values cannot but appear as "queer" or "quasi"-real entities (2003, 311).

Of course, the very problem of the relationship between ethics and ontology would never have come up if we were able to make sense of our moral beliefs exclusively in post-Galilean terms. That would instantly redeem both moral phenomenology and naturalist ontology. However, as Taylor's doctrine of strong evaluation makes plain, at this point in time such theories are nowhere to be seen (2003, 311). This leaves us with the prospect of challenging naturalist ontology. Taylor holds two positions here. On the one hand, he praises McDowell's modified, nonreductive naturalism (as elaborated in *Mind, Value, and Reality*) for having shown "how we can see values as imported into the universe by human beings, without seeing them as merely a matter of subjective reactions or projections which we might peel off things" (2003, 314). That is, we no longer need to think that because a property is human related it must therefore be "projected" onto things, or not be properly "real," or be incapable of yielding a "fact of the matter" (2003, 314). On the other hand, Taylor also criticizes McDowell (and Wiggins) for denying what he calls the "full reality" of strong values (2003, 316). That is, even though McDowell sufficiently redeems "the deliverances of phenomenology (we really discern ethical differences in human life, and these have to be understood as involving incommensurable, higher values)," Taylor holds that he still is committed to the "basic concerns of a naturalist ontology which cannot allow such values into the furniture of the universe" (2003, 314). In this way, he criticizes McDowell for lacking an explanation of the ontological status of strong values:

> We have now lost a reason to consider all significance properties as "queer" or less than fully "real." But there remain the reasons specific to moral properties, namely, that they invoke incommensurably higher values. *These by definition have no place in what I have been calling the "post-Galilean" conception of nature.* So even if we no longer aspire to reductive explanations, we still can balk at the full "reality" of the intrinsically higher. [. . .] There remains the tension between the phenomenology of the incommensurably higher and a naturalist ontology which has difficulty finding a place for this. (2003, 316, italics mine)

Moving toward the end of his paper, Taylor draws attention to an aspect of moral experience that in his view has been addressed by neither Mackie nor Blackburn nor McDowell. More importantly, this is the moment at which Taylor the phenomenologist steps aside in favor of Taylor the ontologist. Or, perhaps better put, this is the point at which it finally becomes clear that these are not two different figures but one and the same. Taylor makes his case by invoking two moral-phenomenological examples. As moral agents, we generally see human beings as "worthy of respect" and we give a "special importance to nobility" (2003, 316, 318). He then notes that such ethical notions have been articulated historically in terms of religious and metaphysical beliefs. In this way, the basis of respect has been understood in such terms as the universal ontic logos that resides in human beings or as our being made in the image of God. It is precisely this type of ontological grounding, Taylor argues, that we cannot and must not dismiss as confused. This is because these articulations of *why* human beings deserve respect did not just provide an "extra rhetorical impulse" to our tendency to treat others rightly, but were meant to *articulate* just "what respect worthiness consisted in" (2003, 317). That is, they offer "further specifications of the concept that is in play here, the one that we can apply rightly or wrongly, and that we therefore cannot see as a simple projection" (2003, 317).

In other words, since ontological accounts provide us with crucial foundations of morality rather than gratuitous subtractions, we cannot simply reject the question of what ontology best explains our moral motivation as a pseudo-question from a distant past. What differentiates us from our forebears is that we no longer see this question as having a single determinate answer. But at the same time, most of us embrace the ethic of universal respect without question. Even if we feel at a loss to say what underpins this motivation because we now have a deeper identity than any of our articulations of it, even the most exploratory vision can orient and inspire if it illuminates our moral experience. In fact, the present discussion now reaches a point at which Taylor's phenomenological and ontological viewpoints coincide with both his critique of naturalism and his overall concern for the status of moral sources. As he says,

> [s]ome of these arguments are, no doubt, mistaken. But are they all? If not, *then the question can arise whether the values we espouse can be supported on the basis of the ontology to which we want to subscribe.* Maybe [. . .] the kinds of things most of us believe about rights call for an articulation that would take us beyond the bounds of a naturalist ontology. The battle between phenomenology and ontology would break out again. (2003, 318, italics mine)

Intriguingly, Taylor implicitly has recourse to the logic of his first essay on ontology (1959) in discussing the concept of nobility as a second example, by emphasizing the "ontological gaps" that this term evokes. He argues that once we see morality as "programmed" in our brains, then unavoidably a "gap" opens up between "the ontology of what we discriminate in our world (which includes the noble/nonnoble), and that of the universe including complex organisms in which we act" (2003, 318). In the end, for all the diversity of the scientific languages that might offer an ontological explanation of concepts such as nobility, Taylor nonetheless insists that it is very unlikely—at present at least—that such groundings will succeed, arguing that "the hoped-for-reconciliation between moral phenomenology and naturalist ontology is, to say the least, somewhat premature" (2003, 319, 320).

However, we should not gloss over the fact that the "gap" between what we experience as moral agents and what we believe ontologically also disrupts Taylor's *own* reasoning. As we have seen in the previous chapters, his endorsement of a nonanthropocentric perspective in debunking naturalism remains underdemonstrated by his central philosophical-anthropological and moral-phenomenological arguments. Perhaps the bottom line is, therefore, that *identifying* ontological gaps is as far as Taylor's ontology can take us. He concludes:

> This much, however, seems clear. We cannot retrieve the original innocent belief of modern, naturalistic philosophical culture that places moral commitments and factual beliefs in different spheres, so that no problem can arise of reconciling phenomenology and ontology. [. . .] The really interesting question that remains is whether the ethic that all of us share, naturalists and anti-naturalists alike, say, the affirmation of universal human rights [. . .] can consort with the evolutionary naturalism that finds such higher goods "queer." (2003, 320)

Ultimately, Taylor does not make any fundamental changes in his view in "Ethics and Ontology." However, this text does press the issue of naturalism even more than in previous writings by shining a spotlight on the yawning gap between what we "really" experience about ourselves and what we "really" believe to be true about the world. Moreover, it shows that ethical naturalism is far from innocent, as it not only imposes its own ontology on all the others, but also undermines central moral values by leaving no ontological room for them except as queer or quasi-real phenomena. In other words, Taylor's paper sufficiently demonstrates that naturalism is not so much a philosophical "thesis" but something stronger, more a fixed horizon of largely unarticulated and unchallenged assumptions than a doctrine that is open to question. By exposing this, Taylor does not alter his moral phenomenology but uses it instead to highlight the problems of naturalism as a *philosophical* program. The thrust of this move is that it shifts the burden of proof.

Although Taylor's attack on naturalist ontology ends with yet another apologizing note,[18] he continues to explore the relationship between ethics and ontology in *A Secular Age* (2007). He does so in three steps—characteristically, steering a course between phenomenology, ethics, and ontology. First, as a phenomenologist, Taylor draws attention to three basic categories of experience that most people want to uphold. Second, as an ontologist, he argues that it will be very difficult, if not impossible, to include these experiences in a naturalist ontology (which he now also describes as "immanent" and "materialist"). Third, as an ethicist, Taylor then uses this double phenomenological-ontological perspective to reraise his doubts about nontheistic moral sources. He argues: "How can one account for the specific force of creative agency, or ethical demands, or for the power of artistic experience, without speaking in terms of some transcendent being or force which interpellates us" (2007, 597)? In other words, for Taylor it is precisely because most people see our creative capacities and responses to worth and beauty as *incompatible* with reductionist materialism that they shy away from naturalist ontologizing. Although one can disagree with the determined way in which Taylor moves from these basic experiences to claims about "the transcendent," his point is well taken when we acknowledge that the question still remains as to whether naturalism can really explain these experiences in full.

The discussion then picks up where it left off in "Ethics and Ontology," when Taylor reraises the issue of how to account for *moral* experience, invoking the question of "what ontology can underpin our moral commitments" (2007, 607). As in the preceding paper, Taylor's approach in *A Secular Age* is one of trying to articulate this problem rather than to solve it:

> This kind of issue continues as a live question for us; parallel to the case of aesthetic experience, we can ask what ontology do we need to make sense of our ethical or moral lives, properly understood. [. . .] I don't want to pursue this point to an utterly convincing conclusion. More pertinently, I don't think I can. I just want to identify the kind of issue at stake here: whether our moral or ethical life, properly understood, can really be captured by the accounts which fit with our favored ontology. (2007, 607–609)

Taylor returns to this topic several pages later when expressing his dissatisfaction with nontheistic explanations of morality, for example by asking whether the ontology of "moral sentiment" (he mentions Hume) can really "match the phenomenology" that makes full sense of our feeling of moral obligation (2007, 693). If we now recall the vigorous debate on theistic versus nontheistic sources (as discussed in section 5.1.2), we can see that Taylor calls into question both the *explanatory* and the *motivational* force of naturalist humanism. That is, he raises the issue of how to align phenomenology and ontology not only to debate metaphysical questions, but also to open up the more *practical* question of what we need, ethically politically speaking, to accomplish what morality demands of us.

This final effort brings together central elements of the present discussion. Moreover, by connecting issues of metaphysical explanation to issues of moral motivation Taylor raises his prior ontological discussions to a new level. In one way, it follows up on the analysis in "Ethics and Ontology"; in another way it goes back to the issue of adequate sources in *Sources of the Self*. As this suggests, Taylor's ontological course has remained more or less the same—notwithstanding the many different uses of the concept of ontology in particular texts and periods. A further advantage of connecting metaphysical explanation to issues of moral motivation is that it makes more concrete Taylor's idea that ontological theses "structure the field of possibilities" (1995a, 183). In this way, he argues that our answer to the question of what best "explains" our moral beliefs will also clarify our underlying "motivation" (2007, 693).

Again, Taylor raises the issue of adequate explanations in crucial reference to the issue of adequate sources because he believes that the answers to these questions are interdependent and mutually reinforcing. In other words, his interwoven argument here is that becoming more *articulate* about moral sources at the same time inspires us to *sustain* them. This is the reason why Taylor continues to insist on there being an important connection between ethics and ontology. Yet this connection becomes altogether invisible once we adopt a naturalistic approach to ethics, which, as Blackburn clarifies, focuses not on issues of moral motivation but on "finding room for ethics, or placing ethics within the disenchanted, nonethical order which we inhabit" (1998, 49). Given this focus, the hope and aim of any naturalism is to clarify moral experience without relying on phenomenological evidence. This translates to building a mathematical proof without accepting any logical truths. Or, as Taylor aptly puts it, it is an attempt to make naturalism compatible with moral experience by making this experience *irrelevant* to it (1989, 60).

The final paper that clarifies Taylor's ontology is "Disenchantment-Reenchantment" (2011b). This text stands out because it is the only piece in which Taylor *explicitly* invokes the ontological implications of the doctrine of strong evaluation. However, he does so not systematically at the beginning but rather suddenly at the end of his discussion, as a kind of hint about where the ontology of strong evaluation eventually takes us. As noted (in section 1.2.3), Taylor's paper raises the issues of how we should understand the process of "disenchantment," on the one hand, and the attempt of those who seek "reenchantment" within this climate, on the other. His central concern is the status of what he calls "human meanings which are "objective," in the sense that they are not just arbitrarily projected through choice or contingent desire" (2011b, 294). Taylor then seeks to clarify the experienced objectivity of these meanings by arguing that moral reactions are best understood as strong evaluations that invoke "truth, reality or objective rightness" and, in so doing, track "some reality" (2011b, 294, 297–98). That is, "our moral reactions suppose that they are responses to some reality, and can be criticized for misapprehension of this reality" (2011b, 297). Against the background of these claims, Taylor then provides—for the first time—a definition of the ontological reality of strong evaluation:

> A response which we understand as a strong evaluation supposes the following ontology: (1) This response genuinely motivates us, it is not simply a cover, or a rationalization, or a screen for some other drive; (2) it can fail to occur on some occasions or in some people, but this betokens some limitation, blindness, or insensitivity on their part; (3) in other words, there is something objectively right about this response; (4) we can and ought to challenge ourselves to cultivate this response, to refine or improve our perception of its proper objects. This four-point feature represents a package, reflecting our sense that this evaluation is founded. (2011b, 300)

In this way, Taylor ultimately draws together the key themes of his ontology, first, by underlining his doubt regarding "purely anthropocentric articulations" and, second, by concluding that we must allow at least *two* explanatory accounts of moral agency, one naturalistically defined in terms of post-Galilean science, and another hermeneutically informed by strong evaluation (2011b, 300, 302). Whereas the former deliberately avoids "purpose or evaluation as causally relevant factors," the latter puts these human meanings precisely in the center of its analysis (2011b, 300). As Taylor concludes, the vital question that remains is "whether we can give an adequate explanation of the phenomena we describe in the 'upper' language (e.g. people reacting to the universe with a sense of wonder) entirely in the terms of the 'lower' language (post-Galilean science)" (2011b, 300). This account, then, at once restates Taylor's insistence on conflicting explanatory languages and ontologies, his analysis of the tension between moral phenomenology and naturalist ontology, and his nonanthropocentric viewpoint. With these points in place, there remain only two more texts that could illuminate Taylor's ontology: *Retrieving Realism* (2015) and *The Language Animal* (2016). Yet, because most of Taylor's commentators could not yet engage with these new books, I first examine the main discussions of Taylor's ontological view in the literature (section 5.3) before exploring his most recent views in the light of these discussions (in section 5.4).

5.3 ARTICULATIONS AND CRITIQUES

Although Taylor scarcely uses the term until *Retrieving Realism*, both his critics and his interpreters have generally been explaining his "ontology" as a kind of *realism*. Fergus Kerr, for example, attributes to Taylor the view that we remain "stubbornly attached to unreconstructed moral realism" since "the ancient belief in the objectivity of the good is still at work in everyday moral behavior" (2004, 92, 84). Carlos Thiebaut identifies Taylor's ontology as an "appellative ethical realism" (1993, 133), whereas Ruth Abbey interprets it as a "falsifiable realism" (2000, 27). Paul Saurette also sees Taylor reverting to "language reminiscent of objective moral realism," while arguing that this is a fundamentally problematic approach (2005, 202). Stephen White advances a very different interpretation by incorporating Taylor within his own terminology. He argues that Taylor, while at first portraying him as "a border runner between strong and weak ontology" (1997, 506), is in the end best understood as being "squarely within the terrain of weak ontology" (2000, 43, note 5). Others provide more critical readings. The objections of Bernard Williams, Michael Rosen, and Richard Rorty all result from philosophical backgrounds that explicitly challenge Taylor's ontological perspective. As noted (in sections 2.3.2 and 5.1.2), Williams mainly takes issue with the metaphysical background of Taylor's "Catholic tale" (1990, 45, 48). Rosen criticizes Taylor for simply "returning" to moral realism (1991, 183), whereas Rorty challenges Taylor's "moral realist urges" (1994, 200). Reflecting on what I see as the most illuminating interpretations and critiques, I first discuss Thiebaut's and Abbey's views (section 5.3.1), while also discussing in more detail White's portrait of Taylor as a "weak ontologist" in the light of these views (sections 5.3.2 and 5.3.3).[19] I conclude by pursuing the closely related nonrealist critiques of Rosen and Rorty (section 5.3.4).

5.3.1 The Interpretive Challenges of Taylor's Ontology

Given the many failed attempts to give a straightforward definition of Taylor's ontology, Thiebaut's review of *Sources of the Self* has the virtue of explaining *why* it is so difficult to place Taylor's ontological position. He first notes that Taylor's conception of a "moral space" is meant to oppose all naturalist forms of reduction as it "possesses a *reality* that does not fit into the fixed molds of the naturalist reduction" (Thiebaut 1993, 132, original emphasis). The first thing to realize in understanding Taylor's moral realism, therefore, is that it is radically different from contemporary forms of moral realism in Anglo-American analytic philosophy. However, Thiebaut explains, given the "empirical accents that in general taint what is understood by 'reality' in analytical philosophy," Taylor's distinctive brand of moral realism is easily confused with the "biological naturalism" that Taylor opposes (1993, 132). Moreover, he continues, since Taylor also rejects "metaphysical" and "psychological" explanations of morality, there remains for Taylor very limited logical space to elaborate on his metaethical position (Thiebaut 1993, 132).

As noted (in section 4.3.2), Thiebaut ultimately explains Taylor's ontology as a hybrid position that constitutes, "outwardly, the good as a component of the real" while also provoking an "inward movement towards the subject, before which alone this reality has any sense" (1993, 134). In Abbey's view, then, there are at least three possible responses to this inward-outward tactic. The first is to attribute to Taylor a "weak realism" that simply boils down to his phenomenology of moral experience, and thus to gloss over his appeal to the ontological reality that makes sense of this experience (Abbey 2000, 27). As we have seen (in section 2.3.2), this is a fitting interpretation for those who concur with Taylor's phenomenology of strong evaluation, but who cannot accept the ontology behind it—for example, Williams and Laitinen. A second response, "strong moral realism," sees Taylor rather as insisting that "moral values do exist independently of human beings" (Abbey 2000, 27). As shown (in section 5.1.1), Olafson endorses this reading by portraying Taylor as a kind of Platonist, and antitheistic critics such as Skinner, Lane, Johnston, and Flanagan (as discussed in section 5.1.2) are likely to join him.

Abbey rejects both these interpretations. The weak realist reading, she explains, despite having the advantage of being "more readily acceptable to more of his readers," misses the point that Taylor's realism only *begins* with describing the way human beings experience morality in terms of higher goods (Abbey 2000, 27, 29). The strong realist reading, then, makes the opposite mistake of overstating Taylor's conception of higher goods. That is, to erroneously attribute to Taylor the view that these goods are "not just a feature of moral life but also a true depiction of the world" (Abbey 2000, 28). Given these points, Abbey ultimately defends a third reading of Taylor's realism as "falsifiable" rather than weak or strong, drawing attention (and rightly so, in my view) to the tentative nature of Taylor's ontological thought (2000, 29). In this way, Abbey makes it clear that Taylor's view is the probing one that we have to assume *some* kind of moral realism to hold on to our moral experience, that is, unless ethical naturalism is able to clearly demonstrate the nonrealist nature of incommensurably higher values.

If anything, Thiebaut's and Abbey's clarifications show that for Taylor there is no room for an exploration of the good that is not also an inquiry into its metaphysical underpinnings, a definition of the real. Unfortunately, though, their subtle interpretations still do not solve the problem with which our analysis of Taylor's doctrine of strong evaluation started (section 2.1.3), namely how to understand the relationship between Taylor's profound philosophical anthropology and moral phenomenology, on the one hand, and his highly tentative nonanthropocentric positions in ethics and ontology, on the other. In the face of this challenge, I consider in the next section whether White's "weak-ontological" interpretation might help to clarify this issue.

5.3.2 White's Weak-Ontological Portrait

Given Taylor's central interwoven mode of argumentation in between ethics and ontology, it should not surprise us that White identifies Taylor as the central inspiration for his project of rehabilitating ontological reasoning in political theory. As noted (in section 2.2.2), White's position responds to two concerns: it accepts that all fundamental conceptualizations of self, other, and world are "contestable" and yet insists that such conceptualizations are "necessary" and "unavoidable" for an adequately reflective ethical and political life (White 2000, 8). In this way, White's main objective is to stress the importance of an ontological vision to morality in a way that understands ontology as "prefiguring," rather than dictating, ethical-political perception and judgment (2000, 11; 2005, 22). His key concept of "weak" ontology, then, is meant to express the contrast with "strong" ontologies that gain their "sense of what is right" in ethical and political life by reference to "'the way the world is,' or how God's being stands to human being, or what human nature is" (1997, 505; 2000, 6). Since such traditional ontologies generally "involve too much 'metaphysics,'" White continues, it is striking of weak ontologies that they do not bear "clear substantive directions for practical life" and yet these ontologies "do provide a figuration of the world that appears to promise at least some orientation or passage to moral-political reflection" (1997, 505–506; 2000, 7–8).

Ultimately, White thus seeks to sustain affirmation of our ethical-political commitments in a way that acknowledges their contingent and nonmetaphysical character at the same time. Because of this focus, it is crucial to weak ontologies that they signal their own limits, that is, they incorporate a sense of their own "contestability, fallibility, or partiality" (2000, 8). Taylor's relevance to White's project, then, is not only that "the way he describes the idea of 'articulating' our 'background pictures' or 'frameworks' is highly instructive," but also that "no thinker today has done more to press broad ontological questions than Charles Taylor" (White 1997, 506; 2000, 42).

As White understands him, Taylor is "squarely within the terrain of weak ontology" (2000, 43, note 5). He therefore defends Taylor against critics that wrongly assume that he is offering a return to strong ontology, that is, "some foundationalist, determinate truth about the shape and direction of self and world" (2000, 43). White seeks to do so, first, by emphasizing the weak-ontological character of Taylor's philosophical-anthropological and moral-phenomenological views; second, by interpreting Taylor's categorization of theistic, naturalist, and expressivist moral sources in a weak-ontological fashion; and, third, by clarifying that Taylor integrates elements of Romantic expressivism with theism in a way that broadly supports the idea of weak ontology. White strategically appeals to these three aspects to argue that Taylor is firmly rooted in weak ontology, but, as will be shown (in section 5.3.3), his weak-ontological portrait, while revealing, only partly explains Taylor's complex position.

White's discussion begins by invoking Taylor's claim that there exists "'a kind of eclipse of ontological thinking' in contemporary moral and political theory" and that we need to "rethink the self as part of a 'richer ontology'" to undo this suppression (White 2000, 42–43).[20] In White's interpretation, Taylor's "richer ontology" emerges at the background of his philosophical anthropology, that is, Taylor's "internal account of 'what it is to be an agent'" and the claims that "the self is always already engaged, embedded, or situated" and that "human agency is partially, but deeply, constituted by this engagement with the world" (White 2000, 44, 45). Invoking Taylor's "phenomenological account of identity" and the notion of "what is of 'incomparable' importance to us," White further explains Taylor's view that "the peculiar force of the experience of attachment is distinctive to human being" (2000, 45–47). Stepping back from what White calls this "ontological sketch of agency," he then poses the question of how we should understand the "exact philosophical status" of Taylor's view on agency to set the stage for his claim that Taylor is best understood as a weak ontologist (2000, 47).

In answering this question, he first argues that "Taylor deploys an argument of conceptual necessity," while noting some pages later that it also has "something of the sense of a transcendental claim" (2000, 44, 47). White hastens to add, however, that "Taylor speaks only of 'transcendental conditions,' being careful to insert scare quotes" (2000, 47–48). Furthermore, White continues, even if Taylor maintains that the picture of agency defended by his naturalist opponents is that of a monster, "Taylor is nevertheless aware that he has no philosophical means of establishing an absolutely incontestable boundary for us/monsters. Accordingly, he admits that his appeal to conceptual necessity is in reality always open to contest" (2000, 48–49).

There seems little doubt, then, that the cautious way in which Taylor crafts his arguments about agency put him "squarely within the terrain of weak ontology" (2000, 43, note 5) as Taylor is fully aware that his view on human agency does not establish metaphysical truths. As White concludes this point, since Taylor is operating "from within the perspective of engaged, embodied agency," he cannot at the same time claim to have discovered a "level of metaphysical bedrock" (2000, 49). In White's view, then, these points testify to the weak-ontological—that is, nonmetaphysical—character of Taylor's philosophical-anthropological and moral-phenomenological views.

White sees a second example of Taylor's weak-ontological aspiration in the historical narrative laid out in *Sources of the Self*. He first draws the larger background from which Taylor's narrative must be understood: "One of the characteristics of a felicitous weak ontology is the persuasiveness with which an array of specific concepts of self, other, and world are located within a broad historical narrative" (2000, 50). He then depicts Taylor's contribution in *Sources of the Self* as a leading example of such a historical narrative by describing it as "one of the grandest portraits of the modern West that has appeared in recent decades" (2000, 50). This portrait, White explains, consists of three basic "ontological constellations": the "original theistic one," the "naturalism of disengaged reason," and the constellation that "emerges out of romanticism" (2000, 50–51). Without getting into the details, it is a crucial point in White's analysis to show how Taylor's narrative "does indeed affirm a certain openness to ontological diversity" (2000, 52) to highlight the weak-ontological thrust of Taylor's view. In this way, White argues that Taylor again takes a nonmetaphysical stance in developing his historical narrative as he "guarantees that his ontological insights, whether relating to templates or full constellations, signal their own limits, contain their own sense of contestedness; in short, they offer themselves as 'weak' in my sense" (2000, 56).

White's third example of the weak-ontological nature of Taylor's position concerns what he calls Taylor's "aesthetic-expressive theism" (2000, 57). In this regard, White convincingly shows how Taylor's theism crucially depends on his view that God, as any moral source, is now "inextricably entangled with subjective articulation," referring to Taylor's complex "interweaving of the subjective and the transcendent" and his idea that "theology is 'indexed' to 'languages of personal resonance'" (2000, 63).[21] At this point, White's conclusion that Taylor's brand of theism "broadly supports the idea of weak ontology" should no longer surprise us (2000, 63).

White's weak-ontological portrait raises a fundamental question: Even if there are certain weak-ontological elements in Taylor's views, does that also mean that he is a weak ontologist through and through? For one thing, it would seem that White's "ontological sketch" results in a too limited account of Taylor's arguments about agency. Many commentators point out that his philosophical anthropology and his moral phenomenology insist on universal—rather than contestable—features of both selfhood and morality. Furthermore, as Abbey emphasizes, Taylor's defense of the inescapability of strong evaluation seeks to show that relativist and subjectivist moral theories are not merely contestable but utterly mistaken (2000, 25–26). These points illustrate that, while it is true in general that Taylor urges caution in developing his narrative about the modern self in terms of human universals, he is quite determined when it comes to defending the transcendental necessity of strong evaluation. Far from "prefiguring," Taylor's ultimate view on agency is that any theory of human action that resists strong evaluation is not just incomplete but also wrong, and cannot but be so after considering his arguments.[22]

Apart from these philosophical-anthropological and moral-phenomenological issues, however, there remains the more fundamental concern that White's weak-ontological reading fails to acknowledge the nonanthropocentric elements in Taylor's ontological thought. For example, to what extent is Taylor's claim in "Ethics and Ontology" (which White does not discuss) that we are best advised to *revise* naturalist ontology in favor of moral phenomenology still consonant with the basic weak-ontological assumption that all fundamental conceptualizations are inherently contestable? Make no mistake: Taylor's point is that his nonanthropocentric phenomenology *rules out* naturalist ontology. How does this attack on naturalist-inspired metaphysics relate to weak ontology's self-declared nonmetaphysical stance and its "fallibility" and "partiality"? (White 2000, 8) In an attempt to clarify these issues, I argue in the next section that White's habit of equating philosophical anthropology and ontology ultimately prevents him from recognizing the full scope of Taylor's ontologizing.

5.3.3 The Limits of Weak Ontology

At the beginning of his analysis, White makes a quick point about terminology (albeit hidden in a footnote), explaining that his notion of weak ontology is "largely appropriate" to capture Taylor's mixed use of philosophical-anthropological and ontological terms (White 2000, 43, note 3). As noted (in section 2.1.3), Taylor himself has made it clear in a reflection on White's *Sustaining Affirmation* that he is thinking along the same lines as White about issues that he labels both as philosophical-anthropological and ontological (Taylor 2005, 35). However, one major disadvantage of equating ontology with philosophical anthropology is that it reduces ontological inquiry in general and makes invisible Taylor's nonanthropocentric view in particular. Moreover, White's holistic approach of clustering philosophical-anthropological, moral-phenomenological, transcendental, descriptive, normative, and theistic claims all under the label of "Taylor's richer ontology" blurs the distinctions between Taylor's different philosophical strategies and, in doing so, obscures the precise nature of their entanglement. In this respect, it would seem that the tension between moral experience and naturalist ontology could neither be articulated nor discussed from within White's weak ontology, because it is a deliberate strategy of this approach *not* to make the crucial distinction between ethics and ontology that allows for the meta-perspective from which their relationship can be assessed. Let me flesh this out.

White explains his holistic view in terms of his key notion of a "stickier" subject (2000, 8). He generally employs this term to oppose what Taylor has called the ideal of the "disengaged" self (Taylor 1989, 21). White explains the difference as follows: whereas the modern disengaged subject (also the "Teflon" subject) "generates distance from its background (tradition, embodiment) and foreground (external nature, other subjects)," it is essential to the *late* modern sticky subject that it "cannot be divorced from the practical embeddedness of reflection, and thus must be approached through an interpretive-existential mode of thought" (1997, 503). It is precisely because of this "stickiness," White explains, that ontological reflection can no longer be seen as an "exclusively cognitive matter, as it was traditionally, and still is for much of analytic philosophy" (1997, 504; 2000, 4). He elaborates:

> Ontological commitments in this sense are thus entangled with questions of identity and history, with how we articulate the meaning of our lives, both individually and collectively. [. . .] Ontological reflection thus becomes inextricably entangled with distinct characteristics of human being [. . .] in the form of deep reconceptualizations of human being in relation to its world. More specifically, human being is presented as in some way "stickier" than in prevailing modern conceptualizations. (2000, 4–5)

At first glance, White's conception of a stickier subject seems perfectly in line with Taylor's tactic of straddling philosophical domains in developing his interwoven arguments. That is, White has fully grasped Taylor's strategy by emphasizing the problem that "at this deepest level many familiar analytical categories and operations become blurred or exhibit torsional effects" (2005, 14). He explains, "the more I pondered the relation between ethics and ontology, the more they seemed mutually constitutive at this level and the less possible it seemed to accord one or the other clear primacy" (White 2005, 14). In fact, he adds, "it was at this point that the full significance of Charles Taylor's *Sources of the Self* began to dawn on me" (2005, 14). This point is well taken when we consider the problem that having recourse to a more conventional vocabulary does not help to clarify Taylor's interwoven claims but, on the contrary, cuts us off from his "sticky" type of inquiry. White's sticky subject even seems to anticipate Taylor's recent contact theory in *Retrieving Realism*, which argues that our "original" way of being in the world reflects a kind of understanding that generally *resists* basic distinctions between "explicit, analytical elements," such as those between "subject and object," "fact and value," and "belief and reality" (2015, 94, 103).

As these points suggest, White's approach makes a strong case for the claim that differentiating between Taylor's views distorts rather than clarifies his ontology. I have been arguing, however, that we must look into the relationships between Taylor's various concerns only *after* having set the boundaries that separate them, and that doing so uncovers a nonanthropocentric viewpoint that would otherwise remain invisible. White seems to attack this approach at its core by insisting on the practical embeddedness of reflection. From his perspective, our current argumentative situation requires not demarcation but an "interpretive-existential" approach that accounts for the ways in which philosophical categories "entangle themselves" (1997, 503; 2005, 14).

Yet it is questionable whether White's highlighting of stickiness really enables us to explore Taylor's multifaceted ontology in an illuminating way. This brings us to some more fundamental concerns about weak ontology. In the end, two major problems press on White's account. First, it imposes on us a *political* model for ontological reflection, stifling all the others. Second, because of this, it becomes very difficult, if not impossible, to accommodate Taylor's question of how to align our ethical-political affirmations with an adequate ontology. This last claim may seem startling, given White's overall objective of sustaining ontological affirmation in the face of what we might call a postmodern climate. Let me explain.

White's implicit critique of employing familiar analytical distinctions (subject-object, fact-value, belief-reality, etc.) is that this does not fully acknowledge that we live in "late modern" times. As he says, "the sense of living in *late* modernity implies a greater awareness of the conventionality of much of what has been taken for certain in the modern West" (1997, 503, original emphasis). As we have just seen, at issue is the "assertive, disengaged self" as the incorporation of the "dominant ontological investments of modernity" (1997, 503). For present purposes, this means that the attempt to separate philosophical categories and domains is somewhat dated in the sense that a strict division between man and world, philosophical anthropology and metaphysics, ethics and ontology, etc., partakes of the (strong) ontology of the disengaged modern self rather than the (weak) ontology of the late modern sticky subject.

However, it is worth noting that although the *emphasis* has changed in the passage to late modernity—from a focus on the things "in themselves" to a focus on the human subject—the central question has remained the same: How does the human being relate to its world? As Thiebaut and Abbey have made plain, it is precisely the attempt to explore both the subjective and the objective elements of our human way of being in the world that defines Taylor's concern for the ontological preconditions of human subjectivity. The problem with White's analysis, then, is that even if it is true that all philosophical problems relate to the wider (weak-ontological) question of what it is to be human, it still is quick to conclude that *all* ontological questions can be discussed under the labels of human nature, philosophical anthropology, or weak ontology. Yet, as we have seen in the above discussions, this is precisely the objective of White's approach, namely to consider "too metaphysical" approaches to ontology to be excessive, originating from a bygone age. This is where the limits of weak ontology start to emerge.

The explicit nonmetaphysical thrust of White's approach reraises the suspicion (first expressed in section 2.1.3) that equating philosophical anthropology and ontology blocks out Taylor's most recent question of what we are committed to ontologically by our moral beliefs. That is, if it has become impossible in late modern times to accord either ethics or ontology or philosophical anthropology "clear primacy" because these domains appear as "mutually constitutive" rather than as distinct analytical categories, then how do we account for the *conflict* between moral phenomenology and naturalist ontology? (White 2005, 14) Put differently, if ontological commitments have become entangled with questions of identity and history to such an extent that we can no longer "cleanly separate self and foundation," then there seems to be no more space left to investigate the metaphysical reality behind this identity and history either (White 2005, 15). Confusingly, this is nonetheless one of the central points of White's weak ontology, which after all "demands from us the affirmative gesture of constructing foundations," albeit in a late modern, nonmetaphysical fashion (2000, 8).

As demonstrated in the present analysis, it is precisely by *differentiating* between various existential realities (anthropological, phenomenological, ethical, ontological) that the tension between moral experience and naturalist ontology becomes accessible. In this respect, what is striking about Taylor's ontology is that it neither deduces ontological givens from the social existence of values nor locates the source of ethics in a "strong" Platonic human-independent reality. White's nonmetaphysical perspective, on the other hand, seems to hold that what Taylor identifies as the metaphysical reality behind our strong values does not exist. Here we come up against the boundaries of White's interpretation of Taylor, for his distinction between strong and weak ontologies leaves room neither for the tension between ethics and ontology in a naturalist climate nor for the way in which Taylor defines his unique ontological position within this climate. That is, whereas White insists that "the cogency of weak ontology is not traceable to a sky hook or metaphysical anchor" (1997, 508), Taylor's concern is precisely the opposite, namely to trace the metaphysical source that makes best sense of our moral experience.

For all the interesting parallels between Taylor's interwoven strategy and White's perspective of stickiness, it seems clear that the challenges facing the late modern sticky subject cannot be made intelligible without "un-sticking" the different realities to which this subject belongs. Yet this result—that we first need to *dis*entangle our various commitments in order to appreciate the nature of their entanglement—seems more troublesome for White's argument than for the present analysis since it is crucial for weak ontology to take these entangled commitments as they are and to hold at bay all metaphysical anchors that could help to alleviate them. Perhaps the best way to move this important issue forward is through the following question: Which approach ultimately carries most *explanatory* force, one that insist on the stickiness and multiplicity of our commitments (White) or one that explores their boundaries by *confronting* them with one another (Taylor)? Difficulties start to emerge for White's weak ontology when we press on this issue of hermeneutic explanation. Although stressing the historical, cultural, and contestable character of weak-ontological commitments might add to the plausibility of entwining ontological reflection with political affirmation, the issue is just how much this explains.

Ultimately, White's view is that weak ontologies are "fundamental" conceptualizations despite their contestability because they are "nevertheless necessary or unavoidable for an adequately reflective ethical and political life" (2000, 8). As he explains, "fundamental conceptualization here thus means acknowledging that gaining access to something universal about human being and world is always also a construction that cannot rid itself of a historical dimension" (2000, 9). At first glance, White here simply seems to follow Taylor's view that we should be wary not to mix up human universals and historical constellations (Taylor 1989, 112). Yet there is also a decisive difference. What White's explanation of the contestability of weak ontology does not discuss is Taylor's belief that we essentially understand self, other, and world in terms of *strong* evaluations that generally refuse to be treated as contestable. The later Taylor makes this very clear:

> Our attributing these meanings makes a stronger claim. It lies in their nature as strong evaluations to claim truth, reality or objective rightness. [. . .] it can fail to occur on some occasions or in some people, but this betokens some limitation, blindness, or insensitivity on their part; in other words, there is something objectively right about this response. (2011b, 298, 300)

This means that even if our experiences and beliefs are contestable and radically undermined in their meanings, the background that makes sense of them is not. In this respect, we might also recall Taylor's claim that strong evaluations can be criticized for "misapprehending" the reality that they seek to describe (2011b, 297), and his Mandelbaumian/Heideggerian view that the experienced objectivity of moral demands cannot possibly come from human subjects alone (as explained in sections 4.2.2 and 5.2.2). In my reading, this is the distinctly *metaphysical* concern underlying Taylor's more politically sensitive claim that "high standards need strong sources" (1989, 516). Put simply, this shows that Taylor's ontology is not merely concerned with political theory, but also with metaphysics.

This point also explains why Taylor ultimately moves away from his initial human-focused perspective in pursuit of his nonanthropocentric position in "Ethics and Ontology," *A Secular Age*, and "Disenchantment-Reenchantment": because adopting a nonanthropocentric perspective breaks open the issue of how to *align* our most lucid self-understandings—either moral-phenomenological or philosophical-anthropological or weak-ontological—with an adequate metaphysics. It is therefore precisely the move beyond a mere weak-ontological perspective that enables Taylor to focus on the metaphysical reality behind moral experience.

For the weak ontologist, however, this move is "too" metaphysical. As a result, White's conception can include neither Taylor's view that the source of value lies beyond human control nor that his ontology freely crosses the boundaries between strong and weak ontologies in White's sense. Since he does not elaborate on this, I find it difficult to see what kind of balance White thinks he has struck by identifying Taylor's fundamental ethical-political orientation, on the one hand, and the recognition of the deeply contestable character of this foundation, on the other.

At this point, it may be helpful to realize that White and Taylor ultimately take their ontologies in opposite directions. Taylor's question is not which viable principles we can derive from ontological inquiry, but which ontology offers the best explanation of our ethical-political commitments. This begs the question of what deserves priority: ethics or ontology? For White, it does not seem to matter as he explicitly states that there is "no privileged starting place" in philosophical reflection (2000, 12, note 13). Taylor implicitly agrees with this view, since his interwoven mode of thought does not lend itself to any simple prioritizing. At the same time, it is clear that Taylor's nonanthropocentric ontologizing reaches beyond White's political project. Therefore, despite the clear parallels between both ontologies, Taylor ultimately adds an extra question—not the practical one of how we can sustain our policies but the more metaphysically sensitive one of what it is that implicitly informs and directs our moral and political claims and actions. The burden on weak ontology as a *philosophical* program, then, is that White's perspective would exclude questions that Taylor's meta-analysis opens up. Operating within a political mode of questioning, White would sustain the affirmations we have been given, whereas Taylor investigates what makes possible such affirmations at all.

Insightful and illuminating as it is, White's interpretation centers on only *one* of Taylor's many employments of the concept of ontology: the political one.[23] It should not surprise us, then, that his weak-ontological reading fails to acknowledge the full gamut of the issues to explore in Taylor's ontology, due to the somewhat rigid distinction between strong ontologies that show us "the way the world is" and weak ontologies that are not so "rooted in in a crystalline conviction of ultimate cognitive truth" (2000, 6; 1997, 506).

Despite these reservations regarding White's interpretation of Taylor's ontology, I do not intend to deny the overall importance of the weak-ontological approach, either for challenging liberal theories that ignore or suppress ontological reflection or for drawing attention to the cost of such strategies. My restricted aim here has been to highlight the need within White's analysis for a fuller account of the nonanthropocentric elements in Taylor's ontology. Until he resolves this issue, White's weak-ontological portrait will continue to be in tension with Taylor's metaphysical concerns for the reality underlying our weak conceptualizations.

5.3.4 Nonrealist Critiques

On the whole, White's weak-ontological reading can be seen as a *nonrealist* approach to Taylor's ontology, locating the source of value in human practices—and in those practices alone. Conversely and yet similarly, both Rosen and Rorty urge Taylor to adopt some form of nonrealism. I discuss their critiques in this final section as they illuminate the characteristic way in which Taylor both opposes and endorses nonrealism in elaborating his ontology.

In his paper "Must We Return to Moral Realism?" (1991), Rosen poses Taylor the question as to whether we must really "return" to moral realism after abandoning reductive naturalism. In so doing, he endorses Taylor's rejection of ethical naturalism but denies that this entails the rejection of nonrealism in defense of a "reasonable non-realist" conception of a social foundation for morality (Rosen 1991, 189). Rosen's argument has three steps. First, he shows how Taylor's moral realism has its foundation in moral phenomenology. Second, he argues that Taylor's moral phenomenology brings him rather close to nonrealism. Third, because of this, Rosen finally presses Taylor to abandon moral realism in favor of his own social version of nonrealism.

Rosen generally approves of Taylor's critique that at least some nonrealisms fail to do justice to the nature of moral experience. However, he continues, it is not self-evident that *all* forms of nonrealism fail to do so: "Is it really true, as Taylor suggests, that nonrealism cannot give an adequate account of the phenomenology of moral experience?" (1991, 188). Noting that nonrealists are bound to remain unsatisfied with Taylor's view since it ignores the more subtle forms of nonrealism that emerge from the works of Isaiah Berlin, Bernard Williams, and Philippa Foot (all of which provide nonreductive explanations of the nature of the good), Rosen nonetheless agrees with Taylor that "there is no justification for the way in which much contemporary Anglo-American philosophy unthinkingly equates the material and the physical with the real" (1991, 189). He then highlights two features of Taylor's ontology that are perfectly compatible with nonrealism. First, Taylor endorses the nonrealist's essential point that values depend on human existence, not on independent metaphysical entities, and, second, he asserts that moral debates may be open-ended since there are no moral truths beyond our own views and experiences (Rosen 1991, 189).

Rosen's final effort, then, is to convince Taylor of the plausibility of a "reasonable non-realism" that rejects both the "metaphysical independence of values" and the idea that this must lead to a "practical skepticism about the objectivity of moral discourse" (1991, 189). In this regard, he argues that moral relativism has very little impact in practice unless we have "reason to suspect that a genuine alternative to our own code exists," which, in Rosen's view, we do not (1991, 193). This position indeed comes very close to what I have been calling Taylor's *ad hominem* perspective (as elaborated in section 3.2), that is, his view that practical reason should start from an internal-evaluative viewpoint rather than take up an external, neutral perspective. As has been shown, as a philosophical anthropologist, Taylor argues that values such as benevolence and justice give us an anchor for practical reason because we would lose the very possibility of being an agent in the full sense without them. In this respect, Rosen and Taylor seem to agree that the absence of an extrahuman basis for judgment does not mean the collapse of ethical evaluation, since our strong adherence to these principles by itself provides sufficient ground for practical reasoning.

However, I also demonstrated that this *ad hominem* focus only partly informs Taylor's doctrine of strong evaluation, as he also explores morality in a nonanthropocentric fashion that reaches well beyond philosophical anthropology. In this way, I argued (in section 4.1) that Taylor's moral philosophy is best understood as a phenomenological clarification of both the "broad" and the "deep" character of morality. That is, Taylor is not just committed to a nonrealist conception of value as embedded in social practices as he also sees ethics through the lens of a Mandelbaumian and Murdochean image of morality that centers on objective moral demands and the sovereignty of good. As these points indicate, Taylor cannot accept the nonrealist view that there is no standard against which to measure the validity of moral beliefs but for the intersubjective preferences of a society. He rejects this outlook precisely because it neglects the reality that human beings principally respond in moral life to the call of demands that are experienced as objective, not intersubjective.

This means that, although Rosen and Taylor equally defend the nonrealist and antirelativist position that a social (or weak-ontological) foundation for morality is "objectively enough" to sustain our ethical-political views, for Taylor this is only the starting point of a more fundamental investigation into the metaphysical status of our values. This is where the allegiance with Rosen seems to end. In his view, it is neither necessary nor sufficient to look elsewhere than in the social realm for the source of value, as he sees the social foundation of morality as "the only possible way of finding a path between the impoverished subjectivity of disengaged reason and the impossible yearning for the ontic logos" (Rosen 1991, 194).

On the whole, Rosen's nonrealist proposal can be seen as a rejection of Taylor's idea that strong evaluations aim at objective rightness rather than intersubjective equilibrium. Rorty attacks Taylor on similar grounds, arguing that Taylor makes "little attempt to explore the possibility of a *non*-reductive naturalism" (1994, 197, original emphasis). In Rorty's view, Taylor's mistake is that he sees "not only naturalism but the Enlightenment itself as intrinsically and necessarily reductive" (1994, 198). Because of this, Rorty continues, Taylor ignores that we can in fact *harmonize* "Enlightenment and Romantic themes" by allowing, on the one hand, that human beings are "indeed, self-interpreting beings, and consequently not Cartesianly transparent," while insisting, on the other hand, that human self-interpretations are "at their best when they are social" (Rorty 1994, 199). In Rorty's view, then, a social-political proposal such as Dewey's provides precisely the intermediate basis in between reductive naturalism and Romantic expressivism that Taylor is looking for: "Why should not the *social* creative imagination be a hypergood? What is wrong with Dewey as an example of how to be both an anti-reductive naturalist and social romantic" (1994, 199, original emphasis)?

These are valid questions indeed. In this respect, Taylor's wholesale neglect of a contemporary follower of Dewey such as Hilary Putnam is telling, since Putnam has been occupying the exact same middle ground between Platonic moral realism and projectivist naturalism by defending a historically sensitive pluralistic moral realism in works with titles such as *The Many Faces of Realism* (Putnam 1987), *Realism With a Human Face* (Putnam 1990), and *The Collapse of the Fact/Value Distinction* (Putnam 2002).[24] As Putnam pursues a project that Taylor should *applaud* both as a moral realist and as a critic of naturalism, it is somewhat surprising that Taylor scarcely refers to Putnam's arguments at all. In my view, this is a missed opportunity because a clear explanation of the subtle differences from Putnam would allow Taylor to be more articulate about his *own* ontological views.[25]

Resuming our initial discussion, then, Rorty's suspicion is that Taylor ignores a pragmatist view such as Putnam's because it is "just not enough to satisfy our *moral realist* urges" (Rorty 1994, 200, original emphasis). He then rightly points out that Taylor generally neglects pragmatist philosophers in favor of Romanticist thinkers such as Rilke and Heidegger (1994, 200). Rejecting the nonanthropocentrism in Taylor's thought, both Rosen and Rorty ultimately urge him to take more seriously the question as to what remains of our moral sense once we cease to believe in this idea that the world makes demands on us and begin to think of the human being as social and self-creating rather than as standing in contact with some extrahuman reality. Yet is that all there is to Taylor's ontology? Is it simply a nostalgic yearning for the ontic logos? I think not. And I think that, while it is true that Taylor does not invest as much effort into nonreductive ontologies as he should— especially pragmatist ones—it is also true that there is no justification for the lack of willingness among his critics to take Taylor's nonanthropocentrism seriously. This is precisely the thrust of Taylor's replies to Rosen and Rorty. With regard to the latter, Taylor admits to being still somewhat embarrassed by Rorty's questions, yet he clearly states that he does not want to stop at "Deweyan social-democracy" because, as Taylor explains, it remains doubtful that Dewey even saw "the issue that I'm here trying to delineate about constitutive goods" (1994b, 211).

This means, in other words, that whereas it is obvious to Taylor that naturalistic views are mistaken and pragmatic ones incomplete, he himself still lacks a more illuminating ontological theory that shows these views to be inadequate. Taylor's reply to Rosen is especially revealing in this respect. In fact, this is the only text in which he explicates the connection between his (human-focused) philosophical-anthropological and moral-phenomenological views, on the one hand, and his (nonanthropocentric) ontological and theistic views, on the other:

> I would want to say something roughly like this: ethics tries to define the shape of the human moral predicament. But there would not be such a thing unless human beings existed. Once we exist, certain ways of being are higher than others in virtue of the way we are (the "Aristotelian" component); certain demands are made on us by other human beings in virtue of the way both we and they are (the "moral" component). [. . .] *I would want to add:* certain demands are made on us by our world in virtue of what we are and how we fit into it (the "ecological" component). And further, I believe that certain goods arise out of our relation to God (the "theological" component). (1991, 245, italics mine)

This at least partly explains Taylor's inward-outward focus in between a human-focused and a nonanthropocentric viewpoint. That is, since he believes that incommensurably higher values originate from a *triangular* relationship between self, other, and world, he has been developing an ontological perspective that allows him to straddle and explore the boundaries of these realities rather than to stop at their limits. However, for nonrealists such as Rosen and Rorty, it is precisely this concern for a moral reality "beyond" human life that causes problems. For Taylor, then, this debate can be opened up only by clarifying the ontological implications of our moral *language*. He argues:

> I have not got the space to set out my (rather hazy) views on this. [. . .] The demand has something to do with what we are as language beings on the one hand, and with the way we as language beings fit into and emerge from our world on the other. [. . .] I want to speak of this demand as something that we discover. And so I want to go on thinking of myself as a moral realist, even though I am uncomfortably aware of Rosen's urging that we both occupy a kind of middle ground between the old Platonic model and naturalist projectivism. (1991, 246)

As we have seen (in section 5.2.2), the problems of Taylor's ontology generally emerge from his Heidegger-inspired picture of morality as "human-related" but not "human-controlled"—what he calls above the "ecological" component of his ontology.[26] That is, he concedes with nonrealists that values make sense in *relation* to us, but then adds that this does not mean that they are necessarily *dependent* on us. Borrowing a term from Thiebaut (1993, 134), this feeds into the "double, simultaneous movement" that values appear only *within* human experience, but that we come up against a *human-transcendent* reality within this experience. Taylor has elaborated on how these elements relate in an interview:

> The concept "independent of human beings" is an ambiguous concept and I maybe did not make it clear enough. If it means that in a world without human beings there would be a right or wrong action, then this is obviously hard to make sense of. If it, however, means something like: there is something beyond

human beings and the best realistic take is to say that we owe something to it, or that we receive a call from it, then how could one ever say that *a priori*? It is just something that one has to see by looking at the way you could best make sense of your most profound and believable moral experience. My personal feeling is that there is something like that. (Taylor in: Rosa and Laitinen 2002, 187)

Although this explanation is slightly more revealing than earlier ones, Taylor's admission that he is expressing a "personal feeling" when saying that moral experience refers to a transcendent source makes a rather thin philosophical argument. This brings us straight back to his unprovable "hunch" that theistic perspectives might be more adequate than nontheistic ones to the affirmation of human beings as worthy of respect and benevolence (1989, 518)—what he calls above the "theological" component of his ontology (1991, 245). The problem is that unless Taylor clarifies his nonanthropocentrism, his ontology will remain incomplete and unconvincing, at best, and misleading and distorting, at worst. However—even in his late eighties—Taylor's work continues to develop. Against the background of the present analysis it should no longer surprise us that, after his attacks on naturalist ontology, his hesitant defense of moral realism, his unease with pragmatist nonrealism, and his tentative exploration of the nonanthropocentric background of our moral language, Taylor's latest projects are, first, to retrieve a more robust type of realism, and, second, to reclaim the full shape of the human linguistic capacity.

5.4 TAYLOR THE HERMENEUTIST

There remain only two more texts that could illuminate Taylor's ontology: *Retrieving Realism* (2015) and *The Language Animal* (2016). Unfortunately for our purposes, the former avoids rather than clarifies the ontology of strong evaluation. Given Taylor's concern for the tension between what he calls the "upper" language of strong evaluation and the "lower" language of post-Galilean science (2011b, 300), it is somewhat disappointing that his defense of "robust realism" argues for the objectivity of the (lower) languages of science, rather than investigating the (upper) languages of ethics. However, although *Retrieving Realism* largely repeats Taylor's well-known view about embodied agency, it also sheds a new light on the present analysis as he presents his position now in distinctive *pluralistic* terms, arguing for a "pluralistic robust realism" (2015, 154). Moreover, Taylor continues to clarify his arguments in *The Language Animal*, in this case by explicitly referring to issues of "strong evaluation" in developing his view that moral language introduces certain "metabiological" meanings in our world (2016, 192, 195). In elaborating on this, Taylor argues, first, that metabiological meanings require us to define ethics in an unusually encompassing sense; second, that this broader understanding of Ethics (with an intentional capital letter) lucidly shows that moral meanings are rooted in objective, rather than subjective, forces; and, third, that reason in this domain must be hermeneutical. In a final attempt to clarify Taylor's ontology, I first discuss *Retrieving Realism* (section 5.4.1) and then conclude by examining *The Language Animal* (section 5.4.2).

5.4.1 Taylor the Realist

The present discussion demonstrates Taylor's tentative ontological view: unless ethical naturalism is able to reveal the nonrealist nature of incommensurably higher values, we have to accept a certain kind of moral realism, that is, one that acknowledges the complex nature of our values as both human related and human transcendent. In *Sources of the Self*, Taylor labels this view the "Best Account principle" (1989, 58). This principle has one major disadvantage: the mere fact that something is the best explanation at a given time does not necessarily make this explanation justified.[27] However, in *Retrieving Realism* Taylor pronounces a stronger argument for his view. That is, he no longer poses a mere principle but defends a "robust" type of realism by having recourse to what he calls a "contact theory" (2015, 17, 132).

Taylor contrasts his contact view with "mediational" Cartesian epistemology that misunderstands knowledge as "arising through some mediational element" (generally understood as internal representations of some external reality), while also showing that contemporary figures such as Willard Quine, Richard Rorty, Donald Davidson, and Hilary Putnam still rely on a similar inner-outer opposition in terms of a "mental-physical" distinction (2015, 10–11, 17, 40–43, 132). For present purposes, I will not delve into the specifics of Taylor's renewed views on epistemology. Rather, I am assuming a familiarity with his embodied-engaged view and turn instead to the realist position that results from it in the last three chapters of *Retrieving Realism*. Intriguingly, as will emerge, Taylor defines his realism in a way that confronts him with problems he already encountered—fifty-six years earlier—in his first paper on ontology (1959). Notwithstanding his subtle attempt to redefine "realism" in a way that avoids "reductive," "scientific," and "deflationary" realism all in one (2015, 160), it would nonetheless seem that Taylor's defense of the objectivity of science is largely irrelevant in understanding his *moral* realism. This is because he makes it very clear elsewhere (1989, 8) that science and ethics must be looked at in their own right, since these are radically different approaches to reality that analyze human life in their own separate ways. In fact, the tension between moral phenomenology and naturalist ontology emerges precisely from the incompatibility of these different languages.

Against this background, it is disappointing that *Retrieving Realism* does not explain how Taylor's defense of the objectivity of both the natural and the human sciences relates to his principal *hermeneutical* argument that human agency cannot (and should not) be understood exclusively in scientific terms. Nor does it clarify the nonanthropocentric background of our moral beliefs and actions in any detail. In this respect, it is telling that Taylor uses only nonmoral examples to make the case that we check our claims against reality, such as looking at a crooked picture and counting chairs (2015, 58, 67).

Implicitly, though, Taylor endorses the phenomenology of Samuel Todes in a way that might indeed clarify his ontology, but since he refers to Todes mainly in relation to sensory perception and bodily orientation, we can only speculate. Taylor argues that we have to "align ourselves with the causal powers of the physical universe to perceive at all," and that the universe in this way "constrains us to get in sync with it, and rewards us with sight only insofar as we conform to its demands" (2015, 135). In this way, we "interact" with reality by "balancing" ourselves in view of the demands that reality imposes on us. In this sense, Taylor explains, our perception can be seen as human related but not human controlled: "The phenomenon of balance shows us that the determination of objects depends on us, but that we can effect this determination *only insofar as we align ourselves with a truly independent reality*" (2015, 137, italics mine).

Although Taylor himself seems reluctant to take this step, it is at least tempting to extend this phenomenological account of bodily orientation to moral orientation; that is, to apply it to his picture of *morality* as human related but not human controlled. In this way, we might wonder: If Taylor's robust realism shows that we must align ourselves with a "truly independent reality" to have normal *perceptual* experiences, does that also mean that we must embrace a truly independent moral reality to have ordinary *moral* experiences? At any rate, the existence of such a moral-phenomenological "fact of the matter" would at once explain how phenomenological claims feed into ontological ones, and, moreover, how moral reactions can be faulty and inadequate and need correction. Contrary to this suggestion, though, the closing chapter of *Retrieving Realism* ("Chapter 8: Plural Realism") seems to underline the boundaries of Todes' phenomenology. Instead of extending the metaphor of bodily balance to moral orientation, Taylor makes room for *multiple* independent accounts of reality, that is, "one describing those aspects of nature as it is in itself revealed to detached observers, and another account of reality as it is revealed to involved human beings" (2015, 153).

Suggesting that there is a "plurality of revealing perspectives on the world," Taylor implicitly reraises his initial topic of how to salvage conflicting ontological commitments and his claim that the "lower language" of scientific explanation should not dictate the "upper language" of ethical and hermeneutical inquiry (2015, 154; 2011b, 300). However, whereas the young Taylor concludes that "we are still perplexed when we try to understand the relations between what we talk about in one stratum and what we talk about in others" (1959, 139), the later Taylor allows for at least three possible ways of solving this problem. The first is to accept that rival accounts of reality are simply "dealing with quite different questions," that is, insofar as "the answers to one don't impinge in any way on our theories about the other," for example "as some people suggest is the case between the issues of natural science and those of religious faith" (2015, 158). A second solution is that "one approach might just supersede the other, showing it to be inadequate," for example "as post-Galilean mechanics relegated Aristotle's theory of motion" (2015, 158). The third, most radical solution is that "one science might offer a general theory, of which the valid findings of the other could be construed as special cases," for example "as Einstein's theory supersedes and includes Newton's laws of motion" (2015, 158). However, when it comes to explaining *human* behavior, Taylor loses no time in rejecting the second and third options:

> Scientists and philosophers have, after all, so far failed to reconcile mechanical theories of physical reality with the seemingly undeniable facts of free will, consciousness, and meaning. Convergence in all these cases would certainly be satisfying [. . .] but we have to leave open the possibility that there is no single privileged way nature works. (2015, 153)

This leaves Taylor only the first option of embracing a plurality of revealing perspectives on the human world, all of which may be true. That is, while the young Taylor already concedes that "we have ceased to say that some particular language is the 'real' way to talk about things" (1959, 139), the later Taylor takes this idea to its final conclusion by arguing that "one has be a pluralist where essences are concerned" (2015, 153). This is where the closing chapter of *Retrieving Realism* picks up both the analysis of "Ontology" about rivaling languages and ontologies and that of "Ethics and Ontology" about the tension between moral experience and naturalist ontology. Taylor brings these inquiries together when he says that the notion of plural correct descriptions of reality stages "the broader question of whether an account of physical nature as meaningless can be reconciled with an account of the cosmos as having a meaning and human beings having a privileged place in it" (2015, 158). For Taylor the plural realist, then, there is no uncertainty, contradiction, or puzzlement in the idea that there could in principle be many such irreducible and incompatible perspectives on the world.

Difficulties arise, however, when we note that this "pluralistic robust realist" affirmation of "*many* languages each correctly describing a different aspect of reality" (2015, 154, original emphasis) is in stark contrast to the more critical perspective developed in "Ethics and Ontology," *A Secular Age,* and "Disenchantment-Reenchantment." As we have seen, these texts argue that naturalist ontology can be shown to be *wrong* on account of moral phenomenology. Here Taylor moves closer to the "superseding" way of salvaging our different languages of self-understanding at the expense of the more pluralistic option of accepting different ontologies. In other words, he presses the idea that one superior approach (in this case, moral phenomenology) can be used to show the inadequacy of others (in this case, naturalist ontology). Far from simply accepting the ontological gap between them, Taylor here demands from us that we *either* enrich our naturalist ontology *or* revise our moral phenomenology to solve the problem of their relationship (2003, 310, 312; 2007, 609).

Anticipating this objection, though, Taylor seems to espouse a more critical line of reasoning on the closing pages of *Retrieving Realism.* Reflecting on the pluralistic character of his realism in the human sciences, he asserts that "not every culture's sense of what is good seems equally acceptable" (2015, 162). Surprisingly, here we find Taylor returning to Todes' phenomenology of balance to explore its relevance for moral theory after all. He asks: "What elements or insights are so solid that they would have to be incorporated into any view of the human essence and the human good which we could find believable" (2015, 164)? Taylor then explores this possibility by applying Todes' account of bodily orientation to issues of human nature:

> Whatever interpretation a culture gives of the place of human beings in a wider reality, it may have to incorporate some sense of having to conform to a power outside our control that requires us to get in sync with it and rewards us when we do. [. . .] It may be that any ethical sense of the good, and any moral sense of the right, and especially any religious sense of indebtedness to a power beyond our control, has to conform to these essential features of our specifically human form of embodiment. (2015, 165–66)

Notwithstanding the exploratory manner in which Taylor makes these last points, this mode of thought brings him closer to the idea of a superseding theory or even of an all-inclusive view than to the pluralist recognition of different perspectives. It should not surprise us, then, that Taylor's final message is not about embracing pluralism but that "there remain deep differences in basic ontology" (2015, 167). The problem is that this restates rather than dissolves the issue of what we are committed to ontologically by our ethical views.

5.4.2 Taylor the Language Theorist

One of the most difficult interpretive challenges in explaining Taylor's ontology is that, although he has consistently been trying to forsake language theory for ontological inquiry since the publication of "Ontology," this move has been guiding as much as confusing Taylor's thinking as a whole. It is here, I think—in the way in which Taylor's conception of language colors and shapes his ontology—that the gaps within his interwoven mode of argumentation start to emerge. In line with his early view that ontological questions not only arise in substantive expressions but also "in connection with concepts in their use as predicates" (1959, 128), Taylor aims to extrapolate ontological claims from our moral concepts most crucially in reference to Heidegger. He says, for example, that Heidegger's philosophy of language establishes that "our use of language is no longer arbitrary, up for grabs, a matter of our own feelings and purposes" because "the purposes in question are not simply human" (1995c, 124, 126). In fact, since "our goals here are fixed by something we should properly see ourselves as serving," a "proper" understanding of our purposes *has* to take us "beyond ourselves" (1995c, 126). However, even in the autumn of Taylor's career, we can only guess how his implicit endorsement of Heidegger's idea of "language speaking" rather than "human beings speaking" informs his ontology (1995c, 101). Because of this, Taylor's double, simultaneous movement from a human-focused hermeneutics to a nonanthropocentric ontology is underdemonstrated, indeed, rather metaphorically argued for.

Given this history, it is perhaps no coincidence that Taylor takes up his undeveloped language theory in his latest work, *The Language Animal*. In this book, he first restates his earlier "Romantic" view on language (as elaborated in "Heidegger, Language, and Ecology") by taking his cue from the "constitutive" theory that sees language as introducing "new meanings in our world" and as opening us to "issues of strong value," that is, "value independent of our recognition" (2016, 37, 195). Taylor then explicitly applies the constitutive view on language to strong evaluation when he says that some of our terms invoke certain "metabiological" meanings that are involved in our experience of strong value (2016, 192). These points set the stage for Taylor's definition of Ethics with a capital "E," which largely restates his earlier view (as explained in section 4.1) that a proper understanding of ethics includes principles of obligatory action as well as a sense of the virtues, goods, and sources that define the good life for us (2016, 201–15). As it turns out, this broad understanding of Ethics brings us right back to the topic of adequate sources (as explained in section 5.1.2) as Taylor uses it to reraise the—highly contentious—issue whether our values are best understood in theistic or nontheistic terms. He argues:

> An issue arises in relation to all these sources. How do they strengthen us? Is it just that they trigger some highly positive reaction in us? Or do they really impart force? For believers, in relation to the religious sources just mentioned,

clearly the latter is felt to be the case. But what is it with the inspirations from Nature and Art? When I am moved by Nature, is that just a fact about me (or less subjectively, about most human beings)? Or is there some force running through Nature which I am tapping into, opening myself to? (2016, 213–14)

Taylor's new claim, then, is not that this issue arises for believers and non-believers alike, but that we "frequently have a sense, in recognizing these sources, of which it is," that is, we have a sense of "which reading, the subjective or the objective, is the right one" (2016, 214, 249). Although there is no doubt that this is the context in which Taylor's nonanthropocentrism starts to make sense—as both believers and Romanticists direct us toward "transpersonal" sources (2016, 214)—it is also the point where his ontological uncertainties emerge in full force. Taylor admits, first, that such nonanthropocentric sources are "often ontically very indefinite," and, second, that "this sense of an independent reality will often be accompanied by the doubt which is inseparable from faith" (2016, 214). Yet despite these reservations, Taylor still sees a structure that applies to all human beings, either religious or nonreligious:

> There is a structure which is constant here, through all the variations in Ethical outlook: we experience a call, be it from our own nature, or from our noumenal self, or from the nature of reality, or from God; we respond to this in trying to live better, and/or in trying to overcome our limitations and blindness, and/or in striving to come closer to God. [. . .] We might surmise that this structure of call and response is present throughout human history. (2016, 215, 216)

Taylor's analysis then continues the line of "Ontology," "Ethics and Ontology," *A Secular Age*, "Disenchantment-Reenchantment," and *Retrieving Realism* when he adds that this universal experience of a "call" raises the vital question "whether some of our intuitions are *consistent* with others, equally strongly held" (2016, 216, italics mine). Although his initial sense of "perplexity" in the face of this problem remains in the background of his analysis, Taylor is in no doubt that reason in this domain cannot but be "hermeneutical" since there are no "knockdown arguments" in making sense of human action (2016, 211, 217). In elaborating on this, he emphasizes that explaining human actions and responses requires not only "identifying their causes" but also "making the actions/responses understandable," and that his own attempt to do so in terms of strong evaluation obviously appeals to "the tradition of empathetic understanding (*Verstehen*) invoked for human sciences since Wilhelm Dilthey," and pursued by figures such as Weber, Heidegger, Gadamer, and Ricoeur (2016, 212, 214, 217, 218).

With these points in place, we can rephrase Taylor's attack on naturalist ontology as an attempt to "make understandable" a *particular* feature of our action—in this case, moral experience—in the light of the overall meaning of the *whole*—in this case, the broader ontological context within which our actions take place. This tactic clearly underlines the hermeneutical nature of Taylor's argument as it follows a logic that is often referred to as the "hermeneutical circle," that is, to "use the sense of the whole to make sense of the part"—just as in the original context of hermeneutics as textual interpretation, where a reading of a particular passage or verse has to make sense in the context of the entire chapter, and ultimately, of the whole book (2016, 218). As we have seen at length, Taylor effectively applies this hermeneutical reasoning to human action by developing a phenomenological explanation of moral experience only for the ontological purpose of examining the metaphysical background of our actions.

Although Taylor's hermeneutical approach is bound to disappoint those seeking knockdown arguments, he nonetheless manages to raise the important question whether we understand fully the meaning of "the whole," that is, the meaning of the ontological framework that makes our actions understandable. Yet even if Taylor claims that our experience as moral agents should lead us to correct the implicit naturalist ontology in our self-understanding, as a hermeneutist, he has no problem in acknowledging that it is perfectly possible to argue in the other direction as well. As he explains, the challenge of the hermeneutical circle is precisely to *balance* potential arguments in *both* directions into an equilibrium in which one makes "maximum sense" of the issues involved (2016, 218). The upshot of this method is—in the ethical domain as much as the ontological—that we are in need of felicitous descriptions: "We explain properly, we make sense of the action/response, when we add to, or complexify, the range of meanings or motivations actually operating here" (2016, 217).

Given these points, Taylor ultimately argues that the domain of metabiological meanings has "its own kind of independent reality," that is, "not that of self-standing objects, but of strong value" (2016, 262). Intriguingly, he implicitly endorses his pluralistic robust realism by making this very claim. In *Retrieving Realism*, Taylor already alludes to a need for "two independent accounts of reality," one of detached observation, and another of involved coping (2015, 153). As a language theorist, then, he strategically makes room for these different accounts by arguing for two different semantic logics, one "designative-instrumental" and another "constitutive expressive," corresponding to two different kinds of "descriptive rightness" that invoke different kinds of independence (2016, 4, 261).

The designative logic is rooted in the rational empiricist tradition of Hobbes, Locke, and Condillac, which sees language as a tool for encoding and communicating information, and endorses the "standard" kind of descriptive rightness of "attributing properties" (2016, 261). The constitutive logic, then, goes back to the thinking of the German Romantics Hamann, Herder, and Humboldt, and asserts that language does not simply describe but also constitutes meaning, and is committed to a "self-articulative" kind of rightness, which "clarifies and transforms the space of human meanings" (2016, 261–62). In fact, Taylor explains, it was the distinctively rigorous approach of the designative theory that has helped to make the distinction between the two major logics more visible. That is, because of the strong concern for clear and consistent definitions, the designative theory—deeply influenced by the "paradigms of post-Galilean natural science"—helped to make clear that there are "contrast cases (e.g., human meanings) which it doesn't fit," that is, "phenomena which are not simply given as are the states of affairs through which we validate our scientific theories," and which, therefore, require an entirely different logic (2016, 259).

If anything, Taylor's distinction between designative and constitutive reason indicates that he has abandoned his earlier project of showing that one superior logic can be used to invalidate others. That is, whereas Taylor explicitly draws attention to the flaws of naturalist ontology on the basis of his moral phenomenology in earlier writings, his renewed language theory concludes that the realities that these different accounts invoke are best understood as essentially incompatible. This means that Taylor, as a language theorist, has definitively opted for the pluralistic recognition of multiple explanatory languages, thereby ruling out the possibility—still open in "Ethics and Ontology," *A Secular Age,* "Disenchantment-Reenchantment," and *Retrieving Realism*—that one superior language could "supersede" the other (2015, 158). This is of theoretical importance, because it marks a shift in emphasis in Taylor's understanding of the relationship between ethics and ontology. That is, instead of criticizing naturalist ontology by having recourse to moral phenomenology, he now has come to accept that rival accounts of reality are "dealing with quite different questions," questions that concern either our "biological" or our "metabiological" relation to the cosmos (2015, 158; 2016, 344). In this way, naturalists and hermeneutists can simultaneously uphold their positions without invading each other's views.

Yet there still remains an issue here. The problem is that naturalistic and hermeneutical approaches to ethics and ontology—far from being concerned with different questions—make claims about the *same* subject matter, and therefore do impinge on each other's theories. As Taylor himself makes clear in debunking naturalism, this is where the tension between naturalistic ontological commitments and moral experience becomes visible, and where the battle between naturalists and hermeneutists breaks out. Yet neither Taylor's robust realism nor his language theory clarifies how hermeneutical reason might help to *solve* this conflict. In fact, his affirmation of plural revealing perspectives only *intensifies* the problem of their relationship and does nothing to fill the ontological gaps between them.

In this respect, Taylor's major question of "whether the values we espouse can be supported on the basis of the ontology to which we want to subscribe" remains unanswered (2003, 318). It is clear, though, that by drawing a final distinction between two major independent realities and logics, Taylor has definitively given up on the "hoped-for-reconciliation" between moral phenomenology and naturalist ontology (2003, 320). But, I would like to add, *as a hermeneutist*, he has good reason to do so. Taylor concludes by underlining the importance of the designative-constitutive distinction:

> We need this in order to avoid, on one hand, the Scylla of declaring, for example, ethics a realm of purely subjective judgments or projections, and on the other, the Charybdis of imposing an alien model of rationality on them. It becomes evident that reason in this domain must take a largely hermeneutical turn; and this brings with it a certain endlessness, a resistance to completion, the impossibility of resting in some supposedly "final" and unimprovable conclusion. Much more needs to be said on this topic, but I hope that this book helps to make a start. (2016, 338)

With these points in place, we must conclude that Taylor's most revealing writings about ontology are also the most problematic ones. These are then the main features of his ontology:

1. It sees ontological problems as unavoidable, yet unanswerable (1959).
2. It covers issues of language theory (1959; 1995c; 2016), philosophical anthropology (1985b, d; 1989), ethics (1989; 1996/2011; 2011b; 2016), epistemology (1995d, e), political theory (1995a), ecology (1995c), phenomenology (2003; 2007), science, realism (2015) and, at the background of all of these, metaphysics.
3. It culminates in the problem of what ontology can underpin our moral experience and results in a tentative defense of the nonanthropocentric origin of value combined with a strong incentive to revise naturalist ontology in favor of moral phenomenology.
4. On the one hand, these views are in line with both Taylor's pluralistic robust realism, which argues for multiple correct descriptions of reality, and his distinction between two major semantic logics that invoke different kinds of independent reality.
5. On the other hand, it leaves his guiding question of what we are committed to ontologically by our ethical views fundamentally undecided. But even if it is by accident, this result is still consistent with the intuition that launched Taylor's ontology from the very beginning: that this question is unanswerable.

NOTES

1. Originally published as Taylor, Charles. 1999. *A Catholic Modernity? Charles Taylor's Marianist Award Lecture*. Edited by James L Heft. New York: Oxford University Press; and reprinted in *Dilemmas and Connections* (2011a, 167–87). I refer to the latter version.

2. Some examples are Williams (1990, 45–48), Hittinger (1990, 125), Skinner (1991, 133, 147–50), Shklar (1991, 105–09), Lane (1992, 46–48), O'Hagan (1993, 74, 81), De Sousa (1994, 121), and Olafson (1994, 193–95).

3. The discussion in section 5.1.2 first appeared in Meijer (2017a).

4. (Parts of) the discussions in sections 5.1.2 and 5.2.2 first appeared in Meijer (2017a) and Meijer (2017b), respectively.

5. I discuss the relation between Taylor's "Ontology" (1959), "Ethics and Ontology" (2003), and *Retrieving Realism* (2015), and the realist position that results from these texts, in more detail in Meijer (2019).

6. "Much of what he says about the character of our moral experience seems to me, up to this point, importantly true, and any adequate account of morality must try to explain it" (Williams 1990, 48).

7. Note that on these very pages Skinner finds it perfectly acceptable to describe religious persons as "grossly irrational" and as "suffering from some serious form of psychological blockage or self-deceit" (1991, 148). This shameless way of mocking people's beliefs while at the same time judging Taylor for having no doubts makes one question the dangerous double standard Skinner is applying here.

8. I have explored some of these in Meijer (2017a).

9. Initially identified as the "third" problem of Taylor's theism at the beginning of section 5.1.2.

10. Most explicitly stated in "Ethics and Ontology" (2003).

11. I discuss these books in more detail in section 5.4.

12. In the period between "Ontology" (1959) and *Philosophical Papers* (1985c), Taylor wrote his *Hegel* (1975), in which ontological issues are also central. In trying to produce a clear account of Taylor's doctrine of strong evaluation, I do not have the scope in this study to examine Taylor's reading of Hegel directly. Yet it is worth emphasizing that he takes a critical distance precisely from the *ontological* status of Hegel's view. As Taylor notes in the concluding chapter of *Hegel*, "his ontological vision is not ours—indeed seems to deny the very problem as we now understand it" (1975, 571). In fact, Hegel's thesis that "the Absolute must finally come to complete, explicit clarity in conceptual statement" stands in stark contrast to Taylor's own Herder-inspired position, for whom "the unreflective experience of our situation can never be fully explicated" (1975, 568–69). Thanks to Guy Vanheeswijck for pointing this out.

13. The term "ontology of the human" occurs only once in *Sources of the Self* (on p. 5); "moral ontology" appears slightly more often (on pp. 8–10, 41 and 72). Besides these scarce occurrences, it is most revealing of their minor importance that Taylor drops these terms altogether after *Sources of the Self*. In this regard, it would

seem that Smith, who writes in his conclusion that "one of Taylor's chief aims is to rehabilitate the idea of an ontology of the human," reads too much into this concept (2002, 237).

14. As we will see (in section 5.4.1), this broad scope anticipates Taylor's latest "robust realism both in the natural and the human sciences" (2015, 148).

15. In *Retrieving Realism*, Taylor also criticizes Rorty, Davidson, and Putnam for being held captive by the same ontological picture in their implicit endorsement of a "mental-physical" distinction (2015, 10–11, 17, 40–43, 132).

16. This raises the important question whether Taylor's ontologizing makes any progress in his latest book on language theory, *The Language Animal* (2016). I discuss this work in section 5.4.2.

17. The only discussion I have found is a conference paper by Nigel Desouza, entitled "Charles Taylor and Ethical Naturalism" and announced for publication in *Charles Taylor at 80*, edited by Daniel Weinstock and Jacob Levy (Montreal: McGill-Queens University Press). In line with the present analysis, Desouza characterizes "Ethics and Ontology" as a paper that raises the issue of naturalism in a way that sees Taylor "moving beyond the discussion in *Sources of the Self*." His claim is that Taylor has not taken seriously enough John McDowell's and David Wiggins' innovative understandings of naturalism, which, Desouza argues, allow for the kind of reconciliation between ethics and ontology that Taylor in fact should applaud.

18. He concludes: "Here, on the brink of the really interesting question, I have to break off, partly through lack of time; and partly because the conceptual means at my disposal are still too crude to explore this in an illuminating fashion. I hope to return to this at another time" (Taylor 2003, 320).

19. This discussion first appeared in Meijer (2017c).

20. The quotations are from Taylor's papers "Cross-Purposes: The Liberal-Communitarian Debate" (1995a, 185) and "Explanation and Practical Reason" (1995b, 39).

21. The quotations are from *Sources of the Self* (1989, 491–93, 512–13).

22. I discuss this in more detail in section 3.3.

23. Instructive of White's political perspective is that his analysis of Taylor's ontology (2000, 42) is launched by a quotation from the paper "Cross-Purposes: The Liberal-Communitarian Debate" (Taylor 1995a).

24. This also explains why Martha Nussbaum considers Putnam and Taylor as equal "close relatives" of her internal-evaluative approach (Nussbaum 1992, 243, note 12).

25. I return to this issue in the Conclusion.

26. In this respect, it is telling that Taylor's reply to Rosen refers to his (at that time forthcoming) paper "Heidegger, Language, and Ecology" for a more detailed explanation of his views on these matters (Taylor 1991, 254, note 4).

27. Note that Taylor himself implicitly acknowledges this weakness by arguing for the inescapability of strong evaluation via transcendental justification on top of his Best Account principle.

REFERENCES

Abbey, Ruth. 2000. *Charles Taylor*. Teddington/Princeton: Acumen Press/Princeton University Press.
Blackburn, Simon. 1998. *Ruling Passions: A Theory of Practical Reasoning*. Oxford: Clarendon Press.
De Lara, Phillipe 1998. "From Philosophical Anthropology to the Politics of Recognition: an Interview with Charles Taylor." *Thesis Eleven* 52: 103–12.
De Sousa, Ronald. 1994. "Bashing the Enlightenment: A Discussion of Charles Taylor's *Sources of the Self*." *Dialogue* 33: 109–23.
Desouza, Nigel. forthcoming. "Charles Taylor and Ethical Naturalism." In *Charles Taylor at 80*, edited by Daniel Weinstock and Jacob Levy. Montreal: McGill-Queens University Press.
Flanagan, Owen. 1996. *Self Expressions. Mind, Morals, and the Meaning of Life*. New York/Oxford: Oxford University Press.
Hittinger, Russell. 1990. "Critical Study: Charles Taylor, *Sources of the Self*." *Review of Metaphysics* 44 (September).
Johnston, Paul. 1999. *The Contradictions of Modern Moral Philosophy. Ethics after Wittgenstein*. London/New York: Routledge.
Kerr, Fergus. 2004. "The Self and the Good. Taylor's Moral Ontology." In *Contemporary Philosophy in Focus: Charles Taylor*, edited by Ruth Abbey, 84–104. Cambridge, MA: Cambridge University Press.
Lane, Melissa. 1992. "God or Orienteering? A Critical Study of Taylor's *Sources of the Self*." *Ratio* 5: 46–56.
Meijer, Michiel. 2017a. "Does Charles Taylor Have a Nietzsche Problem?" *Constellations: An International Journal of Critical and Democratic Theory*, 2017, 24 (3): 372–86.
Meijer, Michiel. 2017b. "Human-Related, not Human-Controlled: Charles Taylor on Ethics and Ontology." *International Philosophical Quarterly*, 57 (3): 267–85.
Meijer, Michiel. 2017c. "Is Charles Taylor (Still) a Weak Ontologist?" *Dialogue* 56 (1): 65–87.
Meijer, Michiel. 2019. "Ontological Gaps. Retrieving Charles Taylor's Realism," *Philosophy Today* (forthcoming).
Nussbaum, Martha. 1992. "Human Functioning and Social Justice. In Defense of Aristotelian Essentialism." *Political Theory* 20 (2): 202–46.
O'Hagan, Timothy. 1993. "Charles Taylor's Hidden God." *Ratio* 6: 72–81.
Olafson, Frederick. 1994. "Comments on *Sources of the Self* by Charles Taylor." *Philosophy and Phenomenological Research* 54 (1): 191–96.
Putnam, Hilary. 1987. *The Many Faces of Realism*. LaSalle: Open Court.
Putnam, Hilary. 1990. *Realism With a Human Face*. Cambridge, MA: Harvard University Press.
Putnam, Hilary. 2002. *The Collapse of the Fact/Value Distinction*. Cambridge, MA: Harvard University Press.

Putnam, Hilary. 2004. *Ethics Without Ontology*. Cambridge, MA: Harvard University Press.
Rorty, Richard. 1994. "Taylor on Self-Celebration and Gratitude: Review of *Sources of the Self*." *Philosophy and Phenomenological Research* 54 (1): 197–201.
Rosa, Hartmut, and Arto Laitinen. 2002. "On Identity, Alienation and the Consequences of September 11th. An Interview with Charles Taylor." In *Acta Philosophica Fennica. Vol. 71. Perspectives on the Philosophy of Charles Taylor*, edited by Arto Laitinen and Nicholas Smith, 165–95. Helsinki: Philosophical Society of Finland.
Rosen, Michael. 1991. "Must We Return to Moral Realism?" *Inquiry* 34: 183–94.
Saurette, Paul. 2005. *The Kantian Imperative: Humiliation, Common Sense, Politics*. Toronto: University of Toronto Press.
Shklar, Judith. 1991. "Review of *Sources of the Self*." *Political Theory* 19: 105–09.
Skinner, Quentin. 1991. "Who Are 'We'? Ambiguities of the Modern Self." *Inquiry* 34: 133–53.
Smith, Nicholas. 2002. *Charles Taylor: Meaning, Morals and Modernity*. Cambridge, MA: Polity.
Taylor, Charles. 1959. "Ontology." *Philosophy* 34: 125–41.
Taylor, Charles. 1964. *The Explanation of Behaviour*. London: Routledge and Kegan Paul.
Taylor, Charles. 1975. *Hegel*. Cambridge, MA: Cambridge University Press.
Taylor, Charles. 1985a. "The Concept of a Person." In *Human Agency and Language: Philosophical Papers vol. 1*, 97–114. Cambridge, MA: Cambridge University Press.
Taylor, Charles. 1985b. "How is Mechanism Conceivable?" In *Human Agency and Language: Philosophical Papers vol. 1*, 164–86. Cambridge, MA: Cambridge University Press.
Taylor, Charles. 1985c. *Human Agency and Language: Philosophical Papers vol. 1*. Cambridge, MA: Cambridge University Press.
Taylor, Charles. 1985d. "Interpretation and the Sciences of Man." In *Philosophy and the Human Sciences: Philosophical Papers vol. 2* 15–57. Cambridge, MA: Cambridge University Press.
Taylor, Charles. 1989. *Sources of the Self. The Making of the Modern Identity*. Cambridge, MA: Cambridge University Press.
Taylor, Charles. 1991. "Comments and Replies." *Inquiry* 34: 237–54.
Taylor, Charles. 1994a. "Reply and re-articulation." In *Philosophy in an Age of Pluralism: The Philosophy of Charles Taylor in Question*, edited by James Tully and Daniel Weinstock, 213–57. Cambridge, MA: Cambridge University Press.
Taylor, Charles. 1994b. "Reply to Commentators." *Philosophy and Phenomenological Research* 54 (1): 203–13.
Taylor, Charles. 1995a. "Cross-Purposes: The Liberal-Communitarian Debate." In *Philosophical Arguments*, 181–203. Cambridge, MA: Harvard University Press.
Taylor, Charles. 1995b. "Explanation and Practical Reason." In *Philosophical Arguments*, 34–60. Cambridge, MA/London: Harvard University Press.
Taylor, Charles. 1995c. "Heidegger, Language, and Ecology." In *Philosophical Arguments*, 100–26. Cambridge, MA/London: Harvard University Press.

Taylor, Charles. 1995d. "Lichtung or Lebensform: Parallels between Heidegger and Wittgenstein." In *Philosophical Arguments*, 61–78. Cambridge, MA/London: Harvard University Press.

Taylor, Charles. 1995e. "Overcoming Epistemology." In *Philosophical Arguments*, 1–19. Cambridge, MA/London: Harvard University Press.

Taylor, Charles. 1995f. *Philosophical Arguments*. Cambridge/London: Harvard University Press.

Taylor, Charles. 1996/2011. "Iris Murdoch and Moral Philosophy." In *Dilemmas and Connections*, 3–23. Cambridge, MA/London: Belknap Press of Harvard University Press.

Taylor, Charles. 1999/2011. "A Catholic Modernity." In *Dilemmas and Connections*, 167–87. Cambridge, MA/London: Belknap Press of Harvard University Press.

Taylor, Charles. 2003. "Ethics and Ontology." *The Journal of Philosophy* 100 (6): 305–20.

Taylor, Charles. 2005. "The "Weak Ontology" Thesis." *The Hedgehog Review: Critical Reflections on Contemporary Culture* 7 (2): 35–42.

Taylor, Charles. 2007. *A Secular Age*. Cambridge/London: Belknap Press of Harvard University Press.

Taylor, Charles. 2011a. *Dilemmas and Connections*. Cambridge/London: The Belknap Press of Harvard University Press.

Taylor, Charles. 2011b. "Disenchantment-Reenchantment." In *Dilemmas and Connections*, 287–302. Cambridge, MA/London: Belknap Press of Harvard University Press.

Taylor, Charles. 2016. *The Language Animal: The Full Shape of the Human Linguistic Capacity*. Cambridge, MA: The Belknap Press of Harvard University Press.

Taylor, Charles (with Dreyfus, Hubert). 2015. *Retrieving Realism*. Cambridge, MA: Harvard University Press.

Taylor, Charles (with Kullman, Michael). 1958. "The Pre-Objective World." *The Review of Metaphysics* 12 (1): 108–32.

Thiebaut, Carlos. 1993. "Charles Taylor: On the Improvement of Our Moral Portrait: Moral Realism, History of Subjectivity and Expressivist Language." *Praxis International* 13: 126–53.

White, Stephen. 1997. "Weak Ontology and Liberal Political Reflection." *Political Theory* 25 (4): 502–23.

White, Stephen. 2000. *Sustaining Affirmation: the Strengths of Weak Ontology in Political Theory*. Princeton, NJ: Princeton University Press.

White, Stephen. 2005. "Weak Ontology: Genealogy and Critical Issues." *The Hedgehog Review: Critical Reflections on Contemporary Culture* 7 (2): 11–25.

Williams, Bernard. 1990. "Republican and Galilean: Review of *Sources of the Self*." *The New York Review of Books* 37 (November 8): 45–48.

Conclusion

Ethics With or Without Ontology?

The main conclusion of the analysis developed in this book is that Taylor's doctrine of strong evaluation especially deserves further investigation with regard to the connection between ethics and ontology, and his central question of what we are committed to ontologically by our ethical views. This means that his central strategy of intertwining different philosophical arguments in debunking naturalism can claim only a partial success as it leaves Taylor's nonanthropocentric position both incomplete and underdemonstrated. It would, however, that the issue of what ontology can underpin our moral commitments is not simply *Taylor's* problem, as it crosses the boundaries of any one established academic discipline, arising as it does on the borderline between common sense, philosophy, and science. Drawing attention to the major metaphysical challenge underlying this problem, I would like to conclude here with a proposal that not only brings this challenge more clearly in focus, but also helps to identify the philosophical controversies behind it.

Although ontological discussions are currently booming in philosophy, the very notion of ontology is seldom clearly defined—neither in philosophy nor in the empirical sciences; it is, in fact, extremely difficult to define. Adding to the confusion, the many different approaches to ontology have grown so far apart over the last few decades that it has become highly debatable whether "ontology" still designates a single philosophical domain. For this very reason, many argue that ontological debates are nonsubstantive, pointless, or incoherent, thereby accepting that there is no objectively best language that accurately describes the structural features of reality. Within this climate, the very attempt to articulate the relationship between ethics and ontology is often contested. This predicament poses for us at least two major problems. First, what is the status of "ontology" within a science-dominated world?

And, second, does this status demand either the exclusion or the incorporation of ontological theorizing into ethics?

The philosophical reflection on these issues can be divided into three main camps: naturalistic doctrines that take empirical science as our best guide to understanding ethics; hermeneutical theories that focus on the interpretation of human meanings; and pragmatic views that insist neither on empirical science nor on theories of meaning but on practical consequences for explaining value. In the last chapter, I briefly mentioned that Hilary Putnam seems to be a challenging interlocutor of Taylor on these very issues. Like Taylor, Putnam has been arguing from the outset of his career against the idea that "there is exactly one true and complete description of 'the way the world is'" in defense of the claim that "there is more than one 'true' theory or description of the world" (1981, 49). His aim is to show that "the mind and the world jointly make up the mind and the world" and to defend a view in between "metaphysical realist views of reality and truth," on the one hand, and "cultural relativist ones," on the other (1981, ix; 1987, 1). The striking similarity with Taylor therefore is that Putnam rejects metaphysical realism, reductive naturalism, and moral relativism at one stroke, arguing, first, that we are "too realistic about physics and too subjectivistic about ethics," and, second, that "taking the agent point of view" in order to evaluate moral judgments does not mean "lapsing back into metaphysical realism about one's moral beliefs" (Putnam 1981, 143; 1987, 77). These points bring Putnam's position so close to that of Taylor that the difference between them can be only a very subtle one. This means that, although rooted in traditions that are often seen as mutually exclusive, Putnam and Taylor have a shared philosophical agenda, namely to show that there is something deeply wrong with naturalistic approaches to value. To make this point, they equally define moral knowledge as autonomous and discontinuous with nonmoral knowledge, resulting in intricate arguments which claim that moral truths—that is, those that do not "fit" into the world picture of science—do not need empirical evidence to be justified.

Yet the assumed alliance between Putnam and Taylor becomes more complex when considering, first, that they scarcely refer to each other's arguments, and, second, that the analytic debates with which Putnam engages generally have no room for a hermeneutical perspective such as Taylor's. However, as noted in the Introduction, many naturalistically oriented philosophers within these debates find themselves in agreement with Taylor to the extent that they also seek to defend the autonomy of morality in the face of empirically informed reductions of the moral. Yet by focusing mainly on what Blackburn aptly describes as "finding room" for ethics within the natural order (1998, 49), most of these views still agree that a reasonable explanation of morality must in the end be compatible with the scientific worldview. Against this background, what is striking about the philosophies of Putnam and Taylor is that they reject the very framework in which these discussions take place.

Although Putnam and Taylor recognize that "naturalism" is far from a straightforward position, their methods involve not so much detailed engagements with naturalist moral theories as the defense of a pragmatist or hermeneutical counterposition that rejects any appeal to scientism in ethics, understood as the application of scientific procedures to areas of our lives in which these procedures do not belong. Put simply, their shared concern over naturalism is that science should not overreach its purview: the scientific approach is legitimate within the boundaries of empirical inquiry, but should not enter into other areas—in particular, ethics—where different standards and criteria apply.

Given these points, it is worth noting that Putnam and Taylor, while they are quite convinced that naturalistic theories are on the wrong track, both lack a clear vision on how to explain the ontological status of our values. Putnam criticizes not just naturalism but any ontological approach to ethics as obsolete, yet he remains silent about the implicit ontological claims that substantiate this critique. Taylor, then, as we have seen, is quick to reject any appeal to naturalism for understanding ethics but struggles to articulate a more fitting explanation for himself. This is where the assumed philosophical affinity between Taylor and Putnam starts to unravel, as Putnam improves his realism in a way that ultimately leads to the direct opposite of Taylor's doctrine of strong evaluation. In *Ethics Without Ontology* (2004), Putnam continues to defend moral objectivity and the fact/value entanglement—as explained in more detail in *The Collapse of the Fact/Value Dichotomy* (2002)—but now adds that the attempt to provide an *ontological* explanation of the objectivity of ethics is "deeply misguided" (2004, 3). In so doing, Putnam endorses what he calls "pragmatic pluralism," a view that combines a pragmatic conception of ethics as concerned with "the solution of practical problems" with a pluralist take on ordinary language as involving "many different kinds of discourses," that is, "different 'language games' in Wittgenstein's sense" (2004, 4, 21–22).

Putnam's pragmatic pluralism then feeds into an antimetaphysics when he explicitly rejects the attempt to provide ontological explanations in ethics as "an attempt to provide *reasons which are not part of ethics for the truth of ethical statements*" (2004, 3, original emphasis). By contrast, Putnam explains, the major advantage of his own nonontological proposal is that it "does not require us to find mysterious and supersensible objects *behind* our language games" as "the truth can be told in language games that we actually play when language is working" (2004, 22, original emphasis). From this perspective, any explanation of moral statements in terms that reach beyond the practices in which these statements occur is ultimately superfluous.

The most significant innovation of *Ethics Without Ontology* is perhaps the way in which Putnam connects a pragmatic-pluralist reconstruction of moral objectivity with a wholesale rejection of ontological modes of thinking. Yet while Ontology as such—note the capital "O"—is said to be at the core of Putnam's critique, his main targets are "inflationary" Platonic metaphysics, on the one hand, and "deflationary" reductive naturalism, on the other (2004, 17–22). Surprisingly perhaps, Putnam stresses that it is in analytic philosophy in particular that Ontology (in both of its main forms) flourishes (2004, 81). Yet Putnam's critique of analytic metaphysics is so sweeping that it leads him to get rid of *all* ontologizing, abandoning the very idea of ontology. This means that whereas Taylor emphasizes the *entanglement* of ethics and ontology in developing his interwoven arguments, Putnam argues that the only option left for us is to embrace ethics *without* ontology.

To give the full stretch of Putnam's arguments the treatment they deserve lies beyond the scope of this book. This much, however, seems clear: Putnam's unusual development from the view that "humanly speaking" objectivity provides us with "objectivity enough" (1981, 168) to the pronouncement of an "obituary" on all ontologizing (2004, 85) is definitely worth confronting with Taylor's distinctive ontological perspective. Intriguingly, it would seem that the problems pressing on their accounts are direct opposites. Putnam sees ontological considerations as neither necessary nor sufficient for ethical theory, but he ultimately overplays his hand in pronouncing his obituary on ontology as he implicitly endorses, rather than overcomes, ontological thinking in developing his pragmatic pluralism.[1] Taylor, on the other hand, sees ontological reflections as vitally important for understanding ethics, but struggles until the very end of his career to clarify their meaning. Put simply, this means that whereas it remains unclear how Taylor can *substantiate* his nonanthropocentric ontology with a solid philosophical grounding, Putnam's problem is precisely how he can *reject* ontology without engaging in ontologizing himself. The really interesting question that remains is whether Taylor's nonanthropocentric moral realism can coincide with Putnam's antiontological moral realism that finds such metaphysics "almost by definition contrary to commonsense" (2002, 124).

In this respect, I agree with Taylor that there still remains a genuine and important ontological issue that needs to be addressed beyond the inflationary-deflationary impasse, namely how to account for the ontological gaps in our different explanatory languages that make sense of our values. Yet even if Taylor is quite right to argue that the naturalist suppression of ontological reflection has fostered a kind of "eclipse" of ontological thinking in moral theory, then what could it mean to *undo* this suppression? If anything, it needs to be made clearer just how a more felicitous ontology could be established, or, to stick with Taylor's expression, how an ontological gap is filled.

Although this is a valid question, the present analysis has demonstrated that far too little attention has been paid to the relationship between ethics and ontology to answer it properly. Because of this, Taylor's suggestion that we might be in need of a stronger ontological foundation for our ethical beliefs than naturalist ontology can provide is a question rather than a statement. Although his position has its own problems, Taylor's suggestion is worth following up.

As we have seen, in Taylor's view, reason in this domain cannot but be hermeneutical since there are no knockdown arguments in making sense of human action. In fact, this is precisely what makes ethical and ontological questions amendable to hermeneutical inquiry. If we now return to the three-cornered battle between naturalists, hermeneutists, and pragmatists, we can see that the role of hermeneutical argument within this discussion is to point out elements that rival views cannot account for. However, the debate gets more obscure when considering the peculiar contribution of naturalistic voices, namely that they boldly exclude other explanatory languages by accepting only the terms of empirical science for explaining human action. In this way, naturalism does not just neglect ontological gaps but denies them from the very beginning. Putnam makes a point like this when he says that "the worst thing about the fact/value dichotomy is that in practice it functions as a *discussion-stopper*, and not just a discussion stopper, but a *thought-stopper*" (2002, 44, italics mine). Recalling the hermeneutical condition that whatever meaning we recognize in ethics has to make sense within a larger ontological picture, Putnam's point is spot on: any monotheistic talk of the one real language stifles rather than encourages further debate and understanding.

This leaves us with the debate between hermeneutists and pragmatists. This debate definitely deserves further exploration when considering that there is a certain void in contemporary discussions regarding the defense of the autonomy of morality that can be filled adequately and accurately through the development of a debate between hermeneutists and pragmatists. As noted above, most types of nonreductive ethics are predominantly articulated from a naturalistic viewpoint to the extent that they focus on the problem of how to locate (notoriously abstract) notions such as rightness and goodness within the natural world. Because of this narrow focus, these theories cannot properly conceive of the very moral experiences underlying this "location" problem. In their strong concerns for moral common sense, philosophers such as Taylor and Putnam seem to belong to the few thinkers being able to give more nuanced explanations of morality.

In one way, their philosophical projects go back to Dilthey's attempt to defend the methodological autonomy of the humanities from the natural sciences and his endorsement of a distinction between hermeneutical understanding and causal explanation. Yet in another way, they take into account that the philosophical field itself has become more than two-sided. As noted, some philosophers come close to giving exclusive stress on scientific hypothesizing and focus on finding room for ethics. Others protest against this scientism and highlight the anomalies of a too-reductive naturalism and/ or the need for a broader understanding of ethical naturalism. Yet Putnam and Taylor reject the naturalistic framework itself in which these debates take place, and have recourse to pragmatic and hermeneutical models instead.

I think we should be interested in all of these debates as there is something ultimately doctrinal and unimaginative about identifying oneself with either side of a philosophical impasse. Although it seems clear that naturalistic, hermeneutical, and pragmatic views rest on radically different assumptions about the nature of reality that are responsive to different explanatory goals, it is precisely the attentiveness to the difference in exploratory focus that could make our grasp of reality more refined. As noted, one way to explore the peculiar status of ethics and ontology in contemporary philosophy is through the development of a debate between hermeneutists and pragmatists. In this way, we can ask, for example, whether Putnam's rejection of Ontology can still accept Taylor's model of hermeneutical reasoning, and his closely related understanding of Ethics in the broad sense. Is there perhaps some space left within pragmatic pluralism for ontological truths that are neither inflationary nor deflationary? That is, could Putnam include in his method the step toward what might be called a "pragmatic metaphysics," which rejects only Ontology, not ontology? But even where the differences between them are irreconcilable, we can still learn from Putnam and Taylor that when it comes to understanding morality, we require neither causal scientific explanations nor pseudoscientific naturalist ones but the development of a distinctive philosophical platform from which to investigate the complex relationship between ethics and ontology. Although I have been focusing here mainly on the ground prepared by Taylor, there are doubtless many other ways of achieving this end.

NOTE

1. In this respect, both David Copp (2006) and Claudine Tiercelin (2006) criticize Putnam for implicitly endorsing ontology and metaphysics in *Ethics Without Ontology*. Yet even if Putnam were indeed to suppress his own ontological commitments, there still remains an interesting question to explore with regard to Taylor, namely the question as to whether (and, if so, to what extent) Putnam's critique undermines Taylor's arguments for the connection between ethics and ontology.

REFERENCES

Blackburn, Simon. 1998. *Ruling Passions: A Theory of Practical Reasoning*. Oxford: Clarendon Press.

Copp, David. 2006. "The Ontology of Putnam's *Ethics without Ontology*." *Contemporary Pragmatism* 3 (2): 39–53.

Putnam, Hilary. 1981. *Reason, Truth and History*. Cambridge, MA: Cambridge University Press.

Putnam, Hilary. 1987. *The Many Faces of Realism*. LaSalle: Open Court.

Putnam, Hilary. 2002. *The Collapse of the Fact/Value Distinction*. Cambridge, MA: Harvard University Press.

Putnam, Hilary. 2004. *Ethics Without Ontology*. Cambridge, MA: Harvard University Press.

Tiercelin, Claudine. 2006. "Metaphysics without Ontology?" *Contemporary Pragmatism* 3 (2): 55–66.

About the Author

Michiel Meijer is Doctor of Philosophy and Postdoctoral Research Fellow of the Research Foundation Flanders at the University of Antwerp.

Index

Abbey, Ruth, vii, 9, 12nn5, 13, 34, 39, 46n15, 57–58, 61, 63–66, 69, 71–73, 75, 79, 84n9, 88–90, 94, 96, 98, 123, 133, 143–44, 175–77, 180, 183
ad hominem, 7–11, 27–28, 32, 43, 87–88, 93, 102, 108–13, 115n10, 117, 122, 187, 187–88;
  and Nussbaum, 94–97;
  and strong evaluation, 97–101
Anderson, Joel, 6, 73, 124
Annas, Julia, 140n4
Aristotle/Aristotelian, 4–5, 53, 94, 98, 100–101, 114–15nn8, 9, 190, 194
articulation:
  constitutive goods, 122–26;
  ontology, 165, 170–73;
  strong evaluation, 36–40, 42–44

Beam, Craig, 12n5
Berlin, Isaiah, 5, 12nn7–10, 187
best account, 65, 71, 113, 144, 160, 192, 202n26
Beyleveld, Deryck, 115n11
Blackburn, Simon, 1, 4, 12n1, 77, 91–92, 114nn5, 7, 169–70, 174, 208
Bohman, James, 5

Catholic/Catholicism, 10–11, 12n10, 35, 143–44, 147, 149, 167, 175, 201n1
Chang, Ruth, 46n7
Christian/Christianity, 5, 12n10, 137, 144–45, 147, 149
constitutive goods, 118, 120–26, 133–35, 138, 140n7, 145–46, 158, 165, 189
Copp, David, 212n1

De Lara, Phillipe, 89, 95, 114n2, 151
De Sousa, Ronald, 12n10, 201n2
Desouza, Nigel, 202n17
disenchantment, 29–32, 174–75

expressivism/expressivist, 137, 140n8, 148, 163, 178, 180, 188, 198

Flanagan, Owen, 6, 33–38, 42, 44, 46nn11, 14, 58, 62–63, 83n3, 94, 98, 104, 112, 114n4, 147, 150, 176
Frankfurt, Harry, 22–23, 32, 107

Gert, Bernard, 140n5
Gewirth, Alan, 115n11

Hegel, 5, 10, 102, 201n12
Heidegger/Heideggerian, 1, 4–5, 12n11, 74–75, 84n13, 132, 134–38, 140n11, 162–68, 185, 189–90, 196–97, 202n25
hermeneutics/hermeneutical, 1–5, 160, 175, 184, 192–200, 208–9, 211–12
Hittinger, Russell, 12n10, 201n2
Horgan, Terry, 140n9
Husserl, Edmund, 1, 74–75
hypergoods, 140n7, 188

Illies, Christian, 102, 106–12
incommensurable/incommensurability, 4, 8, 25–26, 31–32, 35, 38–39, 42, 46n7, 54, 59, 88, 92, 123, 130, 148, 169–70, 177, 190, 192
incomparable/incomparability. *See* incommensurability

Johnston, Paul, 5, 41–45, 46n14, 47nn17–18, 62, 76, 83n3, 92–93, 99, 104–5, 112, 147–49, 176

Kant, Kantian, 4–5, 26, 38, 46n10, 68, 101, 103, 119, 123, 125, 130, 146
Kerr, Fergus, 12n9, 57–58, 60, 83nn2, 6, 84nn9, 12, 133, 136–37, 163, 175
Kymlicka, Will, 5, 84n14

Laitinen, Arto, vii, 5, 12nn5, 13, 14, 43, 46n15, 57–58, 61, 70–74, 76, 83n6, 84nn9, 14, 88–89, 99, 114n9, 124–26, 140n6, 176, 191
Lane, Melissa, 12n10, 147–48, 151, 176, 201n2
language theory, 5, 163, 196, 199–200, 202n15
life goods, 120–22, 124, 138
Lloyd, Christopher, 140n8
Löw-Beer, Martin, 140n3

MacIntyre, Alasdair, 5

Mackie, John, 1, 4, 77, 90–91, 114n5, 169–70
Mandelbaum, Maurice, 11, 117–18, 126–32, 138–39, 140n8, 185, 188
McDowell, John, 2, 169–70, 202n16
Merleau-Ponty, Maurice, 1, 4–5, 21–22, 46n4, 62, 71, 74–76, 84n13, 103, 157–58
metaphysics. *See* ontology
moral phenomenology/moral-phenomenological, 5, 7–9, 11, 17, 18, 20, 24, 26, 31–32, 45, 51–52, 60–61, 65, 140n7–8, 144, 148, 152, 156, 158, 169–72, 175;
and ethics, 117–26;
and Mandelbaum, 126–32;
and ontology, 54–58, 69–83, 134–39, 179–200;
and philosophical anthropology, 138–39
moral sources, 37, 65, 71–72, 89, 118, 138, 140n7, 158, 171–72, 178;
constitutive goods, 120–26;
theistic and non-theistic moral sources, 146–52
Murdoch/Murdochean, 4–5, 59, 67, 84nn7, 12, 17, 132–34, 136, 138, 146, 161, 165, 166–68, 188

naturalism/naturalist/naturalistic, 1–10, 24–25, 33, 35–36, 46n5, 47n16, 56–59, 98, 102, 107–9, 115n10, 117, 122, 130, 146, 155, 161, 176–81, 184, 186, 188–92, 195, 202n16, 207–12;
naturalistic fallacy, 27–28, 30, 98, 109, 110, 128;
naturalist ontology, 8, 10, 31, 59, 60, 69, 72, 74, 77–79, 83, 123–24, 127, 129, 135–36, 168–72, 175, 180–81, 183–84, 191–95, 197–200, 211;
naturalist projectivism, 90–93, 95–97, 100–101, 111–13, 131, 146, 190;

Taylor's critique of, 18–22, 30–32, 77–79, 83, 90–93, 99–101, 112, 123, 132–36, 139, 168–75, 197–200;
Taylor's definition of, 19–20
Nietzsche/Nietzschean, vii, 33, 96, 133, 136, 151, 156, 167
nonanthropocentrism/nonanthropocentric, vii, 8–11, 20, 51–52, 55, 57, 58–74, 78–83, 117–18, 122–24, 132–39, 143, 146, 152, 154, 161, 165–68, 171, 175, 177, 180–82, 185–200, 207, 210
Nussbaum, Martha, 2, 6, 88, 93–100, 107, 111, 114n8, 202n24

O'Hagan, Timothy, 12n10, 201n2
Olafson, Frederick, 5, 12n4, 58, 61, 63, 70–72, 75, 114n4, 145–47, 176, 201n2
ontology:
analysis of Taylor's writings on, 152–75;
criticisms of Taylor's ontology, 186–91;
misunderstandings of Taylor's ontology, 145–52;
moral ontology, 5, 17, 43, 51, 54–58, 60, 65, 67, 83n5, 122, 133, 148, 161, 201n12;
and moral phenomenology, 72–83;
and naturalism, 8, 10, 31, 59, 60, 69, 72, 74, 77–79, 83, 123–24, 127, 129, 135–36, 168–72, 175, 180–81, 183–84, 191–95, 197–200, 211;
and philosophical-anthropology, 138–39;
weak ontology (Stephen White), 177–86

phenomenology. *See* moral phenomenology
Plato/Platonic/Platonism/Platonist, 5, 8, 20, 69, 78, 96–97, 112, 132, 144, 145–47, 152, 153, 164–65, 167, 176, 184, 189–90, 210
practical reason, 7, 27–28, 32, 47n16, 90–92, 98, 100, 110, 120–21, 187, 202n19
projectivism. *See* naturalist projectivism
Putnam, Hilary, 2, 140n9, 153, 189, 192, 202nn14–23, 208–12, 212n1

Rawls, John, 118, 123, 125
realism:
moral realism, 5, 8, 20, 70–71, 73, 75, 78, 82, 97, 112, 132–33, 135–36, 144, 146–47, 165, 175–77, 186–87, 189, 191–92, 210;
(pluralistic) robust realism, 31, 153, 191–94, 198–200, 202n13
Redhead, Mark, 12n13, 35, 46n9
reduction/reductionism/reductionist/ reductive, 2–3, 7, 18–22, 25–26, 31, 35, 41–45, 45n2, 46n5, 47n16, 51, 56, 64, 66, 69, 71, 74, 83, 90–91, 113, 132, 139, 140n4, 146, 158, 169–70, 172, 176, 186–89, 192, 208, 210–12
relativism/relativist, 5, 43, 56, 87, 90, 92, 94–96, 135, 146, 180, 187–88, 208
religion/religious, 5, 10, 12n10, 89, 96, 114n3, 119, 134, 137–38, 144, 167, 170, 194–97, 201n6
Romantic/Romanticism/Romanticist, 32, 134, 137, 148, 178–79, 188–89, 196–98
Rorty, Richard, 2, 6, 46n5, 84n14, 133–34, 175–76, 186, 188–90, 192, 202n14
Rosa, Hartmut, 5, 12n14, 43, 58, 61, 67–68, 99, 191
Rosen, Michael, 5, 133, 175–76, 186–90, 202n25

Saurette, Paul, 12n6, 36, 38, 46n10, 57–58, 61, 68, 83n6, 84n9, 175

secular/secularism/secularity, 10, 119, 143, 149, 152, 167
selfhood, 7, 18, 51, 53–57, 60, 63–64, 66, 69, 87–89, 111, 143, 180
Shapiro, Michael, 5, 12n6
Shklar, Judith, 12n10, 201n2
Skinner, Quentin, 5, 12n10, 144, 147–51, 176, 201nn2, 6
Smith, Nicholas, vii, 12nn4, 8, 13, 20, 34, 39, 45n2, 46n4–15, 57–58, 61, 62–66, 68, 70, 72–74, 76, 83n6, 84n9, 88–89, 94, 98, 123–24, 201
strong evaluation:
  ad hominem argumentation, 94–101;
  criticisms of, 33–45;
  ethical aspects of, 24–28;
  language theory, 195–200;
  moral phenomenology, 126–32;
  ontological aspects of, 29–32;
  philosophical-anthropological aspects of, 22–24;
  Platonism, 145–47;
  robust realism, 192–95;
  Taylor's conception of morality, 118–26;
  Taylor's nonanthropocentric understanding of, 58–61, 132–39;
  Taylor's rejection of naturalism, 90–93;
  theism, 147–52;
  thematic background of, 18–20;
  transcendental argumentation, 101–12
subjectivism/subjectivist/subjectivity, 8, 20, 31, 42–43, 56, 58, 63, 65, 68, 72–73, 76, 78, 87, 90, 92, 95–96, 124, 132–33, 135–38, 146–47, 164–65, 167, 170, 180, 183, 188, 192, 197, 200, 208

theism/theistic, 5, 12n10, 35, 133–34, 143–45, 147–52, 160, 165, 172–73, 176, 178–81, 189, 191, 196, 201n8
Thiebaut, Carlos, 12n5, 135–36, 175–77, 183, 190`
Tiercelin, Claudine, 212n1
Timmons, Mark, 140nn2, 8
transcendental argumentation, 7–11, 23, 62–65, 67–68, 70–71, 77–80, 82, 84n15, 87–88, 98, 100, 101–14, 115n11, 117, 122–23, 139, 150, 179–81, 202n26

utilitarianism/utilitarian, 18, 24–26, 28, 34, 36, 46nn8, 9, 90, 98–100, 119, 146, 169

Verstegen, Ian, 140n9

Weinstock, Daniel, 6, 84n14, 94, 98, 202n17
White, Stephen K., 5, 57–58, 61, 68–69, 80, 84nn9, 10, 175–76, 202n23;
  White's reading of Taylor, 177–86
Williams, Bernard, 6, 12n10, 24, 76, 78, 84n14, 144, 147–48, 150–52, 175–76, 187, 201nn2, 5
Wittgenstein, Ludwig, 75, 103, 162, 209

www.ingramcontent.com/pod-product-compliance
Lightning Source LLC
Chambersburg PA
CBHW021826300426
44114CB00009BA/342